Modern American History

New Studies and Outstanding Dissertations

Edited by
Robert E. Burke
and
Frank Freidel

A Garland Series

LOS ANGELES AND THE GREAT DEPRESSION

Leonard Leader

Garland Publishing, Inc.
New York & London
1991

Library of Congress Cataloging-in-Publication Data

Leader, Leonard Joseph.
Los Angeles and the Great Depression / Leonard Leader.
Includes bibliographical references and index.
ISBN 0-8240-1903-2 (alk. paper)
1. Los Angeles (Calif.)—Economic conditions. 2. Depressions—1929—California—Los Angeles. 3. New Deal, 1933–1939—California—Los Angeles. I. Title. II. Series.
HC108.L55L43 1991
338.5′42′097949309043—dc20 91-25485

Design by Marisel Tavárez

Printed on acid-free, 250-year-life paper.
Manufactured in the United States of America

To Rita
because she is
as she is
knows and senses it best.

What is the city but the people

Shakespeare
Coriolanus

LOS ANGELES AND THE GREAT DEPRESSION

TABLE OF CONTENTS

LIST OF TABLES

Table | Page

GRAPHIC

PREFACE

What are the sources of this study of Los Angeles and the Great Depression?

All my sources are, like Gaul, divided into three parts. One - standard; two - accidental; and three - myself. For many reasons I make a sharp distinction between two and three, for I am not, by any means, an accidental source.

Standard sources: In the beginning there were the books, the learned articles, the dissertations on this and other cities during the Great Depression. To my consternation, I found little had been done by the time I began, many years ago. My disappointment was great, for I was denied models, and even worse, the materials for comparative evaluations. (To this day, people ask me the haunting and inevitable question: "Wasn't the Depression easier on L.A. than on other American cities?") The beginning might have been a good time to quit the subject in some despair, but I had not decided at the age of 52 to get a PhD, with quitting as an option.

Having been a journalist for many years, I first ventured into that frozen, if not dubious, history called the newspaper. I read the Los Angeles Times, in the main, for that blighted 1930s decade. I leaned heavily on the paper's morgue. What an experience was that- to read that Harry Chandler publication, with its constant violations of journalism's ethics, its strident use of virulent adjectives, and worst of all, its policy of printing only the news which could be made to fit its biases. I read other L.A. papers - major, ethnic, labor, libertarian, radical - all in an attempt to correct the biases. I even went into the New York Times' files for Los Angeles stories of the period. Years as a hooked newspaper reader, journalist and editor, made me pay special attention to "letters to the editor" columns, which I believe catch moods, prejudices, concerns and enthusiasms of the times. I believe historians should pay more attention to that part of the newspaper, though one must be wary of the exclusion policies of given newspapers. The Los Angeles Times, in that period, carried no letters praising trade unionism.

Rich sources of Depression information were discovered in Congressional hearings, though not as rich as the parliamentary blue books Karl Marx wove into Das Kapital. But what a blow it is to the historian of Los Angeles' hard times to find that the national hearings on unemployment, welfare and Depression matters were held on the eastern colonial thesis that the Appalachians, in the main, are the western flanks of the nation. There were occasions when the hearings came to Detroit, to Chicago, I even recall one journey to Denver - and didn't they once get to San Francisco? But never Los Angeles. Oh Philadelphia, how well investigated you were. Such anecdotal goodies as one Philadelphia relief worker being asked "how can a person getting relief of three dollars a week be a good Christian?" and the answer coming back: "On three dollars a week, how can one be anything else?" Why wasn't that question asked in Los Angeles?

The omission of Los Angeles was only an illustration of a theme I have developed in my History of Los Angeles course - the city as the fringe of a fringe. The Spaniards, who built a distant empire when they landed in Mexico in 1519, took a quarter of a millenium to reach the founding of Los Angeles - a fringe on that Mexican fringe of empire.

I lost myself in the minutes of the Los Angeles City Council for those years. Months of deadly drabness and dullness of inadequate men (only men), failing to cope with the continuing crisis. A lucky find of some WPA worker's index to the meetings saved some time.

There were seas of reports, city employee magazines, annual budgets, economic letters, miscellaneous pamphlets. There were great days in the Huntington Library, which I have dubbed the opiate of the scholars, for there one comes and leaves all woes, cares, and spouses behind. I have one scholar friend - name not to be given - who never went back to his mate after working at the reading tables. Once I dreamed that I died, and found that Heaven was a carrel in the Huntington Library, and splendid meals somehow appeared from the Footnote, a refreshing spot below. In that library I found pamphlets on church histories, accounts esoteric and ephemeral.

There are diaries there of Angelenos who allowed one to peek into their daily lives, scattering items like seeds for a harvest of footnotes. I developed a warning sign for my UCLA work closet which stated: "Do not get trampled by the footnotes." Diaries, on occasion, will disappoint you. The entry for the day of the 1929 crash, in one, contained naught but a recipe for a pie. Only once did all the diarists come through unanimously - everybody had to tell you where they were on March 10, 1933, when the Long Beach earthquake hit (including the forgotten writer Hamlin Garland, who lived in a house just behind the late Immaculate Heart College). I believe in diaries as a source for histories, for they catch the moment and the mood in a way that memories years later, which rationalize and distort, do not. The diary entry of the day catches it cold; the recollection warms it and rationalizes it away. (Though I consider interviews with men like journalist and reform activist Rueben Borough and John Anson Ford, people's politician, high points, I am also indebted to the old City Hall clerk who recalled when the order came to use pencils on both ends, and adding machine tapes had to have both sides marked before disposal.

I read endless accounts of local lawyers' associations, police advertisement journals, Rotarians, oral histories, the history of the Daughters of the American Revolution, nervous about the possibility of becoming grandmothers of another. One futile day in a sub-basement of City Hall, I examined old, dust covered cancelled pay checks of city workers. We have all done those things.

Letters are a special standard source and favorite research tool of mine. It isn't just that they feed the gossip and the voyeur in me - I realize that no one else shares these traits of mine. Letters are very fresh and immediate - even more honest than diaries, which often suffer from space limitations and posturing. What a good day it was when I found the correspondence of Senator Hiram Johnson and his man in Los Angeles, lawyer Frank P. Doherty, who kept the senator informed for some two decades of the conversations, moods, lunches and attitudes in Los Angeles during the twenties and the thirties, until Johnson's death in 1945. This correspondence in the Bancroft Library, Berkeley, has gaps, but there were days when Doherty wrote two letters. And his letters were perceptive, and so wonderfully Irish, as when he described a luncheon with important fellow Republicans (after all, Doherty was president of the L.A. Chamber of Commerce).

One asked another if he was behind President Hoover, and the answer came back, "how can you be behind him, he has St. Vitus' Dance." Or a description he has of Mayor John C. Porter of Depression-ridden Los Angeles as a man whose knowledge of politics comes out of Sunday School and the Bible. Porter was the first used car dealer to become mayor of a major American city - isn't it ordained that it would be Los Angeles? How many days there were when I wished I had taken the narrow subject of Porter instead of the large theme of this city in a ten-year crisis.

But enough of the standard sources. Let us turn now to the second research source - the accidental stream. What kind of source is that? Of course, one has to be accident prone - that is, to behave in such a way that an accident will befall you. Said one writer: "...failures and successes are not accidents as we so frequently suppose, but the strictest justice." If so, then it was justice that was working in the City Hall branch of the Los Angeles Public Library when I came across the chairman's report on apple sales on the corners of the city in the 1930s. Labor historian Irving Bernstein has called the apple "the absurd symbol of the Depression." 2,174,296 apples were sold in Los Angeles by some 600 women and disabled men, who collectively made a profit of $55,062. And in that accidentally found report were complaints by saleswomen against men who showed more interest in Eve than the apple!

There were also accidents of place. On a visit to the University of Wyoming in Laramie, I idly dipped into the library and found correspondence about the building of the Boulder Dam which contained letters from Angelenos seeking work. On a visit to London, the British Museum offered no accidents - only an old Los Angeles High School senior yearbook.

My luckiest and most significant accident predates my research and academic career. Many years ago, while browsing through the "as is" used books in the Mormon Deseret Thrift Shop on Soto near Olympic in East Los Angeles, I found a thin, worn, pencil-written diary which amazed me, since it had entries for every day of the year. (My personal diaries tended to fade away after January 9th, the latest.) I bought the diary for a dime, for later perusal. It had obviously come there as part of the cleaning out of a person's belongings.

I have it at home - and, of course, it must be given to some special collection for safekeeping after I have had it published. What is it? It is the day-by-day account of a near-penniless seamstress of the age of 60 for the year 1932, in the city of Los Angeles. Diaries are overwhelmingly the record of the famous and well-to-do. But here in the diary of Mary Elizabeth - we never learn her last name - we have what poet Thomas Gray called "the short and simple annals of the poor."

This research find can only be called accidental. Wander through it a bit with me: Jan. 5: "Coming home a newsboy borrowed 3 cents from me - wonder if will ever get back." Jan. 14: "Mended and patched Mrs. Neil's fur coat did a good job and earned five dollars went downtown and got my dinner went to Welfare and got some magazines came home and read to sleep." On Wednesday June 22, she wrote she was "born 1872": "This happens to be my birthday Laura Kessler had me over and had a nice dinner for me and made a birthday cake with pink frosting and candles gave me a bathtowel and wash rag and fancy hanger and we all had quite a few thrills - " (Mary Elizabeth knew little of sentence structure, periods or rules of capitalization.) Out of this rich "accidental source" I learned about rent day, the fact that she went to the movies often - at least six times in January - and paid ten cents admission on March 3. On election night she stayed up very late to hear the returns on radio in California Senator William McAdoo's Democratic club headquarters. She writes, "they served lunch was tired - did not get to sleep until 3 in the morning listening for returns (happy ones)." Came the day before Christmas, she, in her words, "got a lovely Basket from the Examiner...and 2 bags of Food from the Salvation Army Enough to last many days. This was a hard day and am very tired." (Mary Elizabeth capitalized both key words - Basket and Food.)

And then the wondrous last page - it was a full page, unlike all the others which had two days on a page. I give it completely: "Sat December 31 - Finished up some work and got myself ready and went to Long Beach to Miller's and will come back tuesday It has been a year of great depression but with it all I have gotten through nicely and have been able to help others some when they were in distress and considering all God has been very good to me and I am grateful and am sure the new year will be full of good things for all if we trust in Him Mary Elizabeth - <u>That's</u> <u>me</u>." (Do you see why I am chagrined that I did not seek other volumes which must have been there?)

I have not much more to say about accidents as sources - surely you have come across materials you did not think existed.

The third source I offer with a blend of caution and courage. It is <u>myself</u> - the experiential factor - the young man within me who was a teenager, and more, in the Great Depression in the cities of Brooklyn and New York. Aware that experience is valuable, I became nervous about experience's partisanship while reading Arthur Schlesinger, Jr.'s adulatory work on Robert Kennedy. But I can not escape myself, so I must throw it on the table as Schlesinger did. I chose my subject because the Depression was perhaps the single most searing and forming feature of my life, which has included 39 months as a soldier in World War II. What happens to you between 13 and 23 - give or take a year in either direction - has to be mold making. Papa was in the 1905 revolution in the Ukraine when he was 19. He died at 91, but that experience remained a benchmark for all things throughout his life.

I do not recall the crash day - I do recall a rich uncle in Buffalo where I spent the summer of 1930, and I can still see him watching the stock listings, hoping for a turnabout in prices which did not come. I accepted an older cousin's invitation to visit in Washington, D.C., during the famed 1932 Veterans Bonus March and I spent most of a two-week period in the encampment, leaving four days before Douglas MacArthur burned them out of the capitol. It was not long after, as a college student, that I became involved in the turbulent student movement - before graduation, I walked picket lines in front of restaurants and department stores on the road to unionization in downtown Brooklyn. I recall vain efforts to organize clerks in Wall Street, solidarity actions with striking seamen, parades against mounting events in Germany, boycott movements against Japanese silk and against sending our scrap iron to that country.

With the Committee for Industrial Organizations, which became the Congress of Industrial Organizations, I found myself in its first strike in Camden, N.J., Walt Whitman's town. Little did I realize that I was preparing myself for writing about distant Los Angeles and its turmoil of technocracy, the Utopian Society, Upton Sinclair's EPIC switch, when that Socialist writer captured the Democratic nomination for governor in 1934, the Townsend Old Age movement, $20 every Tuesday, $30 every Thursday, "ham and eggs", the parties of Marxism - Socialist and Communist, the KKK and Father Charles Coughlin, the beatings of unemployed demonstrators. My academic degrees of B.A., M.A. and PhD. should at least allow equal honors for a fourth degree, C.I.O.

Barbara Tuchman once said that one can not be bland in writing history. Surely I am not bland - I feel for all those people gone; understand them in their courage and in their confusion; in their righteousness and their wrongness; both the heroic figure and the one who meets Mr. Dooley's definition of a fanatic as "a man that does what he knows the Lord would do, if he knew all the facts of the case."

I am convinced that experience mulled and analyzed is a powerful research source. Admiral Samuel Eliot Morrison was particularly equipped to write naval history. I am aware of the dangers to the struggle for objectivity - and I am also aware of the insights and understandings my life has given me.

Such are some of the sources of my research.

ACKNOWLEDGMENTS

This study has benefitted from the guidance of Roger Daniels, Norris Hundley and Irving Bernstein.

It has drawn from the care and devotion of the librarians at UCLA, Bancroft, Huntington, Los Angeles Public Library, Los Angeles Times, New York Public Library, University of Wyoming and Duke University.

A special thanks goes to my family for suffering a late comer in the academic world. My parents, Harry and Lillian Swerdloff, daughter Wendi Leader (for extra effort), son Lewis Leader and his wife Sandra Nisley Leader - all cheered me when the going became rough. In the last stages, Frank Leone played an important role. Most of all, I thank my wife, Rita Geller Leader, who was inspiration and major helper. The dedication of the work is an attempt to say more.

Foreword

This is a study of Los Angeles and the Great Depression--a chronicle cf the economic crisis as it affected what was then the fifth largest city in the United States. Though spared some of the worst depression experiences of eastern cities such as unpaid employees, wage warrants and fiscal bankruptcy, Los Angeles faced typical private and public relief inadequacies, mass unemployment, starvation and the cutting of city services.

In this study I have tried to examine depression complications present in this city. In the period, the eager welcoming of tourists and newcomers turned into an unwelcoming police blockade; bounteous fields turned fallow as begging urbanites sought food; aliens from Mexico were deported in an attempt to cut relief rolls; an apathetic citizenry turned to cyclonic mass movements and a provincial city leadership found its way to Washington, D.C. to press for federal subsidies. From the decade came a new politics, perhaps not a depression politics in the main--but as detailed in a iatter chapter of this work--a coalition of righteousness.

This study begins with the coming of the depression as most came to recognize it. Though it was not the cause, the market crash was the signal, and thus I begin there and trace the story in outward circles to the major assault, which, of course, was the mass job layoffs. The conditions of the people in the depression and the recognition that hard times had come was reflected in responses down at City Hall. The Mayor and the City Council, at a time when the classic aids of the Community Chest and the religious sponsored charities were proving inadequate and the county public relief system close to overwhelmed, turned to a short-lived and pitiful volunteer city employees payroll deduction plan. Then, in typical confusion, they convinced the citizens to vote a five million dollar emergency work bond. It proved as ineffective as the plans it followed.

Parallel to these efforts, tens of thousands of ordinary people in the city were swept up in myriad ways seeking answers in self help, utopian schemes, and old political shibboleths; and alliances fell by the wayside replaced by daring and impracticable plans, while the knell of the open shop was sounded as labor organization attained new strength. It is the contention of this work that the changes occurred in the interplay between city government, political organization, popular activity of a utopian and labor character, and in a rising federal response to the problems. For this reason I have not delved deeply into the plight of the non active sectors of the city such as the Mexican Americans, the Negroes and the Japanese Americans. Their conditions and special problems are indicated--but they did not mould the city's depression history as independent forces, as did the governmental, political and popular mass movements. Business and industrial elements, as detailed in the chapter on organization, played a secondary and defensive role in the period. Refusal of the Los Angeles Chamber of Commerce to cooperate made for difficulties in presentation, but did not lessen the impact of the central thesis of how change came.

In tracing the major changes in the history of the city in the depression, I have not examined secondary and tertiary aspects such as water, land values, cultural patterns and many other possible elements. At all times my central concern was the interplay of forces described above. The general insufficiency of scholarly work on American cities in the period seems to indicate that there are only beginnings available.[1] It is my hope that this effort takes its place in those ranks.

Some of the best work in urban history has been done in less encompassing studies on such key phases as economic growth, population mobility, the black experience, immigrant accommodations, political machinations, police institutions and practices, religious blocs and other city forces.[2] Period urban history, such as this work, urgently needs such prior studies.[3]

Yet, there is a genuine value in studying a whole city. The historian of Memphis, Gerald Capers, Jr., has made the valid point that cities are "often more representative of fundamental economic interests than artificial political divisions like the state."[4] The Great Depression revealed itself most acutely in the city. It is the city which is a good vessel--perhaps a glass bottom boat--to observe the depression up close. Despite the troublesome conceptual problems of what the city is, we affirm that there was, and is, a geographical and political matrix known as the city of Los Angeles. There are, it is true, certain major problems that spread beyond the city--many involve the county of Los Angeles[5] in such areas as the county's responsibility for public relief; nevertheless, the city stands large and clear in terms of the Mayor, the City Council, the departments of city operation, the unifying straight jacket of the city budget, the way in which the depression unfolded, and how the urban population was affected and reacted.

My urban history is city biography written around the single thread of the Great Depression--an attempt to tell about some ten crucial years in which the city was engulfed with an overwhelming problem. Though Bessie Pierce's monumental history of Chicago is a model overall city biography, I can not presume her completeness on many counts, not the least of which is the backing of an army of interdisciplinary studies.[6] I hope that the prior statement does not place me in the category of the old urban history, for I find myself very close to the "new urban history" with its emphasis on the "social experience of ordinary people" and the attempt to capture the feel of life at the bottom rungs.[7] With more traditional methods I have made a determined effort to find the small urban voices--be they in letters to the editors, rare diaries such as that of seamstress Mary Elizabeth, recollections of old time civil servants or surviving members of vast and faded causes, or the sad jingles of a man who once raked leaves on a Griffith Park relief project.

Whether I have assayed too large a task is hard for me to judge at this point. I have come to the subject honestly as one who grew up in another city, New York, where I lived through and was active in the Great Depression. That experience, and the more than a decade and a half in Los Angeles, are the direct roots of this study.

FOOTNOTES TO THE FOREWORD

1. Though no complete work exists on an American city or cities in the Great Depression there is an attempt, on too general a basis, in James J. Hannah, "Urban Reaction to the Great Depression, 1929-1933," unpublished dissertation, University of California, Berkeley, 1956. Standard city histories devote some, but not too much, space to the period. Blake McKelvey, Rochester: An Emerging Metropolis, 1925-1961 (Rochester, 1961) devotes some 60 pages to the period (Part II "The Great Depression Hits Rochester," pp. 56-115). Bayrd Still, Milwaukee, The History of a City (Madison, 1948) discusses the depression in not much or extended detail. Still's anthology of readings on New York City, Mirror for Gotham--New York As Seen By Contemporaries from Dutch Days To The Present (New York, 1956), has only two relevant selections of some five pages in length; Charles N. Glaab and A. Theodore Brown, A History of Urban America (New York, 1967), a widely used text in urban history courses, asserts that "The general impact of the Depression on the great cities--mass unemployment; malnutrition, disease and even starvation; the exhaustion of relief funds--is a well-chronicled subject in American history. But the Depression did have special urban effects." (p. 299) Yet this text has little on the Depression--some seven pages (pp. 298-305) with no direct index reference, but a parallel listing to the New Deal which locates the material. (Perhaps city accounts want to bypass the hard times. Typical is some 12 lines in Los Angeles--1900-1961 (Los Angeles, 1961) published by the History Division of the Los Angeles County Museum, which reports a reduction in building permits and a slowing of population increase in the period, yet chortles how L.A. still gained more than 250,000 in the decade compared to San Francisco's gain of 142!) Bernard Sternsher, Hitting Home--The Great Depression in Town and Country (Chicago, 1970) offers an interesting collection of relevant articles--some of which are on rural areas. A valuable suggested readings list in this volume (p. 283ff) refers to the classic Robert and Helen Lynd volume, Middletown in Transition: A Study in Cultural Conflicts (New York, 1937). There is much good material in this volume. Of course, the list of urban studies in the depression era by sociologists is quite long. Bernard Sternsher's The Negro in Depression and War--Prelude To Revolution, 1930-1945 (Chicago, 1969) is also rich in pertinent bibliography. An incisive estimate of the crisis' impact on cities is contained in Irving Bernstein, The Lean Years--A History of the American Worker, 1920-1933 (Boston, 1966). Chapters 5-15 are seminal summaries; especially valuable pages on the urban phases are 287-333. In general, scholars do not seem to have come to grips with the Great Depression and the cities. Whether this is a product of insufficient attention, or pressures of post World War II affluence, I can not say. In the light of the

current and growing interest in urban crisis, we may be on the eve of major re-examination of the problem.

2. The bibliography is a long one and can be found in many places. A recent volume, A Teacher's Guide to American Urban History by Dwight W. Hoover (Chicago, 1971), has a good collection of lists.

3. There is a growing body of scholarly work on Los Angeles in the 1930s. See relevant parts of Lawrence Brooks de Graaf, "Negro Migration in Los Angeles, 1930-1950," unpublished dissertation, University of California at Los Angeles, 1962; Nelson Van Valen, "Power Politics: The Struggle for Municipal Ownership of Electric Utilities in Los Angeles, 1905-1937," unpublished dissertation, Claremont Graduate School, 1964; John Modell's study on the Japanese-Americans in Los Angeles, 1900-1940, soon to be published; a forthcoming publication based on his dissertation by Abraham Hoffman on the repatriation of Mexican nationals from the United States during the Great Depression; and some of the work at UCLA now being done by Jerome Woods on the Los Angeles police, and by Greg Singleton on the City's religious blocs.

4. Gerald Capers, Jr., The Biography of a River Town; Memphis: Its Heroic Age (Chapel Hill, 1939), p. viii. Capers asserts further on the same page that Memphis "typifies more clearly the character of the lower West."

5. There are other areas of difficulty: voting records are tabulated by the state on a county basis; the whole county apparatus of government topped by the Board of Supervisors makes for other unclarities in considering the city. Louis B. Perry and Richard S. Perry in A History of the Los Angeles Labor Movement, 1911-1941 (Berkeley and Los Angeles, 1963), viii-ix, comment on the difficulties in their study "confined primarily to the city of Los Angeles."

6. Urban historian R. Richard Wohl, also trained in economics and sociology, wrote that "full discovery of what has passed in a city's history can only be called forth by cooperative inter-disciplinary inquiry." Philip Hauser and Leo F. Schnore, The Study of Urbanization (New York, 1965), p.

7. Stephan Thernstrom, "Reflections on the New Urban History," Daedalus, Volume 100, No. 2, Spring 1971, p. 360. This essay is an excellent statement dispelling some cliche attitudes in the approach to the new urban history. Much good material is being developed. Though it is not relevant to the years of my study, the volume, Nineteenth-Century Cities--Essays in the New Urban History, edited by Stephan Thernstrom and Richard Sennett (New Haven, 1969), offers much in insights.

CHAPTER 1.

AND THE DEPRESSION CAME

On a morning in October, 1929, members of the Los Angeles Breakfast Club were advised by a visiting New York banker that "with wages high, unemployment low, optimism general all over the country, and a safe, sane cautious Californian in the White House there is no reason to worry about a flurry in stock prices." Another banker and visitor, Texan Jesse Jones, told the press he was impressed with Los Angeles' "plans which have been made for the future." Both his city, Houston, and Los Angeles, he said, had an advantage in common--"oil as an export." As if to dramatize Jones' point, two weeks later an oil well blew 250 feet into the air near the corner of Figueroa and 125th Street with an expected daily flow of 1,000 barrels.[1]

On October 21, Los Angeles Mayor John C. Porter attended the groundbreaking ceremonies for the new $1,500,000 Los Angeles Stock Exchange on Spring Street. Local pride was bolstered by the news that there would be "a trading floor next to New York in size;" the crowd enjoyed hearing an old time banker recall that a seat on the exchange, then selling for more than $200,000, had been priced at $50 when the Los Angeles Exchange opened in 1899. Truly, Spring Street would fulfill its "manifest destiny to be the Wall Street of the West."[2]

The Wall Street of the East was seeing market prices "in a dive amid a frenzy," according to the Los Angeles *Times*, which also described the situation as a "madhouse." A financial columnist ventured the opinion that the worst was over and that "margin traders will never look back on the months of September and October of this year with pleasant recollections." (Mr. F.H. Kraft, retired merchant, 57, afflicted with a heart ailment, and owner of 100 shares of a "nominally valued stock" dropped dead on the fateful October 29 in the office of Logan & Bryan, stock brokers at 636 S. Spring Street.)[3] The Los Angeles Record expressed the hope "that Westerners are going to stop gambling around in the deep blue sky over Wall Street and do some real work in their own fertile territory." This anti-Eastern note would be struck many times in the depression years ahead. Will Rogers, humorist-cowboy, made the perceptive remark that the market gamblers "know now what the farmer has been up against for eight years."[4]

In the months that followed, the Wall Street-Spring Street tremors were deprecated as signals of dire days ahead. The Times' annual business review and forecast at the year's end presented top business and financial spokesmen who viewed 1930 as "promising."[5] It was the traditional view backed by the city's history. Earlier economic setbacks such as drought, flood, bank failures and even an epidemic of hoof and mouth disease among livestock had been surmounted. In their time, massive population increases, sunny skies, crop cultivation, discovery of oil, the film industry and land development and sales, had come to the local economy's rescue. As 1929 ended, the city had great expectations, based on the coming of the Boulder Dam with its potential for strengthening the municipal water and power system; plans to raze Bunker Hill, a barrier to city growth; and industrial expansion which was bringing the aviation industry to the area as well as plants of Ford, Procter and Gamble, Pittsburgh Plate Glass, Crane and the National Lead Company.[6] Perhaps the prosperity syndrome was stronger here; surely most people in the city did not sense that they were entering the bitterest and greatest American depression. Diaries of people recording the fall 1929 days show no special recognition of the turn downward.[7]

But, as the English say, facts are stubborn things. The stock market did not rise and ruin and despair affected many investors here. How many Angelenos were hurt in the 1929 market debacle is difficult to determine. A figure of more than 100,000 is possibly accurate based on a national study of stock ownership at the time. It is definite that they did not soon, if ever, recoup their losses.[8] In that sense they were the first to feel the coming of the depression to Los Angeles.

But for the mass of the people the loss of jobs was the announcement of the depression. The sociologists, Robert and Helen Lynd, caught the essential fact of both Middletown and Los Angeles--"one's job is the watershed down which the rest of one's life tends to flow."[9] In mid-December of 1929 a Los Angeles American Federation of Labor official warned that "there is an acute condition of unemployment in this city that is general in its extension and is quite serious in many directions." He had just attended an all day conference on unemployment at City Hall with representatives from the Church Federation, UCLA, USC, the YMCA, the Los Angeles Board of Education, the California State Employment Office, the Los Angeles County Board of Charities, the City Social Service Commission, and the Volunteers of America. Also present were spokesmen for the employment departments of the Pacific Electric Railway, the Union Pacific and Southern Steam railroads.

The Mayor addressed the gathering, the first such citywide recognition that unemployment was a significant problem. An expansion of public improvements by public agencies was proposed as "the city and county, and the Board of Education are probably the largest employers of labor in the vicinity." Other suggestions included a call for the five day week, completion of the new General Hospital, municipal employment of only city residents and organization of a drive to bring industry, "not people," to Los Angeles. The Mayor was asked to call a further conference, and also convince employers in the city not to cut employment or wage levels.[10]

Nevertheless employment fell, and as 1930 opened, the United States Department of Labor was reporting layoffs throughout the county. The Citizen, local AFL newspaper, reported that "a noticeable labor surplus is apparent in practically all lines of industry."[11] As January ended a resolution introduced in the City Council noted that "the unemployment situation is becoming more and more acute each day and many citizens in the city of Los Angeles find themselves in the embarrassing situation of being unemployed." Referred to committee, the proposal favored civil service examinations restricted to city residents.[12] Three days earlier four persons had appeared before the Council in behalf of the unemployed and the creation of a municipal department for the assistance of the jobless.[13]

The growing joblessness was recorded in the declining membership rolls of the unions in the city. The historians of the Los Angeles labor movement, Louis B. and Richard S. Perry, describe the local union movement as entering the depression in an increasingly weakened position. Job losses were felt in the printing trades, railroad and truck transportation, garment manufacture, music and entertainment, culinary, furniture, maritime and metal industries--to mention a few.[14]

In February and March the economic indicators were taking a drastic downward turn. The critical building permit figures dropped two-thirds from February 1929 with $9.4 million, to February 1930 with $3.8 million. By April 1, a Los Angeles bank analyst indicated that "most reports reflected a recession," and there was "no conclusive evidence of up-turn in business activity."[15] The true situation was coming into focus. Sometime in 1930 the depression's tenure seems to have been established.[16] Perhaps the vision of a second and bitter depression winter looming ahead was part of the sobering process, but more pertinent and inescapable were the results of the national administration's unemployment census conducted as part of normal decennial count in April of 1930. That census enumerated the unemployed in the city of Los Angeles and throughout the nation.

That count detailed the magnitude of the unemployment problem.[17] President Hoover's national tabulation of the jobless, the first in the country's history, reported that 50,918 were unemployed in the city. The figure was broken into two categories: "out of a job, able to work, and looking for a job," and "having jobs but on layoff without pay, excluding those sick or voluntary idle." In Los Angeles 44,480 were in the first group; 6,438 were in the second. For all practical purposes the true picture is the summation of the two categories.

The census of unemployment offers interesting data on specific employment phases. Agricultural unemployment in the city was near the general city average of nine percent. Some 8.3 percent of the 13,708 Los Angeles farm owners, tenants, laborers and wage workers were jobless. The slump in the building trades was reflected in unemployment rates ranging from 10 percent for electricians to more than 25 percent for stone mason and tile layers. (Seasonal factors were still part of the picture in April.) Nearly 30 percent of oil and gas well operators were jobless.

Unemployment in the Mexican community was the lot of one out of seven males, the highest rate for any single group. The rate of unemployment among black males was about one of twelve (thus surprisingly slightly lower than the overall city male figure). Negro unemployment swelled at an accelerated rate as the depression unfolded. Crediting the "inter-racial economy of Los Angeles Orientals and their strong family ties," social researcher Jacqueline Kasun stated that they "seemed to have weathered the depression with fortitude and success" by curtailing births, putting their women to work, often in family businesses and sending more of their young people to school.[18]

Compared to other cities, Los Angeles was in much better shape. Of the 21 cities examined, only San Francisco and Birmingham had a lower percentage of its adult work force unemployed. Minneapolis and Seattle had the same jobless level as Los Angeles. (See Table 1.)

The severity of the city's economic situation could no longer be denied. As the year 1930 came to a close, the local labor weekly wrote that "by and large, 1930 was a 'bad hombre,'" and asked for further information on wage-cutting practices.[19] The year went out with few illusions; New York Times correspondent Chapin Hall reported that the Yuletide spirit was having "a heck of a time," and added these somber details:

> A small bank in Hollywood with an array of customers resembling the guest list at a premiere found itself unable to thaw its frozen loans and folded up; the head of a rather sizable building and loan association broke down and confessed that he had benevolently assimilated $8,000,000 of assets for his own enterprises, consisting largely of a series of holes where oil was not, stocks which flopped and trusting advances to friends who did likewise. Only about one motion picture actor in a hundred has even a now-and-then job, and in spite of concerted efforts to jar the worker into a spending mood, merchants are none too happy.[20]

Nine months after the first federal jobless census, in January of 1931, a special national census of unemployment was taken in 21 selected urban areas including Los Angeles. With the single object of counting the unemployed, an attempt was made to hire the same enumerators who had made the general decennial canvass in 1930. In the space of ten months Los Angeles reported twice as many

TABLE 1 PERCENT OF MALE GAINFUL WORKERS IN UNEMPLOYMENT CLASSES A AND B, APRIL, 1930, AND JANUARY, 1931, IN THE CITIES INCLUDED IN THE SPECIAL UNEMPLOYMENT CENSUS OF JANUARY, 1931.

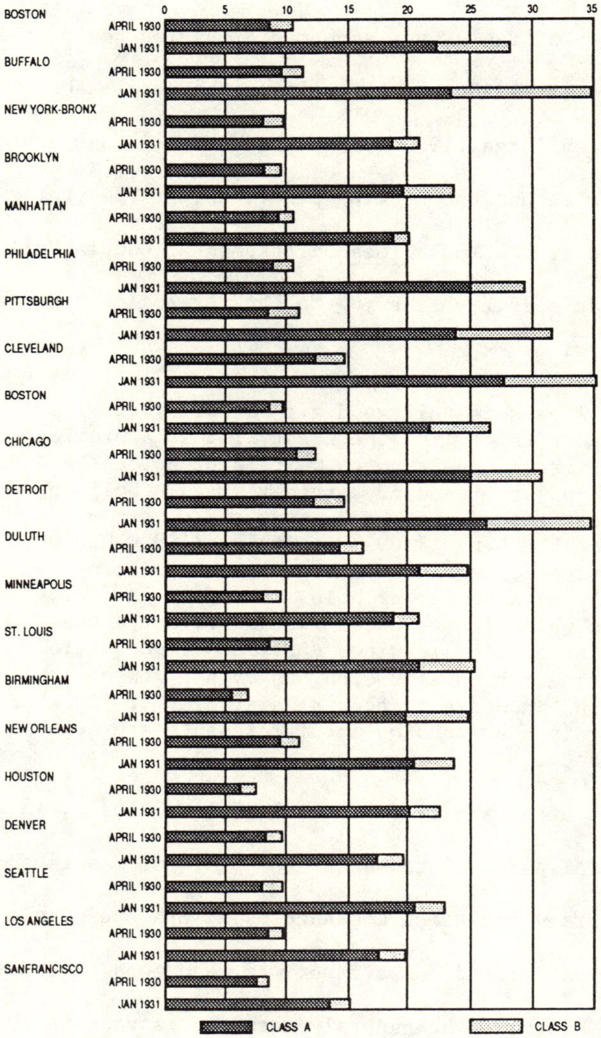

<u>Unemployment</u>, <u>General</u> <u>Report</u>
<u>Fifteenth Census</u> of the U.S., Volume II
(Washington, 1932), page 364.

unemployed.[21] An additional feature of the new census was a tabulation of length of time idle. (See Table 2). More than 30,000 reported that they had been without work for more than four months.

TABLE 2--Unemployment by Sex and Period of Idleness in the city of Los Angeles, January 1931.

	Total	Male	Female
Unemployed	105,220	82,805	23,135
under 1 week	5,249	4,275	974
1 or 2 weeks	10,304	8,024	2,280
3 or 4 weeks	13,747	10,466	3,413
5 to 8 weeks	18,612	14,507	4,105
9 to 13 weeks	15,933	12,618	3,315
14 to 17 weeks	8,596	6,817	1,779
18 to 26 weeks	14,149	11,189	3,060
27 to 39 weeks	6,385	4,978	1,407
40 to 52 weeks	8,398	6,434	1,974
53 to 104 weeks	2,618	2,075	543
105 weeks and over	561	431	-
Not Reporting	678	513	165

Fifteenth Census of the U.S.
Vol. II page 378.

In response to the question--why are you unemployed--the answers were:

Seasonality (off season)	5,736
Personal disability	4,428
Dissatisfaction	3,102
Economic conditions	42,534
Industrial policy	29,122

The last two reasons seem to be most relevant to the depression, and accounted for some 70 percent of the answers (why the 18,599 attributed to "laid off," "slack work," "can't find work," etc. are not listed in "economic conditions" is hard to understand. Had they been so listed, the overall percentage tied to the depression's effect would have been close to 88 percent.)[22]

The new census reported that building trade workers were unemployed in about the same ratios as in the earlier count, laborers had become jobless at a rate of 60 percent compared to the earlier 20 percent (January's seasonal factor is to be considered). Overall, in such occupations as manufacturing, oil and gas wells, transportation, communication and other, the unemployment figure had doubled in the ten months.[23] The sharpness of the slump is best seen in the sensitive catagory of retail trade, an early casualty of the decline in purchasing power. The retail trades unemployed numbering 6,352 in April of 1930, had advanced to 14,032 in January of 1931. "Easter buying has not materialized to the extent anticipated," was the gentle way an April, 1931, bank survey put it.[24]

Thus as 1931 began, one out of five persons seeking work in the city of Los Angeles was out of work. By categories the rate of unemployed to the nearest percentage was:

White		
	Male	20
	Female	14
Black		
	Overall	33
	Male	30
	Female	38
Other Races		24 [25]

The young, between the ages of 15 through 19, with 20 percent unemployed, had the highest rate of all age groups. Los Angeles' rate of male unemployment (Table 1) like San Francisco's and Denver's was in the lowest category compared to the outher cities in the 1931 census. Cleveland and Buffalo, with an unemployment rate of 35 percent, were the hardest hit; Detroit was a close second.

The figures and the charts of the two censuses of unemployment give the large picture; behind each digit there was a person. A man, with a wife and three children, wrote a letter to the Los Angeles Times: "I worked for one firm for seventeen years. They went broke and I went broke with them. I have not bought any clothing for three years." Four days later another correspondent offered consolation with the information that he hadn't bought clothes in six years.[26] Letters from Los Angeles job seekers to the Hoover Dam construction site in Nevada stressed the need:

> Friend Harper. I am writing you for a recommendation as tool dresser and blacksmith. I think I can land a pretty good job soon on the L.A. aquaduct (sic) tunnells (sic) and I think a good word from your office will help quite a little and I sure need the job.[27]

In another, the headmaster of The Harvard School, 1601 S. Western, Los Angeles, put in a request for a good student who

> . . . has been unable to continue his college work because of financial reasons and it would be a tremendous help to him if he could secure work on the Dam project.[28]

To the letters the reply was direct:

> . . . the best advice I can offer anyone who wants to secure employment is to stay away from the Hoover dam, as the percentage of unemployed in that vicinity is probably higher than in any other part of the country.[29]

Maxwell Hatfield wrote directly to the City Council "stating he had heard the statement made over the radio that a number of men would be employed on city work, and asking what procedure to follow in order that he may secure employment"; Irving Hersh petitioned the same body "to permit unemployed men to stand at principal downtown corners . . . selling large fancy apples at five cents each;" E. H. Van Dorn wrote from his San Quentin confinement that a parole awaited him if he could get employment.[30]

Parallel to the increasing joblessness was a rising hunger in the city. "Generous responses have come," wrote the Los Angeles Times, "in answer to the appeal for help for the school children who are in grave danger of starving to death this summer." There was an account of a "little girl who filled her empty lunch bag with wads of paper to hide the fact that she had nothing to eat."[31] "First meal in 17 days sends Malcolm Swenson, 55 years old and jobless to the hospital. Yesterday morning he ate a hearty breakfast of ham and eggs, the first in 17 days, but it proved to be more than his undernourished body could stand and he collapsed in the restaurant at 4108 S. Alameda Street."[32] Older librarians recall readers fainting from hunger in the downtown main library. From the Hollywood Boulevard Association came a plea to the City Council "urging that Hollywood Boulevard, from Vine Street to La Brea Avenue, be kept free from beggars." On February 16, 1931, James J. Long, "A man 70 years of age [wrote] appealing to the Council to help him find something to do to earn his food."

Mrs. M.V. Parker wrote to the same body "to help her and her son to secure employment so that she may be able to keep up her taxes, etc."[33] Her plea reflected the general strains on family life. Marriages, divorces and births declined during the hard times in the city. Kasun's observation that "frustration of vocational ambitions is reinforced by denial of normal family life," has ironic support in the fact that divorce tended to be a luxury in those years, in her words, perhaps because the "warmth and security of the marriage bond may have more importance to individuals during depression when the world outside the family seems particularly cold and unreceptive." Depression conditions saw less children born and parents became such at a later age in the thirties' decade. Family size, the study shows, was restricted more by those less threatened by economic insecurity. There was a higher birth rate in the lower income groups. Los Angeles City figures for 1930 show the Mexican-Americans with the highest rate, better than two-and-one-half times the general and Anglo rate of reproduction.[34]

In the depression years, the city of Los Angeles had less than half as many family dwellings built as during the 1920's. It was a time nevertheless of housing surplus--that is in terms of families' ability to rent. Kasun's study noted that "residents of this area in the early thirties can recall the shantytowns which were built by impoverished families even though the supply of permanent housing was adequate to accommodate all persons in the area at that time. Indeed," she stressed, "the mushrooming of shantytowns coincided with the largest housing surplus" in the 1920-1950 period.[35] Newspaper accounts and resident recollections describe "Hoovervilles" and "hobo villages" in many areas in and around the city. "More than 100 itinerants who had dedicated the summer weeks to home building in preparation for the cold winter rains were routed from their shacks and ordered to move on" along the wash of Rio Hondo and the Los Angeles River banks by the sheriff's office.[36]

On another occasion the Los Angeles Unemployed Voters Association proposed, on behalf of unemployed women and girls, that "at the conclusion of the Olympic Games the two hundred houses of Olympic Village be turned over to this needy class of local residents." Funds were asked of the Council "to be used to establish a Shelter for Unemployed and Homeless colored men on the East Side." Another proposal, never carried out, called for the City's Health Department to take over empty public buildings "to shelter people who are homeless."[37]

The depression meant doubling up of families (with concomitant strains), and, even though rents fell more sharply between 1929 and 1933 than other consumer items in the area, there were dwelling vacancies everywhere. A WPA study in 1937, noting the general absence of crowded tenements in Los Angeles, concluded that overcrowding "sometimes exceeds anything that would be permitted by the Health Departments in our Eastern cities."[38]

Increasingly home owners in Los Angeles were unable to meet their mortgage payments. Even the First Swedish Baptist Church complained about property costs of a location on 12th and Westlake which was bought in better days at "inflated values."[39] Home ownership declined from 37.3 percent of the residents in 1930 to 33.7 percent at the end of the decade.[40]

Those who did not live through the depression find it hard to realize what near pennilessness was like. A diary item of January 5, 1932, written by a poverty stricken Los Angeles woman records: "Coming home, a newsboy borrowed 3 cents from me--wonder if [I] will ever get it back."[41] People walked miles to avoid spending the five cent trolley fare. From 1930 to 1933 rail patronage tumbled drastically. Scholar Robert Fogelson, noting that this was a sharp acceleration of the earlier declines, observes that "for the electric railways...the Great Depression was catastrophic."[42]

The same impoverished woman, mentioned above, wrote in her diary: "I shopped around L.A. all day by myself, getting little needful things and seeing lots of bargains and wishing I had more money but Alas wish again." Two days later she writes that she "had dinner at Boos Bros.,all I could eat for 45 cents was sure nice."[43] The Childs restaurant chain had taken over the restaurant and introduced the "all you can eat" plan as an "anti-depression move" which, according to an official, "greatly increased business."[44] The grinding pressure for money is dramatized in a H.H. Brown's plea to the City Council for refund of $10 paid to the Police Commissioner when he was sworn in as a police officer, "as he is in dire financial straits."[45]

Almost 12,000 "urgently needy unemployed" girls and women were registered at twelve free employment bureaus;[46] a UCLA woman student, whose father in Minnesota lost all in the market crash, was found living under a bridge--she used the college women's gymnasium for her daily shower;[47] the university in its new Westwood quarters was surrounded by mud, raw lumber and sacks of cement as it opened the doors for registrants on September 18, 1929. It was, according to its historians, "a newly launched ship ready to perform on the high seas of academia. The Depression of the 1930's was to be its shakedown cruise for the years ahead with budget cuts and a reduction of faculty salaries."[48]

There was desperation in the city of Los Angeles. "Out of work for months, W.E. Main, 50, engineer, ended his life yesterday in a rooming house at 142 West Jefferson Street by sending a bullet through his heart."[49] Suicide rates were high in depression Los Angeles. The alienated and insecure individual killed himself (78 percent were male) or herself at a rising rate in the first years after 1929. The rate did not drop too much until the war. Reasons included "ill health" (30 to 50 percent), "business failures and financial difficulties" (10 to 17 percent in the early thirties) and a smaller percentage described as "employment difficulties." Economic difficulties and general despondency was given as the key to the 1933 peak in the suicide rate. Alcoholism, often described as another form of self destruction, was another depression aggravated phenomenon but Los Angeles with a 1940 estimated rate of 1,490 chronic alcoholics per 100,000 adults still had a lower rate than San Francisco with 3,191 alcoholics per 100,000, but a higher rate than New York with 1,023 per 100,000.[50]

Suicide was only a critical and more intense expression of the health problems of the city. Levels of hygiene, medical care, economic stability, emotional stability all played their part in a negative fashion. Mental illness tended to increase. The Los Angeles Council of Social Agencies quoted a member agency to the effect that the "current financial depression and . . . insecurity of life in general have made serious in-roads on the mental health of an alarming number of our applicants. . . . the majority of the serious cases have had to go without care."[51] Health services were less available and less used during the depression. Lack of funds meant the cutting of medical and dental care. City funds for public health dropped in the early depression years with an increase in funds starting again in 1933, but not at the pace of the 1920's.[52]

Crime rose as the depression unfolded, more a product of community expansion in the prior prosperity period. As the depression years continued the crime rate decreased somewhat because of a lower in-migration despite continued joblessness and low income. The picture is not completely clear due to inadequate statistics.[53]

Of course, the majority still had their jobs and perhaps their mood is summed up by diarist Ernest C. Steele, school teacher, writing of 1930: "it may have been a year of depression, speaking generally, but I can not say that it has been exactly that for me."[54] Yet even those on jobs had reason to fear, for the unemployed were anxious to step into their jobs. An allegation made to the City Council by M.P. Lloyd, against the Owl Drug Company asserted that when gross sales of their soda counter fell below a certain fixed amount, the Company decreed the man operating the counter "shall be replaced by women at $16 a week."[55]

The depression penetrated every aspect of the life of the city as its effects brought unemployment, poverty, hunger, and insecurity to tens of thousands and caused transformations in family, housing, crime, health and other conditions. Desperation was on the rise affecting the employed as well as the unemployed. It was toward the city, its leadership, government and agencies, private and public, that the people turned for help.

FOOTNOTES

1. Los Angeles Times, October 24, 1929 (eastern banker); October 9, 1929 (Jesse Jones); October 23 (oil well).

2. Ibid., October 22, 1929; the "manifest destiny" phrase appeared in a Times letter by a former Spring Street Association secretary on April 11, 1969. The name Los Angeles Stock Exchange appeared in 1900; prior to that it was called the Los Angeles Oil Exchange.

3. Ibid., October 30, 1929 (Kraft death); October 22, 1929 (margin traders); October 25, 1929 ("madhouse").

4. Los Angeles Record, October 26, 1929. Los Angeles Times, October 25, 1929 (Will Rogers). See Irving Bernstein, The Lean Years (Boston, 1960) for national characterization of the deficiencies of the prosperous Twenties.

5. Los Angeles Times, December 31, 1929.

6. Literary Digest, Vol. 102, No. 2055, September 7, 1929, pp. 19-20. Business Week, No. 32, April 16, 1930, p. 13.

7. Diaries of Selena Gray, Galt Ingram, Marshall Stimson and Ernest K. Steele at Huntington Library, San Marino, California.

8. Direct source for my general computation that 113,816 residents of the city were stockholders in 1930 was Edwin Burk Cox, Trends in the Distribution of Stock Ownership (Philadelphia: 1963). The one out of eight adults calculation is his. The adult population for Los Angeles in 1930 was 910,530 - that is those over 20, (though 21 is the correct breaking point, the census only gives the 20 cut off) Fifteenth Census, U.S. (Washington, D.C.: 1930), Vol. III, Pt. 1, p. 248. The New York Stock Exchange is unable to provide share ownership information prior to 1952. (Letter to author from New York Stock Exchange, June 19, 1970.)

9. Robert S. and Helen Merrell Lynd, Middletown in Transition: A Study in Cultural Conflicts (New York, 1937) p. 7.

10. Los Angeles Citizen, December 13, 1929. The report on the conference was not given in the Los Angeles Times! Quotations here are from the Citizen, account by J.W. Buzzell, Secretary of the Central Labor Council.

11. Ibid., January 3, 1930.

12. Los Angeles City Council Minutes, Volume 213, January 30, 1930, p. 768.

13. Ibid., Volume 213, January 27, 1930, p. 664.

14. Louis B. and Richard S. Perry, A History of the Los Angeles Labor Movement, 1911-1941 (Los Angeles, 1963), pp. 230-236. This volume is source for much of the data presented on the city's unions.

15. Security-First National Bank of Los Angeles, Monthly Letter, Volume 9 No. 2 and No. 3, March, April, 1930.

16. James J. Hannah in his unpublished dissertation, "Urban Reaction to the Great Depression, 1929-1933," (Berkeley, 1956), estimates the time of realization of a full-scale depression as early summer of 1930.

17. An interesting evaluation of the differences in unemployment counts during the depression is to be found in Russell A. Nixon and Paul A. Samuelson, "Estimates of Unemployment in the United States," Review of Economic Statistics, XXII, No. 3 (August, 1940), pp. 101-111. They stress the difficulties of "unavailability and possible unreliability of statistical data" and the variations in the definition of unemployment. Broadus Mitchell, The Depression Decade From New Era Through New Deal 1929-1941 (New York, 1947), asks and answers: ". . . Should wife and young people in the family forced to look for work when the father lost his job, be included in the labor force? (The answer to this would seem to be yes, an instance of the fact that unemployment causes unemployment.)" p. 93. Broadus Mitchell, op. cit., pp. 91-92; Fifteenth Census of the United States (Washington, 1930) Unemployment, Volume 11, pages 160-162. Mitchell's volume warns against the "fallible classifications" of this special census which did not classify many as unemployed who were.

18. Jacqueline Kasun, Some Social Aspects of Business Cycles in the Los Angeles Area, 1920-1950 (The Haynes Foundation, Los Angeles, 1954), pp. 29, 32. This study is an invaluable source.

19. The Los Angeles Citizen, December 26, 1930.

20. The New York Times, December 28, 1930.

21. Fifteenth Census of the U.S. - 1930 - Unemployment, General Report, Volume II (Washington, 1932). Male increase in unemployment was 100 percent, female 102 percent, pp. 494-495.

22. Ibid., p. 378, 382.

23. Ibid., pp. 494-495.

24. Ibid., Security-First National Bank, Monthly Letter, April 1, 1931.

25. Fifteenth Census - pp. 494-495, the age breakdown is on page 388.

26. Los Angeles Times, March 18, 22, 1936.

27. S.O. Harper papers, University of Wyoming, Box 2. Letter from Frank Thompson, 5116 Irvington Pl. L.A. October 20, 1932. (Harper was the Ass't Chief Engineer on the Boulder Dam project.)

28. Ibid., Box 3, Letter dated April 9, 1934 from Harold H. Kelley to S.O. Harper.

29. Ibid., Box 2, Harper to Robin A. Gray, August 8, 1932.

30. Los Angeles City Council Minutes, Volume 217, May 27, 1930, p. 285; Volume 222, November 18, 1930, p. 293; Volume 226, May 11, 1931, 527.

31. Los Angeles Times, June 11, 1931.

32. Los Angeles Examiner, October 10, 1932.

33. Los Angeles City Council Minutes, Volume 227, June 30, 1931, p. 799; Volume 224, February 16, 1931, p. 437; Volume 223, January 22, 1931, p. 747.

34. Kasun, op. cit., pp. 51, 52, 54.

35. Ibid., p. 56.

36. Los Angeles Times, July 22, 1957.

37. Los Angeles City Council Minutes, (hereinafter called Minutes)Volume 235, August 2, 1932, p. 589; Volume 238, December 28, 1932, p. 33; Volume 232, February 4, 1932, p. 341.

38. Kasun, op. cit., pp. 58, 59.

39. Fifty Years in Retrospect, First Swedish Baptist Church of Los Angeles (found in Huntington Library).

40. Kasun, op. cit., p. 59.

41. Diary, Mary Elizabeth (no last name) (handwritten diary in possession of author), January 19, January 5, 1932.

42. Robert M. Fogelson, The Fragmented Metropolis: Los Angeles, 1850-1930 (Cambridge, 1967), p. 183. No one can work in Los Angeles studies without consulting this encyclopedic work.

43. Diary, Mary Elizabeth, January 2, 19, 1932.

44. Los Angeles Times, September 7, 1933.

45. Council Minutes, Volume 223, January 22, 1931, p. 747.

46. New York Times, December 25, 1932.

47. Andrew Hamilton and John B. Jackson, UCLA On The Move During Fifty Golden Years, 1919-1969 (Los Angeles, 1969), p. 73.

48. Ibid., p. 63, p. 65.

49. Los Angeles Illustrated Daily News, December 16, 1930.

50. Kasun, op. cit., pp. 105-110, 114.

51. Quoted p. 102, Kasun, op. cit.

52. Ibid., p. 116.

53. Ibid., Ch. VI.

54. 1930 Diary, Ernest C. Steele, Huntington Library.

55. Council Minutes, Volume 223, January 12, 1931, p. 557.

CHAPTER 2.

FIRST AID IN THE CITY

John C. Porter, son of an Iowa preacher-farmer, was elected mayor of Los Angeles in June, 1929. Seventh in a family of ten, his education and background did little to prepare him for the leadership of America's fifth largest city either in normal times, or as it entered its severest depression. Attorney Frank P. Doherty expressed the fear to Senator Hiram W. Johnson that the new Mayor's "knowledge of city government in general is most mediocre aside from what he learns at Sunday School or gathers from the Bible."[1] Porter's background included education in grammar schools and the Los Angeles Business College, work as a farmer, fifteen years as a railroad telegrapher and the ownership of an automobile wrecking and accessory business. (He was perhaps the first person in the used car business to become mayor of an important American city.)

Neutral in the election between William G. Bonelli and Porter, the Los Angeles _Times_ noted that Porter had "practically no experience in city government or public business."[2] The new mayor had served as a prominent member of an active 1928 grand jury, a post he declared useful to one entering the Mayor's office, for he "will know exactly where to move to clean up the city." He claimed that the grand jury experience had been one in which he "learned very thoroughly the structure of this city."[3]

In a portentous victory statement Porter invoked God "our friend in the past [who] will further direct us;" one supporter hailed the result as an "act of Providence." The religious aura was not out of place, for he had won with Church Brotherhood backing as well as support from the "drys", parts of the labor movement and the Los Angeles Record. Prior to his defeat, Bonelli had seen the handwriting on the wall, and announced that he himself, did "not claim any monopoly of good Christian morals."[4]

Porter did not only win with God's help, he also stressed the fight against crime. He saw his victory as making Los Angeles "the first city of the United States to fully endorse the President's law enforcement program."[5] In triumphal appearances in the weeks after his election, Porter assured the YMCA Brotherhood Club that he would "make a stand against crime in Los Angeles," which he felt had an advantage over the other cities that "are so full of foreigners that it seems difficult to make any headway."[6] To the "greatest applause" at a meeting in the Shrine Auditorium he promised to make law enforcement the main aim of his administration, especially enforcement of the Prohibition Amendment, "if the so-called best citizens would refrain from patronizing the bootlegger."[7]

In his first weeks in office he struck the business and economy chords with directness by cutting $500 from an ordinance appropriating $2,000 for floodlighting the City Hall during the Elks' convention.[8] "I intend my administration to be one based upon strictly business methods, which in the end is bound to be the most successful way to operate a city government." To this Porter added the observation that the Mayor's office is "only the presidency of a large corporation."[9] He soon sold his auto business on Main Street, and brought his son Lee into City Hall as his secretary.[10] In another early move, Porter changed the locks on the City Hall doors, explaining that it was good business practice he had learned in his business.[11]

Association with the new President, Hoover, who had come into office some three months earlier than the mayor, was a point of special pride with Porter. Not only did he back the law enforcement emphasis of the inaugural address, he also went on record backing the concept of "integrity of public officials with honesty and efficiency in all their public acts [and] an economical and businesslike administration."[12] Thus, when hard times came to Los Angeles, it was quite natural for the Iowan who became Mayor to look to the Iowan who became President.

The historian, Albert Romasco, could have had no better model than John C. Porter for the statement that "businessmen, bankers, mayors, governors, and congressmen, social workers, agricultural and labor leaders--all these men and the institutions they represented--looked to the president for their cues."[13] In prosperity or depression, John C. Porter was ready to follow Herbert Hoover. Hoover accepted this responsibility of leadership.

When the President appealed to the governors to undertake street and public building programs "speeded up and adjusted in such fashion as to further employment,"[14] and then followed it with an appeal to the mayors, Porter was quick to respond with a public telegram pledging Los Angeles' cooperation "to the end that unemployment may be minimized." The Mayor promised that "commencing at once [there would be] a mammoth program of improvement work which, during the next year, will be far advanced." There were exact plans pledging $100 million in city projects; to beef up the figure, Porter added a sum of $200 million relating to the Colorado River water project! (There is no record of the city ever spending such sums in the years which followed.) The pledge to the President emphasized that the funds would go directly to labor and materials; none would stay with the middleman and the contractor whose profit and overhead, Porter charged, usually absorbed 25 percent of the funds.

In the months after the telegram to the President, Porter called numerous meetings on the problem of unemployment. In December he appeared at the city-wide conference mentioned earlier. In one urgent message, the Mayor told the Council that "there has come to my attention the matter of unemployment throughout Los Angeles, and that no adequate provisions have been made for the alleviation of this condition." That statement was made four months after the public telegram. The Council was asked to back up a County allocation of funds, with an additional $60,000 to build anti-fire trails and other works in the Santa Monica mountains, adding that, "this money, if made available, could be used at once to relieve a critical situation of unemployment, and at the same time be beneficial in helping to abate a very serious fire hazard."[16] In a communication to the Council a month later, Porter stressed that "the primary need of relief is for unemployed who have reached the age of fifty years or more." He asked the Council to investigate how the city could help.[17]

Porter's awareness of the unemployment problem and the deepening depression became a constant and unavoidable one. The Los Angeles City Council was also spending more of its time on aspects of the situation. In the decade of the twenties, unemployment was rarely introduced into the Council's sessions; beginning with the 1930 meetings it became a matter of increasing concern. A Works Progress Administration analysis of the number of occasions unemployment was a Council business indicates that by 1931, the highpoint year, it was on the agenda 297 times! (See Table 3).

TABLE 3--Unemployment as an Agenda Item at Sessions of the Los Angeles City Council--1927-1937.

Year	Times Discussed
1927	9
1928	19
1929	11
1930	74
1931	297
1932	107
1933	66
1934	22
1935	14
1936	13
1937	22

Many of the proposals on unemployment which came before the City Council were work schemes, invitations to planning meetings and conferences, individual job requests, complaints from unemployed unable to pay their taxes, requests for funds to aid individuals or causes, and applications for permits to hold rallies and parades. There were a host of proposals to create jobs by enlarging the city payrolls, establishing shorter work days and weeks, inaugurating a special employment bureau for veterans, moving transient unemployed into camps or back to their original states--the more than 400 proposals of the years 1930 through 1933 covered a wide variety of hopes, schemes and plans.[18] The drop in proposals after 1933 can be attributed to the development of federal work programs, a failure to obtain much satisfaction from the City Council, and the expansion of other forms of assistance and relief.

The standard handling of such matters by the City Council was a polite hearing, followed by referral to a committee of the Council, or a commission or department of the city. Often the request was just filed with no action. It is surprising how quickly the questions relating to the depression came to the City Council. It was looked upon, in the words of the City Charter, as "the governing body of the city."[19] But to what avail? It was a body of fifteen men beset by problems beyond them. Their classic dilemmas, like those of other cities across the nation, paralyzed their action in the face of the depression's onslaught. Mayor Porter, in the same bind, rode horses in opposite directions. In his annual message at the start of 1931, he claimed credit for reduction of the number of the city's unemployed by 1,000 (at a time when the national census reported that the city had more than 100,000 jobless!). Yet he stressed that the city must abandon public improvement projects to lighten the burden on the taxpayers. The heroic telegram's promises to the President of thirteen months earlier were forgotten. In the spirit of economy, he boasted that his policy of not filling vacated city positions reduced costs and personnel without discharging workers.[20]

This conflict in approaches was characteristic of the city throughout the depression period. The City Council was besieged by contrary demands--enlarge the city's printing plant and give more work, versus don't take away work from private printers; keep costs of city government down, versus establish a city financed employment bureau; a proposal to "speed up the starting of any future work for which plans have been approved," versus the abandoning of projects to save money.[21] An ironic request to the City Council asked that "all public improvements be either abandoned or delayed until business conditions show an improvement." The city was told not to give work to the unemployed--the more pressing problem, the request implied, was the tax paying property owner.[22]

Often the entire question of employment in the city became entangled in acrimonious debate whether non-residents should work on city projects. A non-resident was anyone living beyond the city's border. Mayor Porter, in asking for an ordinance requiring at least one year's city residence before employment, stressed the necessity of the action "at this time when so many citizens are out of employment" adding that its passage would be "for the interest of the city government."[23] To give weight to his request, the Mayor made a rare personal appearance at the Council meeting. Such was the intensity of feeling on the question, that the naming of H.C. Fremming, a deputy state labor commissioner and president of the Long Beach AFL

Central Labor Council, to head a county registration of unemployed in the county's unincorporated areas, was protested because a Los Angeles city resident was not given the post.[24] On another occasion employment of the out of town relatives of city residents was protested.[25] The Council finally passed an ordinance which backed the hiring of city residents before non-residents on all work done by the city or by contractors operating with city funds. Only American citizenship was made a mandatory prerequisite for the workers.[26]

There was a plethora of other ideas--proposing that only city taxpayers be employed by the city, that women as second income producers be fired or that persons with the largest number of dependents receive priority job treatment (even if this approach favored a woman). Latter day Luddite attitudes often were presented to the City Council. "Whereas, the development of labor-saving machinery and abundant electrical energy is constantly reducing the demand for man power, thereby forcing large groups of men into the ranks of the unemployed" began one Councilman's resolution calling for manual labor. Another Councilman was more specific and urged that

> contractors must use men in place of our so called labor saving machines, even though it may increase to some extent the cost of the work. This is to apply to ditch diggers, pavement cutters and the like.

Wherever possible, said another communication, use pick and shovel and replace steam shovels with men and abolish labor saving devices.[27]

The city's Mayor and City Council presented a picture of inadequacy and confusion in the early stages of the depression. Beset by urgent and pressing matters, realizing the need for action, their reactions can only be described as thrashing around the problems--not coping with them. It would be unfair to characterize the Mayor and the Council as more inadequate than prior administrations of the city. There was a tradition of inadequacy. A scholar of the city's 1920's, James C. Findley, characterized the leadership of that decade which ended with the city's population passing the million mark as that "which tended to be, if not provincial, at least unfamiliar with the responsibilities of overseeing the direction of a major metropolitan center."[28]

Perhaps the city's phenomenal growth in the first three decades of the century must be offered as partial explanation for the failure of its leadership. No American city has come up the twentieth century census ladder with the speed of Los Angeles. In 1900 the city at 102,479, was in a class with such hopefuls as Memphis, Omaha, St. Joseph, Fall River, Patterson, New Haven and Syracuse. Of the group, only Los Angeles reached the million mark and became one of the largest cities in the nation. It was, perhaps, too much and too soon for the municipal leadership. The normal problems were large enough for a city that multiplied a dozen times in thirty years--the problems of the depression were overwhelming.[29]

Los Angeles did not stand alone in its inability to meet its problems--but essentially she was one with most cities in those fateful days.[30] Both Mayors Porter and Frank L. Shaw, who followed him, grappled with the problems for nearly a decade. Both looked to

Washington for direction. Porter was anxious to apply the voluntarism answer that Hoover offered. (Shaw's Washington had a different president and a different philosophy.) The need of local voluntary action against the depression was the essence of the series of urgent national conferences the President called in the fall of 1929. He favored expansion of construction and maintenance work and no reduction in payrolls or pay envelopes as part of the national effort. Industrial and labor leaders were called upon to join in the common effort; states, counties, local governments and cities were "to fight their own battles in their own communities" in the war against human want. The President hailed the "local communities [which] through their voluntary agencies have assumed the duty of relieving individual distress and are being generously supported by the public."[31] Local voluntarism would be the answer.

"Our great American experiment," Hoover said, "has demonstrated that the people will of their initiative take care of progress if the Government can remove abuse and help put signs on the road."[32] Successful relief, according to his approach, required one "to mobilize and organize the infinite number of agencies of self help in the community." This, said the President, "has been the American way of relieving distress among our own people and the country is successfully meeting its problems in the American way today."[33] The President's estimate was too optimistic. One had to go no farther than the city of Los Angeles to find out wherein he fell short.

The classic local response to need was the Community Chest; the city of Los Angeles had been part of this movement since 1924. A pre-Christmas, 1929, appeal from the Board of Social Service Commissioners to the City Council that the city increase its contribution to the Community Chest was one of the first depression pleas.[34]

The Los Angeles Community Chest derived its funds from the public in an annual drive, and, in addition, received appropriations from both the City Council and the County Board of Supervisors. In the face of its rising burdens, the Chest leaders introduced an economy drive in their own operations. All salaries in the 100 affiliated Chest agencies were cut 25 percent in the 1930-1933 period. The claim was made that only 4 1/2 percent was spent on administrative costs.[35]

Funds were difficult to raise in the depression years. More and more potential donors became impoverished or even recipients. "Preparations are in the making for the annual unpopular community chest campaign," lamented the New York Times correspondent in Los Angeles in 1931.[36] In that year $3,341,000 was raised; in 1932 there was a drop of $414,000 in contributions; in 1933 there was an additional decline of $223,000. As early as the Spring of 1932, a State hearing on unemployment was told that Los Angeles' Community Chest funds were "practically exhausted."[37] In 1933 the Chest officials explained to the public that their needs were still great, as none of the federal relief expenditures were allocated to their agencies.

A 1930-1931 breakdown of Chest allocations reported that $705,758 of the $3,041,638 which it collected went directly to family relief agencies. The Catholic Welfare Bureau received the largest single sum, $192,926, or 27.3 percent of the total alloted to family agencies. The Salvation Army's share of $150,849 was 21.4 percent; the Jewish Social Service Bureau was third in allotments with $87,393, 12.4 percent. The full breakdown is in Table 4.

The figures represented a substantial allotment over the pre-depression figures for family relief agencies--$511,008 in the 1928-29 period--but the contrast, in light of sharply increased needs, only underlines the inadequacies.[39]

A California Unemployment Commission study made in 1932 evaluated the Chest's share of the depression burden in Los Angeles in the two year period of 1929-1930 and 1931-32. The Chest had raised 5.7 percent of the funds; the governmental funds had accounted for 94.3 percent! The Chest's inadequacy was a national calamity. Jacob Billikopf, distinguished Philadelphia social worker, warned his colleagues that

> we will be guilty of duplicity; we will be betraying the interest of the millions of unemployed who expect us to articulate their needs, if in our vast enthusiasm to fill our community chests, we should give the impression, directly or even inferentially, that all a community has to do is raise its chest quota and the unemployed will be provided for.[40]

Los Angeles' Community Chest effort was in line with the national failure. Allen T. Burns, executive director of the national movement, admitted "that as a whole they play a minor part in relief."[41]

Parallel to the Community Chest drive in the city were campaigns sanctioned by the Department of Social Service, which had been created in 1913 to set standards for solicitations. Agencies not part of the

TABLE 4--Community Chest Allotments To Family Relief Agencies in Los Angeles For The Fiscal Year Ending October 31, 1931.[38]

Agency	1930-31			
	Total	Percent of Total	Regular allotment	Emergency allotment
Total	$705,758 69	100.0	$523,820 85	$181,937 84
Assistance League, Good Samaritan	$19,986 75	2.8	$7,270 00	$12,716 34
Assistance League, Wilmington	4,926 75	.7	4,926 75	----------
British Benevolent Society	11,990 00	1.7	11,990 00	----------
Catholic Welfare Bureau, Los Angeles	192,926 93	27.3	141,088 50	51,838 43
Catholic Welfare Bureau, San Pedro	7,579 05	1.1	7,579 05	----------
Family Welfare Association	59,163 65	8.4	22,768 00	36,395 65
Jewish Social Service Bureau	87,393 99	12.4	67,450 00	19,943 99
North Hollywood Woman's Club	400 00	.1	400 00	----------
Philanthropy and Civics Club	17,027 37	2.4	7,100 00	9,927 37
Salvation Army, all relief branches	150,849 00	21.4	115,364 00	35,485 00
San Fernando Relief Association	900 00	.1	900 00	----------
Van Nuys Woman's Club	242 43		242 43	----------
Volunteers of America	83,543 06	11.8	67,912 00	15,631 06
West Los Angeles Welfare Association	1,285 12	.2	1,285 12	----------
Parent-Teacher Association	67,545 00	9.6	67,545 00	----------
Food Conservation Warehouse	----------	----------	----------	----------

Report And Recommendations p. 354.

Chest collected on their own; on occasion even Chest agencies ran separate campaigns. Major voluntary relief work in the city was carried on by a variety of groups, Chest and non-Chest. Their important work needs detailed examination.

Religious groups in Los Angeles had a long history of family welfare aid before the Great Depression. The Hebrew Benevolent Society, born in 1854, "was Los Angeles' original welfare organization" according to recent history of the Jews in this city.[42] James J. Hannah's national urban study asserted that the churches not only "played a prominent role in the depression," they also had the best organized welfare agencies in many places which "bore the brunt of administration until the municipal departments were organized to take over the task."[43]

The Catholic Welfare Bureau was the largest non-governmental family relief agency in Los Angeles. In 1928-29, a prosperity year, the Catholic body gave material relief to 2,957 families; in 1929-30, 3,211 families were aided, an increase of 254, or 8.6 percent. The 1930-31 figure nearly tripled as the Catholic Welfare Bureau aided 9,172 families for a 185.6 percent increase. The relationship between sums raised and the average allocation can be seen in this table:

TABLE 5. Catholic Welfare Bureau Relief Expenditures, Los Angeles County--1928-1931.

Year	Expenditures	Average Per Case
1928-29	$63,719.00	$21.55
1929-30	62,501.00	19.46
1930-31	112,883.16	12.31

By April 30, 1932, the average dropped to $8.83 per family unit. Of 10,849 families aided, some 2,246 were considered major relief cases.

The Catholic Welfare Bureau, faced with limited funds and rising demands, transferred many cases to other agencies when governmental emergency relief became available in the winter of 1931. Originally geared to cash allotments only, the economic pressures forced the Bureau to send many to the Food Conservation Warehouse (to be described later) for direct issuance of food and other commodities.[44]

There were many days in 1932 when the Bureau was forced by early afternoon, to close its doors to the large waiting crowd. Those already admitted for interviews were more than the hard pressed staff could handle.[45] The agency reported that it was faced with a trebling case load, at a time when its funds only doubled. In an attempt to spread the funds further, the Bureau reduced "the food allowances 10 percent for American families, and 25 percent for Mexican families." Differing food standards was offered as the rationale.[46]

A maximum of $25 per month was alloted for rent, this often, only if eviction was threatened. When necessary, $5 per month was given for light, water and heat in the winter. The Saint Vincent de Paul Society, a church related agency, backed by the Community Chest spent twice its allocation yearly in a desperate attempt to aid those in need of temporary relief. In 1930 the Society aided 2,020 families; in 1931 the aid had gone to 3,644 families.

Church poor boxes and de Paul Society members were the source of funds from 100 parish conferences, 50 of which were in the city of

Los Angeles. Like other agencies, the Catholic Welfare Bureau found itself deluged by its problems.[47]

The problems of indigent Jews in Los Angeles were handled by the Jewish Social Service Bureau, part of the Jewish Federation. The Jewish Bureau's aid program was geared to those unwilling to apply for County aid. An adequate budget was a goal of the agency which presented a typical family allotment schedule for a month. [Table 6.] The claim was made that it was one "which does not fall seriously below those standards the families are accustomed to maintain in normal times."

TABLE 6--Typical Family Relief Budget of the Jewish Social Service Bureau

Food for family of five (man, wife, 3 children 5 to 15 years of age	$39.55 per month
Rent (maximum)	25.00 per month
Gas and light ($5 in winter)	2.00 per month
Incidentals	5.00 per month
Clothing as needed.[48]	

The JSSB offered special aid through a Self-Support Fund which, for example, helped an unemployed chiropodist reestablish an office, or aided refugees from Nazi Germany who did not meet the County's residence requirement. A milk distribution for poor children was a daily occurrence for between 300 to 400 in Boyle Heights.[49] The Jewish agency was motivated by traditional desires to "face our employment situation as a people and solve our problems within the group."[50]

In the early days of the depression in Los Angeles a new organization for aid was developed for those not covered by the Catholic and Jewish family agencies. Called the Family Welfare Agency, it was geared for those who "fell between all the social-work stools." In the past, agencies such as the Red Cross, the Travelers' Aid and the Children's Protective Association tried with difficulty to pick up the slack. Formed by the above three agencies plus the American Legion, Assistance League, International Institute, Philanthropy and Civics Club and Volunteers of America, the association received Community Chest backing. In 1930-31 it was given $59,163.65, some 8.4 percent of the family relief allocations. In the words of Survey it was given "a place in the social-work sun."[51]

Put bluntly, the new agency was to be the central family welfare agency for needy Protestant families formerly aided only by the Volunteers of America, the Salvation Army and some smaller organizations. Typical of the groups was the Assistance League of Hollywood which aided "people who lost their savings in investments, and workers formerly employed in the motion picture industry and clerks and salesmen." The League reported that it spent $3,832 in November, 1931, on 160 major cases, an average of $23.95 per case for the month, "an average higher than any other agency in the city."[52]

Besides the network of family relief activities conducted in the name of the three basic faiths of Los Angeles, there were a host of subsidiary groups, individuals and various institutions offering aid. Oldtimers invariably recall Aimee Semple McPherson and the Angelus Temple where she dispensed evangelism, and the needy found food available. Her husband, David Hutton, was introduced at the City Council on January 12, 1932, and "made a brief address, placing the services of the said Temple at the disposition of the Council in connection with unemployment relief."[53]

The contributions to the wants of an average poverty stricken person are recorded in the seamstress' humble diary for the year 1932. Mary Elizabeth (no last name) tells of visits to Good Will, Community Industries and the Volunteers where she obtained sums of money and worked in return. On the day before Christmas she tells of "a lovely Basket from the Examiner [and] 2 bags of food from the Salvation Army," enough "to last for many days." The life of many in the city is in her daily jottings about occasional sewing jobs, work at an eating place in return for meals, buying as inexpensively as possible, and, at times, aiding others. Her closing item for the year is tribute in part to private agencies:

> It has been a year of great depression but with it all I have gotten through nicely and I have been able to help others some when they were in distress.[54]

The Mary Elizabeths of Los Angeles who were not on relief, were not only helped by the private charities and the obtaining of odd jobs, they also found special places such as Clifford E. Clinton's Cafeteria, that offered a meal for 5 cents to those who could pay. The destitute or those who could pay only a penny were given a bowl of brown rice over which was ladled vegetable soup fortified with vitamins and minerals. Years later, Clinton recalled:

> We became known as the "penny cafeteria." People began to line up until it pained us to see little

families waiting anywhere from one-half to three hours just to get a meal.

He estimated that this policy of feeding the needy in a basement dining room brought 10,000 nonpaying customers in the first 90 days. He had to establish a second cafeteria to avoid pushing out his paying customers and going bankrupt. Established in 1931, the Clifton plan fed some 1,000,000 meals in the crisis years to persons without funds, and operated a credit system for others. He also tried to offer free employment and housing services. It was his proud claim that "no person has ever been turned away hungry, regardless of the state of his funds." In his way Clifford Clinton became a symbol of compassion in this city. He tried to fill the hunger gap that kept widening in the years before massive federal aid entered the picture.[55]

A special place in the private relief picture was held by the Los Angeles Food Conservation Warehouse. Mrs. Mary Covell, head of the Midnight Mission, obtained a former Southern Pacific warehouse, rent free, for a year and opened it in August 1931 as a center for the receipt of nonsalable food surpluses to be given to the needy unemployed. Donations flowed in from farmers, the Bean Growers Association, wealthy donors, "even bootleggers, unwittingly, contributed their share; for sugar in ton lots confiscated by the Federal authorities in their liquor raids, was turned over," and chain grocers put barrels in their stores to solicit food from their customers. As many as 2,500 families a week received supplies from the warehouse. Only families certified by family welfare agencies were eligible, and in many cases firemen in private cars delivered groceries to indigent families. Agencies sent applicants for at least 50 percent of their needed food supplies.

The consensus of the participating agencies was that "without the warehouse they could not have pulled through the winter of 1931-32". From November 1931 through May 1932, some 15,649 different families received supplies at the conservation Warehouse. Of the $73,475 worth of food distributed in that five month period donations accounted for some 32 percent, some 68 percent had been purchased. Community Chest and agencies' funds had picked up most of the tab.[56]

The homeless individual, a wanderer from another area, often ineligible under the residence rules of private and public relief agencies, always on the verge of desperation, with scant familial or social ties, stood as a gaunt symbol of the depression. A City Council resolution, considering a Municipal Lodging House, spoke of the homeless as:

> the great army of unfortunate who traverse our highways and roam our streets, scantily clad and without sufficient food or adequate shelter, is a menace to Society, and at once a challenge to our civilization...[57]

This note of fear was echoed by the city's Board of Health Commission decrying the homeless as "a constant police menace and because of the deplorable unsanitary conditions prevailing in some places where they find sleeping quarters, they constitute a serious health menace as well." The Board's answer was the establishment of work camps, adding quickly that "this discussion does not in any sense refer to our own residents who are at this time out of employment."[58]

The first step for the homeless in the city was registration with the Los Angeles Municipal Service Bureau for Homeless Men, founded in 1928, as a part of the Social Service Department. The original concept was three days work in city parks paid for in meals, maintenance and six dollars in cash. Then the transient was told to get a job or a railroad ticket home. This initial plan was discontinued when the City Attorney ruled that the City Charter made it illegal for men to get relief by working for the city. New procedures continued the three day meals and lodging during which time they were told they must get work and a place of their own to live. Failing this, they were told to go back home or anywhere else they could find work. By the Spring of 1932 the three day period was extended to seven days. Part of the termination ceremonies was the warning that the police had an active vagrancy squad, and that the homeless man was in danger of being arrested. The City Council voted funds at various times to finance departures from the city.[50]

The rising tide of such men can be gauged from the Bureau's registration figures:

1929	-	6,902
1930	-	19,515
1931	-	39,386

Thus the leap was better than five fold in two years. We have monthly figures for the period December 1931 through June 1932 with recurrent registrants listed separately.

TABLE 7--Registrants at the Los Angeles Municipal Bureau for Homeless Men.

Month	Total	New	Recurrent
-	31,272	20,516	10,756
Dec. 1931	4,265	2,791	1,474
Jan. 1932	4,662	2,688	1,974
Feb. 1932	5,732	3,380	2,352
Mar. 1932	4,988	3,358	1,630
Apr. 1932	4,138	2,890	1,248
May 1932	3,761	2,723	1,038
June 1932	3,726	2,686	1,040

[60]

Conditions on arrival at the Bureau were far from attractive. In 1931 the operation was still on its 1928 allotment budget, though the traffic had increased five fold. Medical examinations were hasty--primarily to detect veneral and communicable diseases and to determine ability to work. Conditions at the facility were presented at a hearing in Sacramento:

> At present, the Bureau is located in the basement of the San Fernando Building. This basement has only an artificial ventilation system. When the Bureau was first established, it occupied offices on an upper floor. The management of the building was forced to discontinue this arrnagement, because "the patrons of the building resented riding with 'bums' in the same elevator.

Of the health and sanitation facilities:

> The Bureau has no delousing plant, but uses that of the Union Rescue Mission, a small non-Chest agency, or the Police Department. Not all men in need of this service are able to obtain it, because of limited space and time; and the spread of vermin in overcrowded conditions is serious to health and morale.

It was a Bureau operating without allowances for carfare, meals or emergency relief for men not assigned to agencies. "Frequently old men, exhausted by fatigue and hunger, must walk to their assignments." Funds were spread so thin that carfare was given only to the handicapped going to medical clinics. Often hungry men just coming into the Bureau missed the meals because of bureaucratic rules.[61]

Most of the homeless men in Los Angeles came to the Midnight Mission, the largest shelter in the city. It had as many as 300 beds in one of its dormitories. Under its roof one could obtain free meals, lodging, baths, laundry, barber service and clothing. The claim was made that temporary placements were made by a Mission employment bureau. Daily religious services were held "to rehabilitate men through service and inspirational sermons." Able-bodied transients were given two meals a day, and were required to work four hours a day in return, while three meals a day were given to the incapicated who were not required to do compensatory work. In the Spring of 1932 the transients, as in the city's facility, were allowed to stay for seven days, instead of the prior three days. Exceptions were made for the ill and those waiting for expected work; they were allowed to stay as long as two weeks. After the Midnight Mission stay, the men were expected to leave the city, but it is obvious that there was no certainty that this happened.[62]

In the two years 1931 and 1932 the Midnight Mission supplied more than 800,000 meals and 330,000 nights of lodging.[63] Funding came from the Community Chest and also from the county and city governments. The City Council, by a unanimous vote, met a deficit of $2,500 in 1931.[64] Much food was donated by local cafeterias, markets, butchers, millers, bakers and grocers; blankets were given by the Los Angeles Police Department.[65] The Mission's sanitary conditions passed minimal City Health Department standards but pressure of the Social Service Commission, the Bureau of Housing and Sanitation, Health, Fire and Police Departments finally forced a clean up, in partial answer to the complaints of the homeless men protesting "300 room mates sleeping in one dormitory."[66]

Other groups aiding the homeless men were the Salvation Army, the Saint Vincent de Paul Society, the Jewish Social Service Bureau (which maintained a three to seven days residence called the Jewish Home for Wayfarers), and the Union Rescue Mission, which "allowed them to sleep on benches, on chairs in the chapel, and on the floor."[67]

Such were the initial attempts to cope with the ever rising number of unemployed, their families and the homeless men. It was voluntarism at its high point, a continuation under very difficult conditions of the methods of a more prosperous time. It was based on the belief that all that was required was the Community Chest stepping up its annual campaign, the people of the three great faiths digging down deeper to help their own, and the thin line of professional agencies like the Salvation Army, the Midnight Mission and the Travellers' Aid holding the line.

Under the new pressures of the Great Depression new ideas like the Food Conservation Warehouse would break through, or a troubled and effective figure like Clifford Clinton would appear, but basically the hunger increased and the homeless were still told to "move on", "get a job", or "go home." Failure was written up and down the line and the city's torment, part of a national malaise, did not lessen. A people becoming poorer and poorer was being asked to give more and more as the need rose and the resources became slimmer. Voluntarism was hard pressed and failing in the city, yet new and valiant attempts were being developed in City Hall and among municipal employees.

FOOTNOTES

1. Letter, Frank P. Doherty to Hiram W. Johnson, June 5, 1929, Johnson papers, Bancroft Library.

2. Los Angeles *Times*, June 3, 1929, has his full platform and a short biography of Porter.

3. *Ibid.*, February 26, 1929.

4. *Ibid.*, June 5, 1929 (victory statement); June 6, 1929 ("Act of Providence"); Doherty telegram to Johnson, (estimate of forces behind Porter); Los Angeles *Times*, June 4, 1929 (Bonelli statement).

5. Los Angeles *Times*, June 5, 1929.

6. *Ibid.*, June 21, 1929.

7. *Ibid.*, July 1, 1929.

8. *Ibid.*, July 4, 1929.

9. *Ibid.*, June 6, 1929.

10. *Ibid.*, August 26, 1929.

11. *Ibid.*

12. Ibid., June 3, 1929.

13. Albert W. Romasco, *The Poverty of Abundance: Hoover, The Nation, The Depression* (New York, 1965),p. 9.

14. *Ibid.*, p. 29.

15. Los Angeles *Times*, November 28, 1929. The full text of Porter's telegram is given.

16. Council *Minutes*, Volume 215, March 21, 1930, p. 253.

17. *Ibid.*, Volume 216, April 22, 1930, p. 245.

18. Index in City Clerk's office, City Hall, Los Angeles.

19. City *Charter*, Los Angeles, 1925, Article III, Section 22.

20. Los Angeles *Times*, January 3, 1931.

21. Council *Minutes*, Volume 222, November 17, 1930, p. 259; Volume 223, December 18, 1930, p. 113; Volume 214, February 3, 1930,

p. 107; Volume 224, February 2, 1931, p. 138; Volume 216, May 6, 1930, p. 617.

22. Ibid., Volume 231, December 16, 1931, p. 428.

23. Ibid., Volume 222, November 26, 1930, p. 488, also Volume 224, February 2, 1931, p. 148.

24. Ibid., Volume 222, December 10, 1930, pp. 752-3. This communication was filed saying the City Council had no jurisdiction in the matter.

25. Ibid., Volume 230, October 16, 1931, p. 217; November 5, 1931, p. 588.

26. Los Angeles Illustrated Daily News, April 17, 1931.

27. Council Minutes, Volume 225, March 17, 1931, p. 242; Volume 227, June 30, 1931, p. 815; Volume 231, January 12, 1932, p. 793. This communication was from the Business Women's Legislative Council. Volume 222, November 28, 1930, p. 512; p. 522; Volume 224, February 2, 1931, p. 148; Volume 231, November 24, 1931, p. 94; December 15, 1931, p. 243; December 18, 1931, p. 483.

28. James C. Findley, "The Economic Boom of the Twenties in Los Angeles," unpublished Doctoral Disertation, Claremont Graduate School, 1958, p. 405.

29. Eighteenth Census of the United States, 1960 (Washington, D.C., 1960) Volume I, pp. 1-68. By 1960 the cerca 100,000 population cities of 1900 looked like this: Omaha, Nebraska, 301,598; St. Joseph, Missouri, 79,673; Patterson, New Jersey, 143,663; New Haven, Connecticut, 152,048; Syracuse, New York, 216,038 and Fall River,Massachusetts, 99,942.

30. Romasco, op. cit., has an excellent chapter [8] on the subject of voluntarism and the general problem of cities.

31. Ibid., p. 129.

32. Ibid., pp. 13-14.

33. Ibid., p. 129.

34. Council Minutes, Volume 212, December 24, 1929.

35. Los Angeles Community Welfare Federation, Los Angeles City School District School Publication No. 263 (Los Angeles - 1934) passim for the Chest figures given here and in following paragraphs.

36. New York Times, July 26, 1931.

37. Abstract of Hearings on Unemployment before the California State Unemployment Commission, April and May 1932 (San Francisco, August 1932), p. 17.

38. Report and Recommendations of the California State Unemployment Commission, (San Francisco, November 1932), p. 355; other Chest data is from same report, p. 354. Hereinafter document will be cited as Report and Recommendations.

39. Ibid., p. 356.

40. Quoted p. 160 Romasco op. cit., A contemporary article by Robert W. Kelso, "Banker Control of Community Chests," Survey, May 1, 1932, hits at weakness of professional social workers in Chest Control.

41. Romasco, op. cit., pp. 158-59.

42. Max Vorspan and Lloyd P. Gartner, History of the Jews of Los Angeles (San Marino, 1970), p. 222.

43. James J. Hannah, op. cit., p. 227.

44. Report and Recommendations, p. 339.

45. Ibid., p. 374.

46. Ibid.,

47. Ibid.

48. Report and Recommendations, p. 375.

49. Vorspan and Gartner, op. cit., p. 196.

50. Quoted from B'nai B'rith Messenger, February 28, 1930 in Vorspan and Gartner, op. cit., p. 194.

51. The Survey, November 15, 1930, p. 214. See Table 4 in this study.

52. Report and Recommendations, p. 375-76.

53. Council Minutes, Volume 231, January 12, 1932, p. 791.

54. Diary of Mary Elizabeth, passim. This volume which I found many years ago in a Mormon thrift shop called Deseret on Soto near Olympic is a priceless day by day record by an impoverished woman of 60 in Los Angeles in 1932.

55. Sources for this section on Clifton's are John E. Hogg, "Host to 15,000,000 Diners," Nation's Business, November 1945, pp. 44-45 and Los Angeles Times interview, April 17, 1969.

56. Report and Recommendations, pp. 377-78.

57. Council Minutes, Volume 225, April 7, 1931, p. 699; March 30, 1931, p. 506.

58. Ibid., Volume 223, January 29, 1932, pp. 252-53.

59. Council Minutes, Volume 231, December 15, 1931, p. 421.

60. Report and Recommendations, p. 341.

61. Report and Recommendations, p. 380. U.S. Senate, Subcommittee of the Committee on Manufactures, Hearings on S - 174 and S - 262, Unemployment Relief. 72nd Congress 1st Session. 1932 p. 106. Testimony of Frank Bane, director of the American Association of Public Welfare Officials.

62. Report and Recommendations, p. 381.

63. Ibid., p. 343.

64. Council Minutes, Volume 224, February 6, 1931, p. 289.

65. Report and Recommendations, p. 381.

66. The Survey, December 15, 1930, p. 326.

67. Report and Recommendations, pp. 381-82.

CHAPTER 3.

MEANWHILE BACK AT CITY HALL

The growing unemployment, the rising clamor for some kind of relief, and the inadequacies of private agencies all clouded the city's horizon early in the depression. The personal nature of city government is such that it reaches down every bright street and dark alley and concerns itself with those fainting from hunger, whether it be in the classroom or in the library, for it touches every urbanite when he is born, educated, trained, tested, licensed, relaxed, taxed, married, robbed, arrested, judged, imprisoned, rescued from raging fever or fire, or finally buried. Harry Hopkins' observation that the immediate problem was "on the necks" of the local communities was most accurate.[1] A California report noted that "the city and the county governments, as well as private citizens, realized that some provision must be made at once, to avert suffering among the unemployed."[2]

In the Fall of 1930, the first ameliorative effort was a proposal that city employees donate, voluntarily, one percent of their salaries into a special fund to put men to work. At a Council meeting on November 26, 1930, with Mayor Porter present, a committee was established to arrange "for hiring unemployed citizens of Los Angeles" under the new fund. The committee was to be composed of two delegates from the Chamber of Commerce, two from the Merchants and Manufacturers Association, and one each from the City, County and Federal

Employees' Associations. Two days later a resolution was received from employees of the Health Department backing the one percent plan for the four months beginning December 1, to create jobs "where the greatest number of manual help can be employed."[3]

Emphasis was on the "voluntary" nature of the plan; "absolutely voluntary" wrote the City Employee magazine in its initial belief that some $30,000 a month would result from the donations.[4] The slogan for the drive was: "One Percent of Our Income for Four Months." By January 1931 the publication announced

> Every man and woman in the city service from the Valley to the Harbor, in every department, division, yard and office, has answered the call by a pledge of 1 percent of his or her salary for four months.[5]

The claim was more exuberant than accurate. There was resistance to the idea that all city employees give the one percent; one councilman attempted to restrict the donations to those receiving more than $175 per month. The initial months did see a high participation, and by February 1, 1931, the start of the third month of collections, the plan was grossing some $25,000 a month, only $5,000 short of the monthly goal.

In the 25 months ending December 31, 1932, the fund received some $228,000.[6] Thus the monthly average was not even $10,000, the claim made in mid-May of 1931 that "fully 90 percent of all city employees are actual contributors."[7]

Under the plan, the unemployed were registered for work at the fire department stations, locations considered the most widely and evenly distributed of all the city departments.[8] By March, 1931, some 18,000 had registered under the auspices of the Los Angeles City Employees Association Fund for Male Applicants. The report noted that the figure included "no women, no transients [and] no voteless foreigners."[9] As many as 500 additional unemployed registered daily. Little of the fund's money went into administration as the fire department emplcyees conducted the operation on a voluntary basis. During the plan's life only $83 was spent on administration; many city employees donated overtime and nigh work.

The Fire Department staffs processed applications "with respect to the degree of distress, the matter of dependents, residence in Los Angeles, capacity for manual or other work, and various other items." An official of the department wrote that because of the administrative delays

> many poor fellows are calling in belief their registration has been lost, because they have not yet heard from it, some have registered at several engine houses with the idea that their case might meet the employers' attention sooner.[10]

The Fire Department investigated all applications and was able to report that 80 percent of the initial 14,000 were householders, taxpayers, married men with children. The full magnitude of the condition of these men was noted by the firemen who found "that over 50 percent of the men who had started on the job fell by the wayside after an hour or so work through weakness caused by undernourishment, or, in plain cold American language--HUNGER."[11]

The work plans called for 20,000 men on fire breaks; 500 to work in Griffith Park; 2,000 in the Arroyo Seco bed; 2,000 in the Los Angeles River bed; 500 to sweep and clean the streets and 1,500 to improve the city's parks and playgrounds.[12] Pay was set at $4 for an 8 hour day. In the first nine months of the plan some 7,900 checks had been issued for 28,410 days of work. The report did not tell the number of individuals who had worked (obviously it was less than 7,900), but the average check was a bit above $14.[13] The second year of the plan produced a similar report.

The problem soon became overwhelming, and the Fire Chief complained that "due to the fact that there is so little work we can finance in comparison with the great numbers of men without employment, the jobs are of distressingly short duration."[14] The less than $250,000 did not get very far; Mayor Porter attended a meeting of the Los Angeles City Employees' Association that heard that "the amount collected is trivial compared to the fund which is necessary to adequately cope with the present unemployment situation."[15] The gratitude of the unemployed men was pathetically recorded in verse by one of them, C. Mohr, who wrote:

> We "jobless men" who clear the weeds
> And get our pay, thank your kind deeds.
> We know we gets our jobs and pays
> From you good city employees,
> Who labor for Los Angeles in very many useful ways.[16]

There was an unsuccessful attempt to bring other than city employees into the one percent donation plan. The Mayor called upon the bankers, businessmen and stockholders to donate one percent of their profits and dividends.[17] _Times_ publisher Harry Chandler and a group of 100 businessmen asked their employees to join. The plan's auditor reported only $705 from those sources in the first nine months of the appeal. In the same spirit approximately 200,000 letters were sent to club women and PTA members appealing for jobs for the thousands registered at the fire stations. The appeal brought 126 temporary jobs, "often for a few hours."[18] There was little public response to various "Give A Job" and "Clean Up Week" campaigns.[19]

City employees alone carried the one percent plan, and it is understandable that the City Employees Association struck back in anger, in December of 1932, at the Community Chest's charge that they were poor contributors to the annual drive. They not only stressed their plan, but added the somber note that they had suffered pay cuts ranging from 10 to 50 percent.[20]

Another less ambitious City Employees Association drive revolved around the apple, which has since become, in historian Irving Bernstein's apt phrase--"the absurd symbol of the Great Depression." Selling of apples by the unemployed on the streets of the city was a frequent proposal at the City Council. The Chamber of Commerce had called for a test "on a small scale in order to determine the local reaction." At first the Council's Public Welfare Committee vetoed the plan; at another time it was feared that the fact that the apples came from the state of Washington would be unfair competition with local fruit merchants and "throw further people out of work." But finally the simple apple was favored over the proposal of flowers or shopping bags as street sale items.[21]

In the Spring of 1931 the apple sellers took to the streets of Los Angeles. For nearly two months some 600 individuals, mostly women and a few crippled and disabled men, sold 2,174,296 apples earning a profit of $55,062. Each seller was restricted to three days a week with a goal of $15; the average participant earned approximately $90. The campaign though it was called an "extra-ordinary success" by its sponsors, seemed to have fallen far short of that description. Times columnist Lee Shippey thought that "munching of an apple on the street is a badge of honor [because] it shows that the muncher has helped a worthy worker in an honest effort making a living."[22]

On a more direct path, food baskets were given to thousands from funds raised by a city employees' Food Relief Fund. In a Christmas distribution, baskets went to 8,700 families classified "in three groups" as "Americans," "Colored," and "Mexican." Some 35,000 individuals benefitted, and due to the work of the Christmas Clearing Bureau, organized in 1914, duplication was avoided. It was reported that this special Bureau's alertness had prevented 2,425 families from receiving more than one basket! In a four months period ending May 31, 1931, the Relief Fund raised and spent $5,215. March 24, 1931, was set aside as a Food and Relief Day on which city employees brought foodstuffs to City Hall. Firemen brought in some $41,000 worth of food. The Food and Relief Day was described at the Employees' Association meeting as the "final gesture of the employees."[23]

The city employees' plans had been dedicated and determined. Their best effort, in the one percent plan, had given short time work with small remuneration to no more than 7,000 men; the apple sales hadn't even involved a tenth of that number; the sundry schemes had given charitable food baskets and clothes to a few. The meagerness of the results stood out as the second Federal Unemployment census reported 105,200 jobless in the city in January of 1931. A Municipal League fall survey that year of 1,500 major Los Angeles business establishments, which employed 15 or more persons, reported that 33 of every 100 persons working on their staffs in the fall of 1928 were no longer with them. A large proportion of the remaining 67, of the original 100, had been forced to take cuts in their wages, or were on part time. (See Table 8.)

TABLE 8--Survey of 1,500 Los Angeles Firms Employing 15 or more. Fall 1931.

	Employees
Fall, 1928	217,270
Fall, 1930	175,211
Fall, 1931	152,108

These firms accounted for a drop of more than 65,000 jobs in the three year period.[24]

The problem of need was too big for private solution; voluntary philanthropy had failed and the belief grew that only the government could provide the large funds needed. That direction had gone far in the 1920's, so that by 1928, 71.6 percent of all relief in 15 major cities came from public funds. Nationally this trend was accelerated by the coming of the depression. Harry L. Lurie of New Yorks' Bureau of Jewish Social Research told the 1931 National Social Work Conference:

> The development of public relief may be considered as a definite reaction against the validity of the principle of private responsibility for poverty.[25]

This awareness was expressed in a City Employees' Association resolution describing their plan as "only scratching the surface," and calling for a $5 million dollar city bond to finance the employment of some 25,000 men, at half time, at $4 per day for four months. The Association magazine editorialized: "Why not put in a bond issue for needed public improvements to meet this grim emergency?"[26] Public pressure for special city funds to aid residents mounted. The list of groups endorsing the idea included the Chamber of Commerce, the League of California Municipalities, the Los Angeles Municipal League, American Legion posts and an endless stream of petitioning individuals.[27]

The City Council unanimously voted to place a $5 million bond issue on the March 5, 1931 ballot. The monies were to be alloted to street construction and maintenance--$3 million; park improvements and playground improvements--$1 million each. The official resolution proposed that the

> primary object of the proposed bond issue be for the employment of labor, and that only American citizens who have been residents of the City of Los Angeles for at least one year shall be employed on any of the proposed work.[28]

High hopes were held for the efficacy of the bond, and all individuals and groups petitioning the City Council were told to "wait for the bond vote."[29]

There was no campaign against the bond, and the roster of supporters covered a wide range of groups, including the American Red Cross, the Socialist Party of Los Angeles, the Jewish Welfare

Federation, the Salvation Army and the American Legion. "No concerted opposition to the bonds has developed," said the Los Angeles Times; it carried a luke warm statement by Anthony Pratt for the good government Municipal League which stated it "would not put a straw in the way," but that "we find ourselves with no enthusiasm for this politically conceived scheme of the present administration to ride back into office by taking advantage of an unemployment crisis."

The Mayor's pre-voting day message raised great hopes if the bonds passed:

> Every dollar of these bond issues will be expended to alleviate the present unemployment situation, thus, to an appreciable extent relieving the economic depression in this vicinity.

In a like vein on the eve of the vote the Times carried an enthusiastic front page cartoon implying that the voters' X would cross out the un in Unemployment.[30] Similar endorsement came from the Los Angeles City Employee:

> It is now squarely up to the voters, and they are being watched by the gaunt eyes of the aged, and by the hungry eyes of the little ones.

In answer to taxpayers worried about costs, it was noted that on a $6,000 piece of property, the tax rise would be 50¢ a year, and the total no more than $20 in a 40 year span.

Less than 25 percent of the eligible voters voted on the bonds, endorsing them by a close margin. Victory required a two-thirds endorsement; a shift of 2,000 votes would have defeated all three bond measures. The Daily News described the result as "safe, but small margins." Attorney Frank Doherty wrote that "it required some courage for the public to vote such a large bond issue during this depression." The vote on the three bond issues was:

		Yes	No
#1	Street improvements ($3 million)	82,447	36,094
#2	Park improvements ($1 million)	81,357	36,443
#4	Playground improvements ($1 million)	81,094	36,794

The mood of high hope was caught in the City Council's resolution of thanks:

> the proper municipal authorities now possess the means of alleviating to a considerable extent immediately the unemployment conditions among citizens and taxpayers.[32]

Advice poured in on how to spend the $5 million. Soon the bond fund was in a swirl of controversy with demands such as one to allocate $500,000 in direct aid to jobless women, (to which the Director of Budget and Efficiency answered that the monies were "for construction purposes and not for the employment of either men or women."[33]); wage scales were bitterly contested, with the general settlement on $4 per day; and arguments developed over whether the funds were "intended solely for the purpose of employing labor" or whether major sums could be spent on construction materials. General agreement favored as much of the funds as possible, going into pay envelopes.

Initial plans called for jobs for the more than 18,000 city residents who were registered at the fire department employment bureaus. Though it was conceded that some time would elapse before the bonds were marketed, the Mayor promised to borrow the money in advance from the coffers of the Department of Water and Power.[34]

What was accomplished with the $5 million dollars? The Park Department reported that, in less than a year, its one million dollars had given jobs to 3,500 unemployed men, some 1,750 on alternating weeks, and that they had built some 13 miles of new bridle trails and mountain roadways in Griffith Park. Areas for picnics, future park development, expanded parking space and work at the Park's Fern Dell and Bird Sanctuary had been accomplished as well as needed improvements at Elysian Park. (Boyle Workman recalled a similar public project there during an 1880's depression!) Better than 15,000 trees were planted, 12,000 of them on city streets, and nearly 15,000 new park shrubs and plants had been added. The report emphasized that 83 percent of the park funds had gone to pay labor and the rest for materials and tools.[35] The one million dollars allocated to playground expenditures had gone into the construction of 17 community houses, 5 gymnasiums, 6 swimming pools, 3 bath houses, 10 baseball diamonds, 57 cement tennis courts, 3 children's wading pools, lights for night use of 10 baseball diamonds and 7 tennis courts, a lifeguard station and other needed facilities.[36]

A formal report on the $5 million work relief bond presented to a State Commission on unemployment noted that there was no exact knowledge of how many had been put to work ("approximately 18,500"). The figures for the expenditures in 1931, when most spent, were:

a) Labor	$3,141,247.91
b) Materials, rental of trucks, supplies,etc.	963,451.93
c) contracts let, covering labor and materials	173,242.46
Total expended in 1931	$4,277,942.30
The balance was disbursed in 1932	

The operation of the city's bond was the subject of a letter of Doherty to Senator Johnson commenting on a proposal for a national bond of five billion dollars to aid the unemployed. He wrote that he

> did not want to trust that much money into Mr. Hoover's hands. We had a recent experience in matters of that sort in Los Angeles. We voted five million dollars to relieve unemployment. The city administration had no program for the use of this money, consequently they put crowds of men to work cleaning off sidewalks and removing embankments from private property and other similar work which the city ordinance requires the property owners to do themselves. Very little, if any, real constructive work was done with the five million. The men just took their time and worked for $4.00 per day when probably it would have been just as healthy for them if they were taken out to the public park for an airing and given setting up exercises.

Contained in the estimate are foreshadowings of attitudes to New Deal work projects.

The <u>City Employee</u>, full of hope in March, was lamenting in October:

> In a few short weeks the 1931, $5,000,000 unemployment bonds will have been exhausted. Then--what?...this is going to be a tougher winter than the last one.[39]

By November the bond issue wasn't mentioned in the City Council; it had come and gone, with no meaningful effect on the larger crisis in the city. Some 18,500 men, perhaps 10 to 15 percent of the city's unemployed, had found work for at best a half year, and earned perhaps $300. In all it was reported that the city of Los Angeles had expended, in direct funds and with city employees' aid, a sum of $5,548,469 in the less than two years ending in the middle of 1932.[40]

Resentments on the bond proposal had been expressed from many quarters. Typical was a protest communication received from a resident who opposed

> the levying of any further tax for the relief of unemployment. Stating that the bond fund voted by the people for the relief of unemployment did not help the middle class such as clerks, teachers etc., but only the unskilled laborer, the majority of whom are not tax payers and stating that they are unable to bear any additional taxes.

In desperation, Mayor Porter called new conferences on the unemployment problem in October; a councilman saw taxes on gasoline, amusements, checks, soft drinks, cosmetics, tobacco, wine tonics, etc., as a possible new income to provide unemployment relief.[41]

When the funds from the $5,000,000 bond issue were gone the City Council was beset, as before, with proposals and analyses. The California Manufacturers Association opined that:

> the only permanent solution of our unemployment problem must come from employment of our own idle workers by our own industries and urging that the Council instruct the Purchasing departments of the City that at least during this great emergency they give preference to, and purchase, products manufactured in Los Angeles, quality and suitability being equal.[42]

They obviously had little stomach for special work relief operations.

As the funds ran out pressures rose to develop other sources of money. Detailed examination of possible funds left in a 1922 sewer bond allocation was undertaken. At one point the city turned to its reserve fund, normally not touched and assigned only to dire emergencies or as a needed temporary backup before tax revenues came in. A sum of $61,000 was taken out of that fund to provide for the following relief needs:

a) For food for the needy unemployed	$ 5,000
b) For food for indigent children	15,000
c) For water and electric light bills incurred by families of the unemployed	31,500
d) For meal tickets on restaurants for the homeless	2,500
e) For temporary care for homeless children	2,000
f) For transportation of unemployed	5,000
Total from city reserve fund	$61,000

[43]

In reality, the city itself had little experience in giving public aid; historically, the relief of the needy had been a county responsibility in Los Angeles since 1915. Prior to that relief, the little there was, had been the city's task. After 1915 the County supported and controlled the whole relief system with a two fold approach - direct material relief and the provision of medical and custodial relief to qualified patients. The Bureau of Indigent Relief handled the former; the General Hospital, Rancho Los Amigos and Olive View Sanitorium took care of the patients. Both aspects were under a County Department of Charities.[44] The County's office of the Superintendent of Charities is rooted in a county charter of 1912 approved by the State of California Legislature in 1913.[45] The licensing and regulation of private agency fund solicitations and the providing of some supplementary aid was left in the city's jurisdiction.[46] The County handled all direct material relief in the decades from 1915 on; it is still at the job, more than a half century later.

The county's task was formidable. In a California study of 1932 the summation was pointed:

The Los Angeles County Welfare Department is the chief family relief organization; but its relief budget for 1930-31 was not calculated to meet a sudden economic crises, and the department was unable to extend relief immediately to all those who found themselves in distress.[47]

The magnitude of the relief problem was expressed in the number of cases handled on a monthly basis by the County's Department of Charities. In the fiscal year 1928-29 the number of cases on hand by end of an average month was, at most, 6,435; a year later, the top month, March 1930, listed 10,784 cases and by the years 1931 and 1932 the number of cases were:

	1931	1932
Jan.	16,666	26,801
Feb.	18,640	30,283
March	20,393	33,641
April	19,907	33,960
May	20,001	31,267
June	15,973	30,758
July	15,005	31,597
Aug.	15,144	32,599
Sept.	15,603	34,037
Oct.	17,053	35,702
Nov.	19,000	38,046
Dec.	22,742	40,867

In the four years from January 1929 with a case load of 6,013, to December of 1932 with its case load of 40,867, the burden had increased more than 600 percent.[48] The County Department of Charities spent $15,020,319 in 1931-1932, a sum "constituting approximately 50 percent of the total expenditures from funds included in the general County level." By 1933 the city of Los Angeles had exhausted all its special funds, and the County was staggering under the relief load.[49]

The County's inadequate and desperate situation is best understood in terms of the allotments in the individual cases. In the pre-depression year of 1928, $90.64 was the average spent on a family; in the two fiscal years following, the sum rose to $99.94, but by 1931-1932 the average per family fell to $83.82. Said a state analysis: "These amounts are entirely inadequate to keep a family with children in health and to supply them with even a minimum of the necessities of life." By June of 1932 the County was spending $15.97 per family per month or a little more than 50 cents a day![50] This was the scale on which relief families were aided in the city.

John Anson Ford, who served many years as a Supervisor, recalled, years later, the temper of the times:

> [the]Welfare Department was all but overcome by the magnitude of its burden. Something like 375,000 people were on one form of relief or another during the peak of the Depression...At times, the meetings of the Board of Supervisors were crowded with distraught people who demanded that we do more than was being done for the benefit of hundreds of thousands of unemployed.[51]

To face the immense problems, the County supervisors had established an Employment Stabilization Bureau to register unemployed in unincorporated areas of the county; this had no impact on the city's jobless. Some county road work programs offered jobs which city residents obtained after investigation in what one Angeleno described as the "Inquisition building."[52]

Supervisor Frank Shaw, later to be mayor of the city, sponsored a County conference to which 40 prominent business, government, labor, civic and newspaper personages came, and adopted a six point program expressing popular outlooks and attitudes:

> (1) Create a four, or five-day work week, holding actual lay-offs to minimum

(2) Start a "buy-now" campaign.
(3) Urge local firms to display and advertise locally manufactured products thereby stressing the general public's responsibility to buy locally produced goods.
(4) Create a sane and humanitarian program for providing emergency aid to bona fide residents-not charity cases-suddenly impoverished by unexpected unemployment.
(5) Devise a practical method of saving equity of home owners from confiscation of their property through inability to pay assessments and taxes because of temporary financial stress.
(6) Aid all employers in the county in working out their particular business problems and adopting a uniform program assuring worthy and efficient employees continued employment over a period of the next six months to a year at reasonable wages.

Susan B. Dorsey, a former Los Angeles City school superintendent, told the conference that women could play a great role in combating unemployment, by adopting the slogan: "Every home employ at least one woman a week."[53]

Public relief was in a growing crisis as 1932 drew to a close. On a state scale there was approval of a $20 million bond issue for emergency relief to cover 1933-1934 needs (the County of Los Angeles received $12 million of it on loan), but this solution, like the earlier ones, was too little and too late. It was symptomatic that the relief problems grew, it seemed, geometrically, and the solutions, arithmetically. Only federal funds would aid the County's relief dilemma.[54]

Though not isolated from the relief problems it was fortuitous that the City of Los Angeles did not have the burden the County had. Some other American cities had the responsibility, and their experiences were devastating; in a majority of cities, poor relief was an obligation of the county or the township.[55] Yet relief was only one vital aspect of the depression's impact on the American city. The financial storm brought with it urban wreckage affecting property taxes, declining assessed values, loss of city income, wage cuts, firing of city employees, tax delinquencies, budget deficits, declining borrowing capacity, weakening of city services, and a host of related difficulties.

FOOTNOTES

1. Paraphrased in Josephine C. Brown, Public Relief, 1929-1939 (New York, 1940), p. 140.

2. Report and Recommendations, p. 361.

3. City Council Minutes, Volume 222, November 28, 1930, p. 522.

4. The City Employee, publication of the All City Employees Association, December 1930, p. 12. Hereinafter referred to as City Employee.

5. Ibid., January 1931.

6. Report and Recommendations, p. 351.

7. City Employee, May 1931.

8. F. Shirley, "The Los Angeles Fire Department and the Unemployed," City Employee, January 1931, p. 35.

9. City Employee, February 1931.

10. Ibid., January 1931, p. 35.

11. Ibid.

12. City Employee, March 1931.

13. Ibid., December 1932, p. 7.

14. Ibid., January 1931, p. 35.

15. Ibid., May 1931.

16. The apple selling proposal to the City Council Minutes, Volume 222, November 1930, p. 293; Mohr's poem, Los Angeles City Employee, December 1930, p. 2.

17. City Employee, October, 1931, p. 5.

18. Ibid., February 1931, p. 31.

19. Council Minutes, Volume 222, November 14, 1930, p. 255. The endless hope that private beneficence could meet the problems of the needy ironically was illustrated in the City Employee publication reprinting the famed Eight Degrees of Charity of Maimonides in its January 1931 issue.

20. City Employee, December, 1932.

21. The apple seller is portrayed on the cover of the recent Studs Terkel volume, Hard Times (New York, 1970) as a symbol of the Great Depression. Many volumes have selected it as the special symbol. The national hoopla is detailed in Bernstein's, op. cit., p. 294; The economist was Broadus Mitchell, op. cit., p. 87. The apple sales plan was mentioned or discussed at City Council Meetings on November 18, 1930 (Volume 222, p. 293), November 19, 1930 (Volume 222, p. 357), December 19, 1930 (Volume 223, p. 143) The protest on behalf of local merchants - Council Minutes, Volume 232, January 13, 1932 p. 3, apples favored, Minutes, Volume 225, April 8, 1931 p. 724; Volume 229, September 23, 1931, p. 646.

22. Homer C. White, chairman Apple Selling Committee, "Apple Selling Campaign an Extraordinary Success," City Employee, April 1931.

23. City Employee, November 1931, February 1931 and April 1931 for the various campaigns; Council Minutes, Volume 224, March 8, 1931, p. 752.

24. City Employee, October 1931, p. 4, Council Minutes, Volume 224, March 8, 1931, p. 752.

25. National Conference of Social Work, Minneapolis 1931 (Chicago 1931), p. 215.

26. City Employee, February 1931, p. 2.

27. Council Minutes, Volume 221, October 27, 1930, p. 708 communication from LAC of C; Volume 222, November 13, 1930, p. 193, from League of California Municipalities; November 19, 1930, p. 335 from the Municipal League; Volume 223, December 29, 1930, p. 298 from Eagle Rock American Legion. There are many more.

28. Ibid., Volume 224, February 9, 1931, pp. 316-317.

29. Ibid., Volume 224, February 27, 1931, pp. 692-3; March 4, 1931, p. 752; Volume 225, March 17, 1931, p. 242, March 18, 1931, p.271.

30. The Pratt statement and the cartoon was in the Los Angeles Times of March 5, 1931. Exuberant front page cartoons of the Times were not an exception. A November 16, 1930 article heralded the coming national cashing of $700 million in Xmas Club savings as putting "depression on the run." The Mayor's statement: Los Angeles Illustrated Daily News, March 5, 1931

31. City Employee, March 1931, contains the advice to taxpayer; The Los Angeles Illustrated Daily News, March 5 and 10, 1931 concerns the vote; Frank P. Doherty to Hiram Johnson, September 30, 1931, Hiram Johnson Papers, Bancroft Library.

32. Council Minutes, Volume 225, March 6, 1931, p. 34.

33. Ibid., Volume 225, March 9, 1931, pp. 37-38; March 27, 1931, p. 462.

34. John C. Porter, Annual Budget Message, May 8, 1931, Budget July 1, 1931-June 30, 1932 - p. 1; Promise to borrow from Department of Water and Power in Los Angeles Times, March 6, 1931.

35. Dana R. Tyson, "Report of Development Work Accomplished With $1,000,000 Unemployment Relief Moneys," City Employee, November 1931, p. 23.

36. Roy Smith Wallace, "Ups and Downs of Public Recreation," The Survey, July 15, 1932, p. 330.

37. Report and Recommendations, p. 361.

38. Doherty to Johnson, June 24, 1931, Hiram Johnson papers.

39. City Employee, October 1931.

40. Report and Recommendations, p. 363.

41. Council Minutes, unemployment conference call, Volume 229, October 1, 2, 1931, p. 776, 789; tax proposal, Volume 230, October 13, 1931, p. 162; tax protest, Volume 230, October 19, 1931, p. 256.

42. Council Minutes, Volume 228, September 2, 1931, p. 340.

43. Ibid., Volume 229, September 17, 1931, p. 574; Report and Recommendations, p. 362.

44. A detailed accounting of the early history can be found in Ronald M. Ketcham, Inter-governmental Cooperation in the Los Angeles Area, a Bureau of Governmental Research publication, UCLA (Los Angeles, 1940), pp. 41-42.

45. Helen R. Jeter, The Administration of Funds for Unemployment Relief by the Los Angeles County Department of Charities Prior to November 24, 1933 (Los Angeles, 1933), p. 1.

46. George W. Bemis, Public Relief Administration in Los Angeles County, (Los Angeles, 1938), p. 48.

47. Report and Recommendations, p. 361.

48. Bemis, op. cit., pp. 101, 102.

49. Ibid., p. 88.

50. Report and Recommendations, pp. 348-349.

51. John Anson Ford, oral history volume (UCLA Special Collections), p. 87.

52. Perry and Perry, op. cit., p. 227; Los Angeles Times, Letter to Editor signed W.H.R., March 22, 1936.

53. Los Angeles Times, November 26, 1931.

54. Bemis, op. cit., p. 88.

55. Frederick L. Bird, "American Cities and the Business Depression," National Municipal Review, November 1931, p. 633.

CHAPTER 4.

"THE SAME SAD STORY."

The city of Los Angeles was faced by the same sharp pressures as other American cities in the Great Depression. "One of the most amazing aspects of our topsy-turvy time," wrote an analyst, "is the threatened collapse of municipal government [and] almost everywhere we hear the same sad story of soaring civic costs, shrinking revenues, and staggering loads of debt."[1] A quick overall attempt in early 1932 to delineate what was "the effect of the depression on city budgets and municipal policies" noted that "conditions are changing so rapidly that reports are sometimes outdated before they can be assembled." A report on 26 of the country's largest cities told of such budget problems as:

> NEW YORK - some action may be necessary because bankers have demanded drastic revisions before granting additional credit. Approximately $100,000,000 worth of new building projects have been deferred as not urgently needed.
>
> CHICAGO - In the words of its mayor, Chicago "faces its most serious crisis since the fire which destroyed it in 1871." School teachers have received only one and a half months' pay in cash since April, 1931. There is serious talk of closing the schools. Salaries and wages of all other employees have undergone reductions ranging up to 27 percent. The personnel has been greatly reduced and it is now proposed to eliminate 2,479 more.

Philadelphia's condition was described as "chaotic," with the city facing "budgetary curtailments and emergency measures" involving wage cuts and layoffs for city employees, and cuts in service; Detroit's finances "demanded a policy of drastic retrenchment;"Cleveland's reduction of the city tax levy making "necessary a policy of retrenchment in municipal expenditures," ("All married women...have been asked to take a year's leave of absence"); from Milwaukee, Buffalo, Minneapolis, Cincinnati ("curtailments have been made in reducing waste and garbage collections from twice to once a week"); Newark, Kansas City, Seattle, Indianapolis ("personnel eliminations have been made throughout the city services"); Rochester (elevator service discontinued in the city Museum), Portland, Houston, Toledo ("city plan commission office was closed"); Denver, Oakland, St. Paul, Syracuse ("three probation officers, married women, have been eliminated to save $3,500")--the list continued.[2]

A broader and more statistically oriented survey made in 1931 by urban specialist, Frederick L. Bird, considered 135 cities in the United States and Canada and the way in which they were "weathering the present financial depression." He concluded that "the majority of American cities are not thus far meeting the emergency in their financial affairs with a sufficient degree of foresight and good management."[3] A later study by Bird warned that "indiscriminate cutting of salaries and ruthless slashing of department appropriations" was a poor answer and that city authorities should "look beneath the surface to the need for fundamental reorganization of administration."[4]

Throughout the United States, cities large and small, were in a vise of declining assessed valuations of property, tax rate shifts and increasing tax delinquencies. There were declining municipal revenues causing difficulties for municipal budgets, reserves, personnel and services. The pressure for more funds rose as they became harder to obtain by either taxation or borrowing. It was the worst of times for American cities. In the blunt words of an election tract written in behalf of Los Angeles' Mayor Frank L. Shaw's re-election in 1937:

> Most American cities have been between the devil and the deep blue sea in the past three or four years. Property values went down with a bang, and the depression created a lot of new expenses.[5]

How did the government of Los Angeles measure up in the economic storm? The major source of the city's revenue was the general property tax, based on the assessed value of a given property. As property values fell in the depression, the city's tax income fell with them. This parallel decline was a theme in Mayor Porter's fiscal 1932-33 budget message:

> Throughout this period of economic adjustment there has been an ever increasing demand upon the finances of the city for social relief purposes. At the same time the insistence of property owners for a reduction in the valuation of property has resulted in a decrease of anticipated revenues from taxes.[6]

He warned of an expected evaluation drop of $5,350,000. Starting with the pre-depression fiscal year estimate of 1929-30 the net assessed valuation figures for the city of non-operative (land, improvement and personal property) and public utilities (operative property) were:

1929-30	$2,089,174,370
1930-31	1,983,830,878
1931-32	2,019,918,163
1932-33	1,628,080,666
1933-34	1,363,668,333 [7]

Mayor Porter's 1933-34 budget was based on an evaluation in property values which had dropped nearly 35 percent since the 1929-30 period.

In a study of earlier years of the depression Frederick L. Bird made for the Municipal Administration Service he noted that in eleven cities of 500,000 or more residents, only Los Angeles showed an evaluation decline! The other ten increased their assessed valuation from 1929-1931. (Chicago did not reply to the questionnaire.) Neighbor San Francisco's figure increased by nearly a half a billion dollars, while Detroit, in the same population range, raised its valuation some $200 million. Most cities, 83 of the 135, had increased valuations; 26 had remained approximately the same, only 26 in the general group had lowered valuations, with Los Angeles the most significant. Los Angeles could not be charged, as were the other cities, with having a "valuation machinery...slow to reflect the deflation of property values."[8]

"It is, of course, misleading to consider valuation figures except in relation to tax rates," observed Bird's study, adding that "a declining assessment accompanied by a rising tax rate carries no relief for the taxpayers."[9] In Los Angeles, however, there was a drop in the city tax rate parallel with the drop in property valuations. The city tax rate, per thousand dollar in assessed property valuation was:

1928-29	$ 1.79
1929-30	1.63
1930-31	1.60
1931-32	1.64
1932-33	1.53 [10]

As a result of the drop in valuations and the tax rate, the tax levies fell better than 40 percent from fiscal 1928-29 to 1933-1934. The tax levies, which include more than property taxes, were:

1928-29	$ 33,361,074
1929-30	30,583,318
1930-31	28,495,374
1931-32	28,953,279
1932-33	21,331,670
1933-34	19,815,582

In the city's reports of tax rates and assessments declines, there was always a competitive approach to the Los Angeles County's figures. The County's tax rate rose from the constant 83 cents base of 1929 through 1933 to $1.20 in the 1933-34 period and its tax levies showed a drop of slightly more than 14 percent in the same period.[11]

Again, in comparison to other cities, Los Angeles stood in a unique position. Of the top twelve cities with populations of

500,000 or more Los Angeles showed, for the period ending in 1931, the greatest drop in tax rates--10 percent. Philadelphia's fell nine percent, and Detroit's fell six percent. Buffalo's tax rate went up 12 percent in the same period, and San Francisco edged up 2 percent. Only four cities on the list of 135 had a greater drop than Los Angeles in their tax rate ratio in the three years, 1928-1931. It was one of the five cities which lowered both the valuation and rate figures. Seventy-one cities, by raising the valuation or the rate, had actually increased taxes![12]

The financial plight of Cities in the depression was further worsened by an additional aspect--tax delinquency. This was a matter which caused problems, apart from valuations and rate drops, in cutting the income of the city. In the prosperous fiscal year 1928-29, Los Angeles had a 4.27 percent delinquency rate. It was not as bad as the highest delinquency, New York with 14.2 percent; nor as good as the lowest, San Francisco with a mild 1.18 percent. It was a poorer delinquency rate than the 6.82 percent of eight top cities surveyed. Certain key cities are missing in this particular study--for example Chicago, which was one of the 191 cities of the 326 over 30,000 in population, did not answer. (The sample was, nonetheless, considered representative, though the study conceded that "it is probable that the cities which failed to reply include an abnormally large proportion of those which are in serious financial condition."[13]

A Los Angeles tax delinquency of 6.61 percent in 1930 meant that better than $1,700,000 was not forth-coming in a year when the levy itself had fallen more than $2 million - thus actual income was nearly $4 million less!

Another type of municipal revenue showing a sharp decline were receipts from varying fines. In 1928-29 fine income from Municipal Court, Motor Vehicle and Street Traffic sources amounted to $1,582,739. By the 1931-32 fiscal period the sum had fallen to $505,815--a drop of better than two-thirds. The court incomes, falling from $890,806 (1928-29) to $109,592 (1931-1932) had an 88% decline.[14] It is possible that the sharp rise in unemployment cut the usage of vehicles. Even incomes from business license fees finally reflected the turn downward. By mid 1933 the licensing fees drop was $90,000 below the 1929 figure, yet enterprising efforts and struggles caused a rise in the 1930, 1931 and 1932 figures of as much as $62,000 above the 1929 figure.[15]

How then, in the light of the earlier described pressures on the city, and the declining incomes, did the city of Los Angeles sail between "the devil and the deep blue sea"? The first depression budget that Mayor Porter presented in office, for the period July 1, 1930-June 30, 1931, was accompanied by a message "cognizant of the subnormal conditions now existent, due to economic conditions." He stressed "a policy of economy and retrenchment" and pledged the holding of general taxation "to the lowest level" with the hope "that no department of the city government should lack adequate funds."[16]

Porter warned in his 1931-1932 budget message of:

> potential dangers to municipal fiscal resources which may become so formidable as to require

> further decreases in assessed valuations, full dissipation in the Reserve Fund, registry of unpaid demands and salary warrants, salary decreases, elimination of revolving funds, and the curtailment of many activities.[17]

The desperate search for new revenue sources was expressed in the 1931-1932 message of the Mayor who asked for allotment to the city as part of the gasoline tax collected by the County and raised the possibility of more income from "more rigid enforcement of traffic laws and increases in license, permit and service fees."[18] In a budget message two years later, Porter estimated that the city's share of the county gasoline tax was approximate $3 million dollars; he pressed for it as the city's due, and also urged the repayment by the County Board of Supervisors of a total of $2,735,835 for street maintenance work made at the city's expense.[19]

In his last budget message (his failure to win re-election made it that) Porter referring to the 1931-1933 period wrote:

> Los Angeles can well be proud of the fact that during the past two years it has continued successful operation and has met all obligations, including bond redemption and interest requirements, without resorting to either the registration of warrants or the securing of short-term loans.

He claimed that neither employees nor essential municipal services were eliminated.[20]

The Mayor's claim, to be analyzed in greater detail in the next chapter, was not accurate, for he trimmed the city budget quite severely during his administration. Under his predecessor, Mayor George E. Cryer, the city's budget had gone from $18,293,962 in fiscal 1924-25, to $25,660,000 in fiscal 1929-30. Those budgets, which increased some 40 percent in the five years from July 1, 1924, to July 1, 1929, reflected a rapidly growing city.

Porter's budget figures were:

1930-31	$25,000,000
1931-32	24,650,000
1932-33	19,300,000
1933-34	17,000,000

The budget had dropped $8 million dollars, some 30 percent from his first fiscal year in office. The city did not attain a $25 million budget until years after the depression. The Shaw administration which followed Porter's, after an initial drop to $16 million enlarged the budgets.[21] Actual expenditures during the years exceeded budget estimates, and required shifting of monies from special funds to meet the higher expenses. The extra $12 million the city finally received as its share of the gasoline tax also helped fill the gap.[22]

There were four deficit years in the 1929-1936 period. The figures, as given in a survey of the time, lists surpluses and deficits as follows:

Fiscal Year Ended June 30	Surplus	Deficit
1929	$21,285,599	
1930		$1,612,407
1931	5,845,665	
1932		11,531,668
1933		6,531,935
1934		2,707,604
1935	1,543,664	
1936	5,325,000	

[23]

The ancient worry of government budgeteers that there would be an unbalanced budget and that the city would face annual deficits plagued Los Angeles as well as other municipalities. Financial experts consider a debt burden as a weakening of the independence of the local government, and in the case of default a threat to credit standing, operating ability, financial solvency and critical weakening of general competence to cope with social responsibilities.[24]

The first difficulties in floating city bonds came early in the depression when no bids were received on an offering of $3,000,000, part of $38,800,000 bonds voted in 1930. Deputy Controller Daniel O. Hoye, later the Controller, expressed the shock:

> ...no bids were received which was somewhat surprising. In a very recent issue of Moody's Investor, the City of Los Angeles was given a rating of AA, whereas heretofore the same publication gave our city an AAA rating and we wonder why this change.

Hoye thought the problem lay in the general lack of confidence in municipal finances, which he called a "hysteria of the moment." City bonds, in his opinion, were much more attractive than railroad, utility or industrial securities which were depressed and had uncertain outlooks. Cities, though never in danger of disappearing as entities as business establishments can, nevertheless find the floating of bonds during the depression an increasingly difficult enterprise.[25]

The city of Los Angeles tended to keep on top of its bonded indebtedness and had a declining obligation throughout the critical years. A compilation, drawn from budget messages of the pertinent years, offered this indebtedness picture:

1930-31	$191,726,233
1931-32	186,136,187
1932-33	180,517,625
1933-34	174,763,062
1934-35	168,809,500
1935-36	162,716,937
1936-37	156,487,275
1937-38	150,210,362

The city did not falter on its bond payments.

The city's general strength on the bond market was buttressed by the special attractiveness of its water and power bonds. The Department of Water and Power, operating a successful utility with an expanding market, received strong banker approval. In 1937, a City Councilman, who was part of a negotiating team marketing a $23,000,000 Power Revenue bond described their reception in the East:

> The Los Angeles delegation was received with open arms by the Wall Street brokers who declare that Los Angeles credit continues very high. Los Angeles municipals are holding up extremely well in a soft bend market.

In 1938 a $15,250,000 DWP offering was sold to the public "a few hours later."[26]

A year later, in 1939, there was a temporary change in the bond market's attitude to the city (and California), as financial circles feared a possible victory for the "$30 Every Thursday" plan, widely known as "Ham and Eggs." The plan, subject of a later chapter in this study, called for payment of $30 weekly in state warrants payable to all unemployed citizens over 50. Funds were to come from a three percent gross income tax. Though the Department of Warer and Power announced it would not accept the warrants in payments, a $3,000,000 General Obligation Bond of DWP suddenly found itself in deep distress:

> The bond houses which usually are eager to acquire Los Angeles promises-to-pay for resale to their clients, and which are aware of all the facts, are conspiciously uninterested.

Defeat of the plan removed this threat to the bonds of the city and a councilman commented that the "bond market now is in better shape"; less than two weeks after the vote, eight financial houses were in the bidding.[27]

There were other difficulties with the electorate which also affected the voting of bonds. School bonds in Los Angeles faced a particular difficulty during the depression. Three bond issues in 1934 for elementary, high school and Junior College needs failed to receive the necessary two-thirds support; yet a year later, a school bond was voted by better than three to one. The ups and downs of school bonds at the ballot box reflected more than the economic straits; in 1934 school board disunity was a factor in defeat; in 1935 the understanding of the 1933 earthquake damage to the schools gave strength to the pro-bond side. That vote was also sweetened by a Public Works Administration offer of more than $10 million as a matching gift, if the city passed the more than $12 million school bond. In the same election a bond to finance electric transmission costs from the Colorado River was also passed.[28]

Street improvement bonds were caught in the vise of declining tax payments by homeowners and foreclosure threats. The Street Improvement Bonds were never defaulted by the city throughout the depression; this was another impressive accomplishment looked upon with favor by the financial community.[29]

The city of Los Angeles, as did other cities, had a tempting reserve fund. Created by the charter as a source of emergency and revolving funds when tax revenues were delayed, the fund had a basic vitality throughout the hard times. Over the years the sums in reserve at the beginning of the fiscal year, as reported in the budgets, were:

1929-30	$4,682,995
1930-31	6,086,235
1931-32	5,672,034
1932-33	5,059,873
1933-34	4,535,380
1935-36	4,085,987
1936-37	4,085,987
1937-38	5,329,714
1938-39	3,614,260

An estimate in late 1933 noted that "Los Angeles is one of the few large cities in the United States which has accumulated a cash reserve fund" and though there were times when the reserve fund was low, there was no need of the city issuing warrants (promissory notes in lieu of wages) to city employees. This was done in other cities and a major cause of trouble in Chicago. Norman M. Tucker, of the California Municipal Statistics, Inc. of San Francisco, and later associated with the World Bank, made these points about the city's reserve fund:

> In every recent year there have been times when there is only a small balance in the reserve fund. The amount in the fund at the start of this fiscal year was equivalent to 26 percent of the current year's general budget, against 26 percent of the 1932-33 budget, 23 percent of the 1931-32 budget and 24 percent of the 1930-31 budget at the start of those years. Thus, the budget and reserve fund have declined in about like proportion.[30]

The city also had tangible assets in its own property which grew in value throughout the period. The Controller reported that Los Angeles, as a city, had its property grow from a June 30, 1929 figure of some $290 million to a June 30, 1938 figure of some $442 million--an increase of nearly 50 percent. In a like manner the city's school lands, buildings and equipment rose, in the same nine year period from $8,675,785 to $9,787,846--an increase of more than 12 percent.[31]

Estimates of the financial condition of the city of Los Angeles thus remained on the positive side. By 1933 when many city governments had suffered economic paralysis and disarray, Los Angeles remained on an even keel. Mayor Porter's September, 1932, estimate that "in comparison with other large cities in the United States, the financial condition of Los Angeles is satisfactory" seems correct. A year later a New York Times analysis listed Los Angeles among those "which have [an] improved financial outlook."[32] Financier Tucker described the city as having a high credit standing in October 1933 and called its financial position "satisfactory." Especially satisfactory to the financial community was "the drastic curtailment in government expenses." It was his opinion that the 1933-34 budget represented "close to an irreducible minimum, considering the expanding population, rising prices and severe curtailment of services."[33]

Three years later, a Pasadena based financial research organization, came to similar conclusions about the city's economic stability, and though it was only 1936, noted that "the City came through the depression with less difficulties than most cities, and is again on the upgrade."[34]

Thus on many difficult fronts the city of Los Angeles averted some of the worst aspects of the "same sad story." The pressing question is how did Los Angeles' government come through the depression in such fair financial shape? At what sacrifice and at what cost to the city, to its personnel and its services were bonds kept attractive to the bankers and saleable, deficits low and reserves solvent? What was the human price?

FOOTNOTES

1. Lothrop Stoddard, "Why Cities Go Broke," Forum, LXXVII, June 1932, p. 375.

2. Harry H. Freeman, "How American Cities Are Retrenching in Time of Depression," supplement to the National Municipal Review, XXI, No. 4, April 1932, pp. 267-281 is the source for this material.

3. Frederick L. Bird, The Present Financial Status of 135 Cities in the United States and Canada, (New York, 1931), p. 1, hereinafter referred to as Present Financial.

4. Frederick L. Bird, "American Cities and the Business Depression," National Municipal Review, Volume XX, No. 11, November 1931, p. 634.

5. Mayor Frank K. Shaw - The Executive - The Man, (Los Angeles 1937), p. 15, Joseph Shaw Papers, UCLA Special Collections, Box 11.

6. Budget, Fiscal Year, 1932-1933, City of Los Angeles, California (Los Angeles, 1932), p. xi.

7. Ibid., 1940-1941, opposite p. 94.

8. Frederick L. Bird, Present Financial, p. 4.

9. Ibid.

10. Budget, Fiscal year 1941-1942, City of Los Angeles, California, (Los Angeles, 1941), p. ix.

11. Ibid.

12. Bird, Present Financial, p. 4.

13. Ibid., pp. 1, 4-5. The time periods are not the same - some are fiscal and some are calendar years.

14. Annual Budget Message, Mayor of the City of Los Angeles, Fiscal Year 1933-34, (Los Angeles, 1933), p. xi.

15. Controllers' Annual Reports, City of Los Angeles, California, for the fiscal years ending June 30, 1929, 1930, 1931, 1932, 1933.

16. Annual Budget Message, Mayor of the City of Los Angeles, California, Fiscal Year 1930-31 (Los Angeles, 1930), p. 3.

17. Annual Budget Message, Mayor of the City of Los Angeles, Fiscal Year 1931-32, (Los Angeles, 1931), p. 2.

18. Ibid.

19. Budget Message, Fiscal Year, 1933-34, p. xi. Porter in his 1930-31 message asserted that city residents were the source of 60 percent of the County's gasoline tax income.

20. Ibid.

21. Figures taken from various budget messages. A formal $25,000,000 budget was not to be reached until 1943-44 during World War II.

22. Los Angeles Times, June 4, 1938 and September 30, 1938. As late as 1939 Water and Power funds were being considered on a temporary loan basis for budget balancing - Los Angeles Times, May 9, 1939. In a November 28, 1938 message to the City Council, the newly elected Mayor, Fletcher Bowron, hit at the past borrowings from the Power Revenue Funds and deplored the constant $2,500,000 to $4,000,000 per year spending beyond the announced budget figure.

23. Young & Koenig, Inc., Los Angeles: Its Economic and Financial Position (Pasadena, 1936), p. 18.

24. Source of general picture is Carl H. Chatters and Albert M. Hillhouse, Local Government Debt Administration, (New York, 1939), see pp. 388-389.

25. Daniel O. Hoye, "Municipal Bonds," The City Employee, April 1932, p. 29.

26. Los Angeles Times, October 8, 1937; December 7, 1938.

27. For the refusal to bid aspects see the Los Angeles Times, September 23, 1939; the term "funny money" scheme is in the same article; the reports on the changed attitudes and bidding are in the Los Angeles Times, November 11, 1939 and November 21, 1939.

28. The 1934 vote: Los Angeles Times, March 21, 1934; 1935 vote: Los Angeles Times, November 20, 1935; the contrast with San Francisco and the PWA promise: Los Angeles Times, October 17, 1935.

29. Los Angeles Times, April 5, 1936.

30. Los Angeles Illustrated Daily News, October 26, 1933, reprinted by Office of City Controller, Los Angeles, California. This was in the files of the Municipal Library, Los Angeles City Hall.

31. See Controller's Reports for relevant years.

32. Los Angeles Times, September 5, 1932; New York Times, August 13, 1934.

33. News, cited in footnote 30.

34. See footnote 23 above.

CHAPTER 5.

"NOW WE HAVE NO DOCTOR."

A Los Angeles city employee during the depression lived in two worlds. In one, there seemed to be an immunity to the hard times, for civil service was considered a safe harbor; in the other, the economic pressures on the city were intense, and the continuing cry for economy tore at both the wage and salary schedules, and at the very existence of the jobs and the civil service system itself. Popular cliches were "elimination of government services...not of essential value to the general public," "elimination of employees whose duties have been rendered superfluous," "retrenchment," and the like.[1] From the beginning of the downturn, the concept of "drastic economies" pervaded all statements and approaches. The budget cuts, described in the previous chapter, outlined the overall direction. The specifics became painful, and on occasion, pathetic.

Economy in government was a constant theme of Mayor Porter, who, on one occasion, refused the city's new car, stating that he would continue to use his 1925 Lincoln.[2] The City Council's Finance Committee reflected the same mood in an answer to the California Realty Association's plea for economy:

> The City Council is in sympathy with this movement [and] the Finance Committee of the City Council is doing their best to keep the expenses down and that the city affairs are now operated as economically as possible.

On the other side, the City Council also heard a call for an increase in police personnel from the Aviators' Post of the American Legion, and still another communication "protesting any increase of personnel in the Health or Police Departments." The hard pressed City Council, by unanimous vote, informed the Los Angeles Washington Bicentennial Commission that it was unable to grant $5,000 for the 200th George Washington birthday celebration as "the City has no funds available for the purpose."[3] Ideas to meet the tightening budget included the City Employees' Association proposal for sales taxes on luxuries, vacations for city workers without pay, and no replacing of people in "uneeded jobs."[4]

City workers' wages were under constant attack. The anger of city employees precipitated talk of a boycott against leading firms allegedly backing such wage cuts. Fear of such action prompted Safeway, Adohr Creamery, Harris and Frank, and Langendorf Bread to disavow any such implications in statements to The City Employee.[5]

General pay reductions across the board were not possible. Under the charter, various departments such as library, park and playground, water and power, and harbor set their own wages scales independently of city council control.[6] One much favored economy move was the establishment of a five day week, lowering wages proportionately from the prior five and one half day scale.[7] Mayor Porter's salary, in a symbolic spotlight, was cut from $29,439 in his first year to $23,706 in his closing year, fiscal 1932-33. Mayor Shaw's first year salary increased more than $2,600.[8] By fiscal 1936-37 the Mayor's salary was back to the more prosperous 1929-30 figure. The $7,000 annual salary of City Councilman did not change throughout the decade. Other salaries of officials showed an overall gross decline reflecting phasing out of jobs due to attrition or elimination of posts.

In the city government generally, the salary and wage bill figures for the pertinent years were:

1928-29	$19,948,050
1929-30	20,579,039
1930-31	20,759,569
1931-32	19,686,727
1932-33	16,812,544
1933-34	15,757,157
1934-35	15,849,626

After fiscal 1934-35, the upward trend began again with a jump of nearly a million and a half dollars.

A more detailed breakdown (See Table 9) of two fiscal years, 1929-30 and 1934-35 offers a five year contrast between the beginnings of the depression and a later period. The salary and wage

TABLE 9--Los Angeles City Employees Under City Council Jurisdiction

	No. on payroll	Total salary & wage	Average
June 30, 1930	9,827	$20,579,039	$2,094
June 30, 1935	6,451	15,849,626	2,457

figures indicate a better than 17 percent average wage increase, and a drastic drop of 3,376 jobs--more than one third smaller than the pre-depression staff. The salary and wage increase figure is surprising, and perhaps reflects mandatory increases in certain categories at a time when many others were taking cuts, voluntarily and forced. The year 1935 may have been looked at as a year of better times. The drop in personnel is the sharpest indication of the depression's effect on Los Angeles city employees and services. In the accompanying table certain key departments are highlighted. (See Table 10). Of special importance is a 25 percent cut of custodial wages, generally among the lowest. Neglect of maintenance, cleanliness and renovation, in years when the need was most urgent, is also obvious in the decrease in custodial allotments. The Bureau of Engineering with its tremendous responsibility for street improvements, bridges, storm drains and sewer systems saw its wage-salary allotment cut by more than half. Bureau of Engineering personnel was cut 30 percent. It is this Bureau which was responsible for designing and estimating street improvements, bridges, storm drains, and sewer systems. (Federal allocations by 1935 will be considered in Chapter 11.) The Building and Safety Department saw a sharp decline in emphasis with a drop of more than 40 percent in personnel. Some of this is to be explained by the decline in new building and construction. Most disturbing decreases occurred in such depression geared departments as Social Service, which was forced to take a cut of 45 percent in the 1929-1935 period. Even decisive city functions such as Department of Public Works and the Bureau of Street Lighting saw 9 to 10 percent cuts. Mayor Porter in his

TABLE 10-Seven Selected Departments of the City of Los Angeles
Comparison of Los Angeles City Wages, Salaries and Number of Employees, in the Five Year Period June 30, 1930-June 30, 1935.

	Wages-Salaries		Number of Employees			Average Salary-Wage*		
	1930	1935	1930	1935	% change**	1930	1935	% change**
Custodian Bureau	$391,332	$266,112	291	262	-10	$1,345	$1,016	-24.5
Dept. of Building & Safety	722,021	392,648	318	189	-41	2,271	2,072	-4
Dept. of Health	613,309	546,070	342	334	-2	1,793	1,605	-10
Dept. of Public Works	64,830	64,421	22	24	9	2,947	2,684	-9
Dept. of Social Service	20,200	12,029	11	6	-45	1,836	2,005	9
Bureau of Engineering	6,131,525	3,043,449	3,241	2,249	-30	1,892	1,309	-31
Bureau of Street Lighting	125,024	88,464	60	47	-22	2,084	1,882	-10

* to the nearest dollar
** to the nearest half percent

Sources: Employment figures: Los Angeles Civil Service Commission Reports, June 30, 1930; June 30, 1935. Wages and salaries: Los Angeles Controller Reports, June 30, 1930;June 30, 1935.

1932-33 budget message warned that Health Department reductions were "severe."[9]

As of June 30, 1935, there were 1700 persons in the Los Angeles Fire Department. Their annual salaries and wages amounted to $3,856,421. On an average, this meant that each individual received a bit more than $2,268 per year. Five years earlier, June 30, 1930, there were 1,740 on the department's roll, and the salary and wage allotment was $4,275,861 which meant that the average annual pay was $2,457. In short, there had been a $189 decline, or some 7 1/2 percent. A comparative study of firemen's maximum pay of 15 typical cities in the United States for the years 1929 and 1932 showed that Los Angeles' department's maximum remained static along with that of six other cities; seven saw wage maximums rise--only one, Atlanta, Georgia, dropped its maximum.

Figures in the Police Department were:

	Number in Department	Wage & Salaries	Average Income
June 30, 1930	2,676	$6,311,494	$2,358
June 30, 1935	2,616	5,793,330	2,214

There was a general six percent cut in wages and salaries among police. Charter provisions protected the salaries in both fire and police departments, but "volunteer" cuts, with time given off, resulted in lower wages. Examination of other departments also shows cuts, with differing percentages but all tell of wages, and the number employed in decline. A Stanford study of that period rated the city's fire department as providing top protection, compared to a like category of California cities; Los Angeles was only bested by San Francisco and Fresno.

The Board of Civil Service Commissioners was a particular example of the depression dilemmas of the government of the city of Los Angeles. Founded under the 1903 Charter, Civil Service procedures had grown from a jurisdiction over 630 to that over 19,588 in 1936. It was a 30 fold expansion, greater than the city's phenomenal population growth. In 1903 nearly two thirds of the city posts (1190) were exempt from civil service; by 1936 only 178 of the city's 19,765 positions were exempt.

This vast pool of employees was processed by the Civil Service Board, which prepared and graded examinations, and helped choose the future city employees. All the normal pressures increased as the city entered the depression. It was an understatement by the president of the Board of Civil Service Commissioner in 1933, when he described the year as one "fraught with so many unusual problems of work and management." The General Manager reported that a decided increase in the number of applicants has made the problem of examinations a difficult one." In the year ending June 30, 1933, there had been 61,337 inquiries and 11,901 applications. It also was a year complicated by civil service problems concerning "suspensions for lack of work and lack of funds throughout the city departments." A Charter Amendment, passed in May, had established a new lay-off procedure and added to the work burden by "a noted increase in inquiries and protests, both verbal and written regarding layoff list status." The special depression problems also included a heavy pressure on the Commission for knowledge of grades and status on the lists. The 1933 report recorded 10,000 eligibles on Civil Service lists plus a registration roster of 4,255 laborers "each of whom is interested in immediate employment."[11]

During these years the salaries and wages schedule, drawn from Controllers' reports, gave this picture of the Civil Service Department:

1928-29	$93,602
1929-30	99,118
1930-31	103,226

then as the depression deepened:

1931-32	94,699
1932-33	54,074
1933-34	49,848
1934-35	51,055

By 1935 the number of persons working in the Civil Service Department had been cut from 55 to 27! The warning was given that the Civil Service System itself was in danger. The call was made for extra funds for processing "the thousands of additional candidates in examinations caused by the depression." The report warned "those of us who believe in the merit system are alarmed."

A sad illustration of the Department's crisis was the city's decision to eliminate the commission doctor's full time status, though the law made it mandatory for the Commission to give physical and medical examinations for candidates. From part-time status, with the allotment dropping to $200 per year, the post was finally eliminated--"so that now we have no doctor," read the 1934-35 report. Doubt was expressed whether the decision was an economy, or an illegal act forcing other departments, especially police and fire, to hire their own doctors. The city also faced potential liability claims from workers hired without medical certification. Costs in that direction could prove very high, the Commission warned. Thus the Civil Service economies were potentially the most expensive of all, and highlighted the kind of panic approach the city government was applying as part of its survival technique.[12]

One of the clearest examples of the depression's effect can be found in an account of the fortunes of the library system. It is a record of a sharp rise in demands for the library's services, and a deep decline in its income for salaries, books and periodicals. There had been more funds in less demanding times. There was perhaps the added dimension that the librarian quickly met the unemployed and in great numbers, for they were unable to afford other types of diversions.

The depression was a time of economic assault on city library systems. Rochester cut its library appropriation by 30 percent in 1932; Philadelphia considered partial closing of libraries; Detroit cut library book expenditures drastically; Syracuse cut $30,000 in its library appropriation, necessitating lesser hours, forced leaves of absence for six married women, practical elimination of new book purchases and abolition of the post of assistant librarian. Throughout the nation, city library systems saw wage cuts, firings, cutting of services and materials and, of course, little construction

[13] of new facilities.

The operation and problems of the Los Angeles Public Library during the depression years offers, in microcosm, an insight into the budgetary and human problems of the city. The construction of the Library's central building downtown was hailed as one of the architectural and cultural landmarks of the 1920's. Dedicated in mid-1926 the new building and the library's status in the city was reinforced by the new 1925 City Charter which granted an increase in the fund allocation from 5 cents to 7 cents on each hundred dollars on the assessed valuation of "all real and personal property of the city as assessed for city taxes." All funds received by the library in the form of "fines, sales, gifts" were placed in a library fund not to be used, except for the Library Department.[14]

This Charter allocation was both boon and bane-boon because it was a permanent income, bane because it tied the library's income to a declining elevator in the depression. As assessed valuations fell in the depression, the library's income fell in the following manner:

1929-30	$1,313,394
1930-31	1,260,091
1931-32	1,235,810
1932-33	975,958
1933-34	825,649
1934-35	810,440

In five years there was a drop in income of some 37 percent--more than a half million dollars.[15]

This was at a time when the library staff publication described 1931 as a year in which "the intellectual breadline at the Receiving Desk grew longer daily."[16] For the abnormal use of the library in the depression time flowed from the forced leisure of unemployment which increased the demand for books. Unemployment increased the special interest in books about social and economic problems. (A 1933-34 report indicated the top ten subjects in demand were NRA--National Recovery Act, Alpha army tests, sales tax, home plans and home loans, wine making and weaving, use of leisure time, youth movements, free lectures and classes, and books about Upton Sinclair, "a candidate for governor."[17] Do-it-yourself books vied with civil service examination manuals in reader demand. "Never in all its history has the Public Library meant more to the community than during the twelve months just closed," read the 44th Annual Report for the year ending June 30, 1932.

In 1934 the library reported that 24,000 books were circulated for each librarian; only Milwaukee, of the first size cities in the nation, could boast a higher figure. Librarians recall lines so long that entry had to be regulated at the main library entrance. By mid-1935 City Librarian, Althea Warren, noted that "few urban regions in the United States display such avidity for reading as that shown in Los Angeles;" circulation had dropped "at the rate of one million borrowings per year." Increased employment and consequently less leisure was given as one reason for the drop; the decline was also attributed to "decreased library funds and fewer hours of service," but, in her words, "the one leading cause of the drop in circulation is lack of books." Four years of cuts in book budgets resulted in less than 20,000 volumes being added in a depression year as compared to the prior normal annual accretion of 100,000 volumes. (See Table 11 for the ten year period.)

In ominous words the librarian summed up the situation:

> We can no longer say that our book collection meets the accepted minimum standard set for public libraries--one and one-half books percapita - as our today's total of 1,466,773 is approximately one and one-tenth books per capita.[18]

Salary cuts had been instituted on January 1, 1934; building enlargements were discontinued; the post of maintenance superintendent was abolished; and the central building cafeteria was closed. (It was reopened in the summer of 1937.)[18]

It was, in the librarian's words, a period of "falling budgets and depressed spirits," with drastic economies, wage cuts and an overworked staff. In desperation, the library tried to get 50,000 books from the public as gifts in the spring of 1933; only 14,180 volumes were donated. The pay book system instituted to raise income for new books made the public unhappy. Cards were limited to residents of the city, and others were charged a fee.[20]

Other expedients included the cutting of the allowance for each borrower from five to three fiction books; a reduction of 45 percent in the number of new books purchased; the raising of postal charges for reservation of books to five cents; an increase of the number of

TABLE 11--Chart showing percentage gain or loss in books in the Library, books circulated and book budget during the ten year period 1925-1926 to 1934-1935.

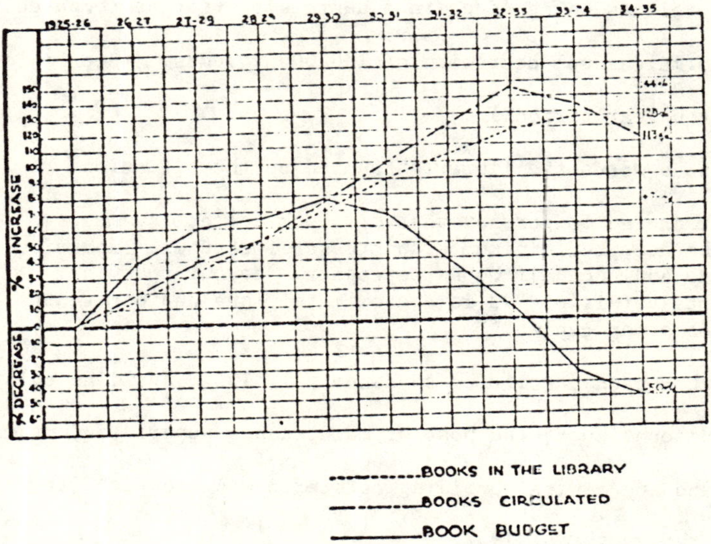

	1925-1926	1934-1935	TEN YEAR GAIN or LOSS
BOOKS IN THE LIBRARY	643,977	1,466,773	128 % GAIN
BOOK CIRCULATION	5,521,889	11,798,518	113 % GAIN
BOOK BUDGET (exclusive of Pay Revolving Fund)	$ 139,168	$ 69,078	50% LOSS

Los Angeles Public Library
Forty-Seventh Annual Report
1934-35 (Los Angeles, 1935),
p. 15.

books on the pay loan basis of five cents per week; and a combination of morality and economy in "rejecting best sellers containing too many offensive passages."[21]

The library staff made a determined and dedicated effort throughout the trying period in the face of a declining budget and few additions to the staff. A 1933 annual survey reported that "with the equivalent of sixteen additional full-time employees, the Library cared for one million and a half increase in circulation, the largest reading room crowds we have ever known and the biggest registration in its history."[22]

Consideration by Library officials of a $1 million bond for citizen approval on the May 1931 ballot was withdrawn when the project was frowned upon by city councilmen. An attempt to obtain part of the $5 million bond issue passed in 1931 to be applied to needed library construction also failed. Some federal project funds were given for library purposes.[23] There is no doubt that the depression years were especially cruel to the city's library. (See Table 12)

Wage levels and positions were critical questions generally in the ranks of city employees. At no point did the city workers ever mount an effective campaign to protect themselves. There was more of a tone of supplication in the publication of the Los Angeles City Employees Association, and formal trade union organization made no significant advance in the municipal ranks.[24] Special attacks against women working in civil service were blunted and a move to dismiss working married women was defeated.[25]

TABLE 12 –The Los Angeles Public Library

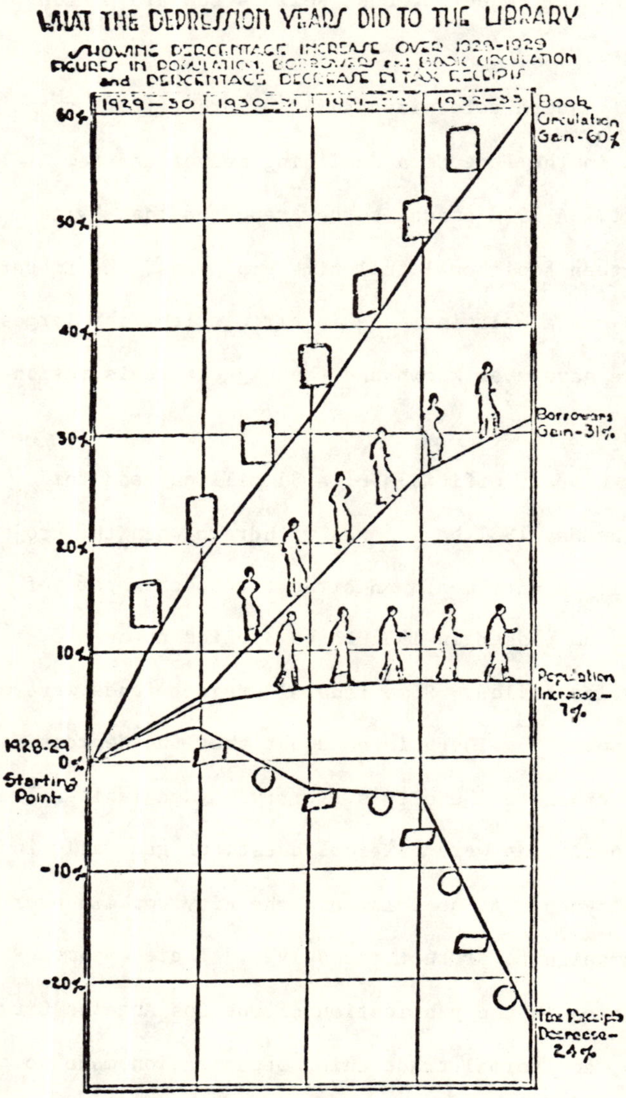

Forty-Fifth Annual Report
Los Angeles Public Library
For Year Ending June 30,
1933, p. 2.

In certain critical areas the City Council felt it was forced to raise salaries. Employees of the City Attorney's office received increases, as did lower paid City Hall elevator operators (raised from $105 to $114 a month); the City Engineer lost his plea for department wage increases in the summer of 1936, even though he stressed that he was losing his best men to the higher paid federal service. A councilman countered with the view that younger men "would be glad to work for lower pay."[26] In the ongoing debates on city wage scales one Councilman said the "city should set the pace," while another countered that it would be "a disgrace that the city should pay more for salaries than other concerns, either public or private."[27]

The restoration of wages of municipal employees was begun in the second half of the Thirties and continued into the Forties. Police and firemen who suffered reductions from mid-1932 through the first three months of 1936, sued in 1944 and won reimbursement for cuts they charged were made illegally according to the city charter.[28]

The city's services were sharply impaired by the economies of the depression years. The drastic cut by one-third in the overall personnel working for the city, with some departments losing as much as half their staff, alongside of the rising demands upon the city resulted in a deterioration of many key departments such as the civil service commission, the library, and general maintenance. It was a time of not only lowering or stagnant wages, but more important, a severe lowering of morale. The city employees who had made the first steps to aid Los Angeles' indigent, found themselves unable to help themselves. Outside in the larger city the hard pressed populace began to turn elsewhere, to self help and other movements in an attempt to meet their pressing problems.

FOOTNOTES

1. Harry H. Freeman, "How American Cities are Retrenching in Time of Depression," Supplement to the National Municipal Review, XXI, No. 4, April 1932, p. 270.

2. Los Angeles Times, April 19, 1930.

3. City Council Minutes, Volume 223, December 18, 1930,p. 113. Finance Committee statement; Volume 223, January 22, 1931, p. 747, Legion statement and protest; Volume 231, December 23, 1931, p. 575, Washington Bicentennial vote.

4. City Employee, May 1932, p. 2.

5. Ibid., p. 57.

6. Los Angeles Charter, Sec. 428, Sec. 66.

7. Annual Budget Message, 1933-34, (Los Angeles, 1934), p. xi.

8. Controller's Annual Reports, 1930-1934. Budget reports and controller accounts are not easily laid out for comparative purposes. One finds certain categories renamed, re-shuffled and, at times, disappearing. There are many intriguing mysteries such as the fact that expenses for the city kept rising constantly during the depression years, or side paths like how did prisoners fare? Meals for prisoners: 1928-29 - $31,036: 1929-30 - $150,850; (five fold increase); 1930-31 - $110,346; 1931-32 - $68,477 - what happened? Then no reports given - possibly under some other budget?

9. Budget Message, Fiscal Year 1932-33, City of Los Angeles (Los Angeles, 1933), p. xii.

10. John A. Vieg et. al., California Local Finance, (Stanford, 1960), p. 91. The comparative firemen figures are in Clarence E. Ridley and Orin F. Nolting, ed. What the Depression Has Done to Cities (Chicago, 1937), p. 37.

11. Thirty-First Annual Report of the Board of Civil Service Commissioners, July 1, 1932 to June 30, 1933, (Los Angeles, 1933), pages 5-19.

12. Civil Service Commission 33rd Annual Report, 1934-35 (Los Angeles, 1935), p. 14.

13. Harry Freeman, op. cit., Rochester, p. 276; Philadelphia, p. 268; Syracuse, p. 280.

14. City Charter, Sec. 158. The 1902 Charter started the automatic appropriation with a sum of four cents on the dollar; in 1918 it was increased to five cents. The late Reuben Borough, in an interview with the author, considered it one of the many progressive aspects of the City's Charter.

15. Budget, Fiscal Year 1940-41 (Los Angeles, 1941) opposite p. 94.

16. The Broadcaster, published by the Los Angeles Library Staff Association (Los Angeles, California 1947), p. 12.

17. Los Angeles Public Library, Annual Report 1930-1931 (Los Angeles, 1931) p. 24. The philosophy and religion items are on p. 25. Interestingly enough the 1934-35 annual report lists Philosophy as having the highest book turnover of any Dewey System category - 8 percent compared to the nearest, 4.3 percent for travel. History is way down with a 2.4 percent. Fiction, of course, led with 14 percent; periodicals had an 11 percent turnover. See p. 13 of the report for other aspects.

18. Ibid., (1933-34), p. 14.

19. LAPL Report, 1934-35, p. 6, Cafeteria re-opening announced in The Broadcaster, September 1937, p. 2. In October 1937 news was released in The Broadcaster that wage increases were to be given to 80 on the staff, first since 1929-30.

20. LAPL Report , 1933-34, 1934-35 passim.

21. Los Angeles Public Library Report, 1932-1933 report, p. 13.

22. LAPL Report, 1934-35, p. 12. Miss Warren also noted that the city led the nation in number of books circulated and area served. (p. 5)

23. Los Angeles Illustrated Daily News, April 16, 1931.

24. The City Employee, September 1930, p. 1 and passim; Perry and Perry, op. cit., pp. 489-490.

25. The City Employee, February 1931.

26. Los Angeles Times, August 18, 1936.

27. Ibid., August 27, 1936. The City Attorney's office had people working said one Councilman, for "about half that of similar employees in San Francisco," Ibid., September 16, 1936.

28. Ibid., September 25, 1944.

CHAPTER 6.

A TIME FOR JOINING

In the nation it was a time of messiahs, promoters, visionaries, revolutionaries, schemers and dreamers and a series of plans to aid the millions trapped in the depression. Names like Senator Huey Long, Father Charles E. Coughlin, Dr. Francis E. Townsend were known nationally, and their supporting armies were large, devoted and growing. The residents of Los Angeles were more than just part of the national milieu, often they were at the cradle of such movements, more often they nurtured even wider, more extravagant movements, making effective challenges to the established government. It is the aim of the next two chapters to avoid the well travelled paths through the movements, to search out the unique Los Angeles aspects and flavors - to give a historical feel of what these movements were like in the lives of the people of the city. It was, in the old tradition, a time for joining.

In the city of Los Angeles and its Southern California environs, the depression years saw more movements and more solutions for the economic woes of the people than perhaps any other area of the country. A soil that nourished a thousand different plants, trees and fruits was also fertile enough to be the base for a melange of causes and needs, "final solutions," "scientific answers," "realistic utopian" schemes,[1] new societies, new glories, new instant answers, succor for the poor, the homeless, the hungry, and above all the aged. Prophets, dreamers, seers, promoters, all were on hand to lead with plans involving free land, free money, free hope - all the freedoms the American past is strewn with. In it all was the smell of ripening Iowa corn, touches of engineering miracles, economic alchemies, remnants of immigrant and European pasts.

Why here? Two contemporary analysts of California's "psychological" state catch the flavor:

> "Always in every emergency before something had happened; always the boom was around the corner. The same energy, the same methods that had brought the snows of the mountains to the desert, that had built the railroads and dredged Port Los Angeles would find a man and a plan. The same luck that had discovered the gold in the hills, the oil beneath the orange groves, would not fail. If leaders had proven false, success was certain for a messiah was bound to come."[2]

Los Angeles itself was populated by many searching for answers. The peopling of the city, like that of the larger United States, was a product of those willing to experiment--to seek change. The others had stayed home. In this period there was a willingness to consider big changes - even the end of the profit system. The routine businessmen's answers had failed in the eyes of most. Los Angeles had many vacuums for, as Carey McWilliams has noted, it was a city where normal political aspirations were systematically suppressed, where politics itself was a mixture of vagueness and subject to ebbs and flows of cross filing, recall, referendum and initiative, where such sturctures of strength as the eastern political machine and a strong trade union movement were missing.[3] Tradition was honored in its breach; when it was necessary "the dispossessed masses of Los Angeles were quick to invent new forms of action and new forms for the expression of social discontent...new and untried political techniques,"[4] while at the same time trying to root themselves in the California around them.

One of the first popular anti-depression movements in this period was the one which seemed best to continue the native tradition of self reliance and individual effort--self help cooperatives. Bootstrap, self-help, ideas were presented early in the depression with the Los Angeles Chamber of Commerce's "Buy Los Angeles County Products" drive and Supervisor Frank Shaw's "Man-A Block" scheme in which neighbors on a block were to chip in to provide a $15 week job for ten weeks for one man on the block. Both plans proved ineffectual.[5] The self help cooperatives had a more vital history.

In the accepted American tradition, some of the city's unemployed, anxious to keep off any charity or relief rolls and not be a burden to relatives and friends, turned to self-help plans. There were, of course, incalculable self help operations such as rent parties, taking in boarders, begging, borrowing, and rummage sales. Some of the most primitive self help involved expeditions to the farm areas for donations of unsaleable vegetables. Often farmers allowed picking of crops unharvested for lack of a market.[6] Such pickings often led to monotonous diets, and one such surfeited individual has left us this ode:

> But carrots, carrots, carrots,
> Are nine-tenths of all you eat,
> Your "inners" got to hank'rin

For a good old chunk of meat.
So I can't refrain from lifting
This prayer to God on high,
Grant me one more leg of chicken
On my plate before I die.[7]

There were areas of shack residents, known as "Hoovervilles," which were another type of self help community, though they were not looked on with favor by authorities worried by problems of health, sanitation and policing. Clark Kerr's impressive study offers one of the few views we have of a Los Angeles unit:

> "Hoover City," the first "jungle" cluster of the dispossessed in Los Angeles, came into existence in February 1931, on the Southern outskirts of the city, but only two years later did the "citizens" organize for collective barter.[8]

Kerr saw the self help organizations as a combination of relief agencies, workers' cooperatives, and "a social movement expressing the desires and attitudes of the participants." They were a "reaction of some workers to their first period of prolonged unemployment at a time when 'charity' was anathema." In the immediate sense the movement resulted in an independence from charity, increase in incomes and also served as a channel for self expression. Kerr characterized the self-help movement "productive enterprises of the unemployed," especially those evolving from earlier barter or exchange organizations.

The Barter Associations were established first and had backing which included liberals, church leaders and veterans groups. Conceived as an elemental search for excess or low grade fruit and the mutual exchange of basic services such as barbering, shoe repairing, recreational and social activities, these bartering operations were hot house growths mushrooming in three to four weeks. Using abandoned stores as bases, they frequently provided for 50 to 70 percent of the minimum food budgets and much of the basic services of their participants. But, as the depression lengthened, the barter approach was unable to supply increasing needs, and faced attacks that they were "spoiling the market;" in its later stages "usually degenerated into salvaging junk and collecting donations of unsaleable merchandise from commission warehouses, bakeries and dairies."[9]

Scrip exchanges were a second form of self help developed in this city and elsewhere. Urban centers, having little to exchange in the way of agricultural products, concentrated on the exchange of services such as that offered by typists, doctors, music teachers and plumbers. In these exchanges they used scrip, "depression money" certificates, as a medium of exchange. The Los Angeles Cooperative Exchange, organized in the summer of 1931, was the first local scrip center. Their activities were described aptly by Kerr as members taking in "each other's washing."[10]

The exchanges were considered illegal operations, although generally they were not prosecuted. Both labor and government looked unsympathetically on their roles as unlicensed employment agencies. Nationally the scrip exchanges faded out about 1934, though California still had some as late as 1938. Failure of the scrip system was a product of lack of adequate controls, mismanagement, often racketeering, and the final debacle when the scrip, minus any security backing, became worthless pieces of paper as the exchanges folded.[11] The barter and scrip exchange period, 1931-33, gave way to the production phase of 1934-38; with federal and state aid this latter effort reach its height in California. Originally the productive enterprises involved such operations as gardening, sewing, canning and the cutting of wood for fuel. In 1933 federal funds became available for equipment and repairs as Congress authorized the Federal Emergency Relief Administrator to make "additional grants to States applying therefore to aid in assisting cooperatives and self help associations for barter of goods and services." The Civil Works Administration undertook projects to aid self help cooperatives, employing many of their members with needed cash "which kept the cooperatives going during their most difficult period."[12]

The city of Los Angeles' self help movement developed in the summer of 1932. Urban groups, where unemployed did not know each other, were also handicapped by their distance from food supplies. Thus the first three metropolitan units were on the town's northern, eastern and southern fringes with eight more developing within the city by the end of August. One had a Negro membership; another consisted of Mexicans.[13]

One city unit was the Cooperative Wholesale Association located at 1615 West 9th Street. It was organized on the Rochdale cooperative plan and operated as other wholesale grocery establishments with subsidiary stores, and even had a house publication. Some 40 retail organizations were connected with the Cooperative Wholesale Association. One such retail operation was the Elysian Heights Cooperative.

Organized in 1935, it was located at 2301 Echo Park Avenue and had 100 members. This group purchased about 50 percent of its supplies from the Association, and the rest from producers' cooperatives and on the open market. Prior to the Elysian Heights group's location in a store, they had operated in a private home. (The first week's sales amounted to $15.54. By the Spring of 1936 they were averaging $250 per week.)[14]

Kerr estimated that some 80 productive enterprises of the unemployed functioned in Southern California. Few were inside the Los Angeles city limits. He lists groups in San Fernando, East Los Angeles, a gardening project "in congested Watts" which moved to a rural area to facilitate hog raising, a South Los Angeles group called Goodyear, a Venice spaghetti and macaroni plant and a unit which manufactured shirts. The shirt making group was the only group, located in metropolitan Los Angeles, which survived through 1938. On the whole the productive enterprises led perilous and short lives, and made no decisive economic impact in the depression period.[15]

How strong was this self-help movement in Los Angeles? Kerr's figures emphasized the state. California's self-help movement, the largest in the nation, involved some 100,000 individual family heads from 1932 to 1938. Los Angeles County figures compared to state totals were:

	No. of units in L.A. County	Percent of State Total	No. of Members	Percent of Total
June 1933	115	65.2	23,200	77.3
June 1935	121	72.4	6,200	70.9
June 1938	58	77.4	1,980	88.4 [16]

It is obvious that Los Angeles County with 39 percent of the state's people, contained a disproportionate share of the state's units and members throughout the period. In the first depression years it was estimated that the County also had nearly 45 percent of the nation's self-help groups. The maximum membership in the County was estimated at about 75,000 in families receiving 50, or even 75 percent of their minimum food budget from the self-help operations.[17] Kerr concluded that "at no time was their active membership a significant portion of the unemployed." With the coming of the first Federal work projects in 1933 the movement waned.[18]

There was general community approval for the self-help movement. Kerr's study indicates that the morale of the productive unemployed was higher than that of relief recipients. They had a sense of ownership and personal responsibility and an immunity from unpleasant relief administration prying. On one occasion, the City Council hailed "in particular Unit Number 33 in their efforts to become self supporting rather than to become recipients of the dole."[19] The groups intensively active in production had little energy left for protest. Appreciated was the saving in relief dollars which Kerr estimated as comparatively small, though it "averaged two to three dollars of compensation to members for one dollar of net cost to public funds, not including expenditures for government administration." Mayor Porter contended that the organization was "feeding and sheltering sixteen people for what it costs the county to support one."[20] At one time, in the 1932-1933 period, the city of Los Angeles was one of the 34 California towns and cities which gave direct aid to the cooperatives in the form of gasoline, oil, payment of utility bills and donations of groceries.[21]

Thus, the self-help associations sailed on a sea of favorable public opinion. (The left attacked them as dulling the desire for a revolutionary solution, and the right was suspicious of their endless discussions.) The labor movement welcomed them as a possible limitation on the ranks of would be strikebreakers.[22]

Self-help as a movement was a chimera, promising an idyllic return to a simpler productive and back-to-the-land life and had within it some of the bloom of the current commune movement. Bernstein's phrase--"a soybean - spinning wheel civilization" puts it well. Both for the few participants and the larger populace it gave the impression of an unabrasive solution to society's woes. The movement fell victim to its own meagre numbers and capital, to all the pressures of the market place, inner difficulties, and eventually to the overwhelming funds of the federal relief system.[23]

This movement can not be written off in a consideration of the depression's history. It came out of the same soil as many of the utopian and political movements of the period. Perhaps it was a simultaneous expression of the anti-business moods sweeping the state, but surely it was part of the mental matrix of the hundreds of thousands who flocked to Technocracy, gigantic Utopian Society rallies and helped Upton Sinclair capture the Democratic Party and nearly the governor's chair. Kerr's estimate that at least 250,000 individuals had been members, or dependents of members of Southern California units by 1934 easily leads one to his conclusion that this "wide-spread self-help experience greatly strengthened the numerous liberal movements in Los Angeles and vicinity during 1934 and 1935." Truly they were an "introductory course in liberal political action."[24]

Yet there is an irony in this, for the original concept of back to the land and self-help was that it was "the solution to panics, strikes, financial depressions, and eventually wars" and that "slef-help takes people off the soap boxes."[25] But were not the threads of return to the land, cooperative enterprise, doubts about the prevalent economic system, non-monetary returns and a people's effort outside of the government--the material going into the political tapestry being woven in Los Angeles?

One cooperator was quoted as saying:

> "...we are entering into a Garden of Eden, hoping for the death of Wall Street and the prosecution of all unfair business tactics."[26]

Perhaps he best expressed the larger relationship this movement had to the new movements. Technocracy was one such cause which hit at unfair economic tactics.

The current in the crusades which rose and fell in Los Angeles in those years had its source in Technocracy, Inc., a movement born in the 1920's under the leadership of Howard Scott and a group of theorists and engineers working on studies at Columbia University. They asserted, in Veblenian spirit, that the politicians and profit makers were preventing the achievement of a truly high standard of living for all. The country was ready for such an explosive idea in the summer of 1932 and the winter of 1933. Even though it was a time when Great Engineers might have been especially suspect, a great engineering idea to cope with hard times was welcome. The Technocrats proposed a scheme of abundance based on "each operative working 4 hours a day, 4 days a week for about 165 days a year between the ages of 25 and 45, with complete leisure after his 45th birthday."[27] It was in the hiatus between Roosevelt's election and inauguration that Technocracy and Howard Scott "flashed across the country."[28] (Was there another omen in the death of Calvin Coolidge in that same interregnum?)

The movement flashed brightly over the city of Los Angeles with a rising abundance of Technocracy meetings. The flavor of one in the city is contained in this:

> A speaker inquires how many of the three hundred intellectual and scientifically minded Technates can extract the square root. Eight answered in the affirmative. How many could extract cube root? Five answered. We were among the minority and felt a little abashed - we do not know anything about energy determinants. But this is Hollywood.[29]

Technate material and discussion were full of "facts"-:

> -In five years [approximately 1941] "there will be no private banks"
> -"there will be 35,000,000 unemployed in 1940"[30]

A meeting of the Hollywood Technates, held in the Hollywood Chamber of Commerce Building, had 300 or more "very respectable and intelligent persons" in attendance. With a woman as chairman, the meeting was half female, with older folks absent (old folks have gone to Townsendism). A lecturer talked with charts, graphs and spoke of energy flow, potential productivity, money, credit, banking, energy determinants. Young people spoke in the discussion - "one girl in her teens, the other a youth just reaching his majority [and] impregnated with elan vital. They have the spirit of the heavens; they are definite, determined and sincere."[31]

In Los Angeles major support came from Manchester Boddy and his Illustrated Daily News. His support was described as that of one who could "whip Los Angeles into a frenzy of excitement."[32] Day after day Boddy devoted his front page column, and often part or most of his front page to Technocracy. Inside, as a feature, he ran Edward Bellamy's Looking Backward in daily chapters, and reserved the column alongside for notices and reports of Technocracy speakers and meetings. The message was presented to groups as varied as the American Legion Wilshire Post 319, the Unique Club, Southwest Realty Board, Ionic Lodge, Beverly Hills American Legion and the Los Angeles Chamber of Commerce's Construction Industries Committee (Boddy was their speaker). Meetings were also held in theatres.[33] Boddy promised to:

> print complete news concerning Technocracy itself as the principles it has expounded find their way into the economic structure of the new era.[34]

A page one banner headline announced TECHNOCRACY CAN END THE DEPRESSION,[35] and inside the paper Boddy's column insisted that the

New Deal, soon to be inaugurated, would be "based on the facts and theories of Technocracy."[36]

The maximum strength of Technocracy in Los Angeles is difficult to estimate. A dissident group in the movement, the Continentals, boasting a more humanistic approach than the original Technates, reported that they had as many as 2,000 members as late as 1936. One can only surmise a strength of a few thousand.[37]

By 1934 Technocracy was not in first place amongst Los Angeles crusades. It was under competitive pressure from the Utopian Society, Upton Sinclair's Epic and the rising Townsend movement. "No matter what its conditions may be elsewhere technocracy is not dead in California" was the opinion of a popular analysis in 1936. Its continued life was seen in its underlying theories which had "become a fundamental part of the dogma of Townsendites, Epicites, Utopians, Fourth Cyclers, Social Crediters, Christian Crusaders, Crusaders for Democracy, International Researchers, Silver Shirts, Socialists and even Communists."[38]

Even though Technocracy was critical of the various organizations or movements of the day,because "they all retain the essential mechanics of a Price System,"[39] its patterns became widespread. The crusade promoters understood, "attended various meetings of organizations like the Technocrats, staying long enough to gather a smatter of what it was all about and some of the patter, and then went out and organized." The desertion from Technocracy as a movement lay, in part, to its long range approach and its lack of immediate answers or actions. In the words of a contemporary observer, Technocracy

> fired the fuse which led straight to the Utopian movement, to Upton Sinclair's EPIC Plan, to Dr. Townsend's Revolving Pensions Plan and to acceptance of Huey Long's Share-Our-Wealth program by wide masses of people.[40]

It truly was "a harbinger of things to come," for its ideas, promoters and members would move right on into other causes. It is apparent that many of the same people, like interchangeable parts, were involved in one, two or three of these movements--sometimes simultaneously, and sometimes seriatim. It was not a big step from Technocracy to the Utopian Society of America.[41]

The Utopian Society of America, one of the movements with a large Los Angeles membership, was proud that its initials were USA. A contemporary journalist noted that USA's

> chief significance in current politics is the fact that it demonstrated the vitality of the purpose to abolish the "profit system" among wide sections of the American public. It picked up where the Technocrats originally failed and under disinterested and sincere if rather sapless leadership, took the Technocratic religion and made it a semi-political force sufficiently powerful to be an important element in the dramatic campaign of Upton Sinclair for the Governorship of California.[42]

USA was, indeed, a link between Technocracy and EPIC.

The term Utopia was not strange to the area, one that had seemed a fantasy to the first travellers and an experimenting ground for those who followed seeking their own nirvanas; recently

Carey McWilliams described the state as having "always been utopia-prone."[43] The Los Angeles Public Library reported in 1934 that there was a great increase in interest in books on Utopia.[44]

USA did things Technocracy failed to do. It introduced secrecy, symbolism and religious tones, all long part of American fraternal society history, yet it called for a socialistic world, a

> Technocratic Utopia, [where] the people own all the means of production. Each citizen gets a certificate of production entitling him to an equal share of all the necessities and luxuries of life that are produced and this certificate must be spent within a year.[45]

Utopian Society ritual stated that one must "look for the causes of governmental, social, and economic wrong in the system rather than in the individuals who apply it."[46] The Utopian Society's concept of social organization called for a planned life path of educational and physical training until 25, self chosen occupations from 25 to 45, and retirement at age 45 if one wished.[47]

The Utopian Society of America filed incorporation papers under California law on January 29, 1934. The papers described it as USA, Inc., Western Branch, and listed social, benevolent and altruistic aims. The charter envisioned a national organization. Leadership was in the hands of a triumvirate who were described as trustees in complete control, aiming at "some sort of an insurance benefit organization, with provisions for adequate financial returns for themselves." Eugene J. Reed, former banker and political economy instructor was the chief founder; W.G. Rousseau, "distant relative of the famous Jean Jacques," was the promoter;[48] Merritt

Kennedy, once a stock salesman for the fraudulent Julian Petroleum Company of the twenties, completed the original leadership.

To become a member one had to be an American citizen, 18 years old or over, and willing to abide the normal fraternal order secrecy vow. After completing the five "cycles" induction sequence, members became "Hermits" and received numbers in place of their names. Growth and meeting attendance was phenomenal though "Utopia called largely to the middle aged" with the Society having little success in winning the young. A class of deaf mutes was organized. The intensity of personal attachment to the Utopian cause can be found in the dilemma of an insurance salesman (signed 7X15779) in the Utopian News

> I no longer have any desire to sell life insurance...I call on prospects to sell insurance and wind up by trying to convert them to Utopian plan, if they are not already members!

The answer, noting that the society has many salesmen in its ranks, pointed out that

> Utopians do not hope to bring the new economy into being overnight...seek another livelihood... or cultivate a convenient mental parking space for your Utopian ideals while you are selling insurance.[49]

Newton Van Dalsem, later to be an active figure in the Utopian Society, who had first heard of Technocracy at his Masonic Lodge in 1933, described an evening in 1934 when he was invited to a "house induction meeting," as part of a group of 14 interested in the Utopian Society of America. His account, too long to reprint, tells of the meeting's messianic and moralistic tone:

> The first evening's Cycle performance opened with a 5th century scene, a little band of destitute pilgrims wandering along the highway in vain search for food and raiment, appealing for help and meeting with rebuff and defeat at the hands of the Grain Merchant, the Dealer in Cloth, the Money Lender, the Constable and the Magistrate, and eventually finding themselves on the highway as before, with the added burden of debt in the form of chains upon their ankles. Later they find the Hermit Reason, who gives them shelter, and offers to lead them to a land of plenty.[50]

There is a Bunyanesque touch to it with the latter cycles introducing the "Forgotten Man," the "Coordinator of Government," and finally, in the ritual's words:

> Trained engineers, executives, and experts from every mine, field and factory stepped up to head positions. Others stood by to carry out their orders. "PRODUCTION FOR CONSUMPTION!" was their battle-cry. "Let profit be forgotten, lest our people die!"[51]

Individuals organized house meetings and committees of others, who went out and did likewise, with pyramiding of memberships running into many thousands.

From such small meetings the Society expanded, until the Shrine Auditorium with its 6,000 seats was required for inductions; in one period nine meetings were held there in a week. The Better America Federation, a conservative Los Angeles group, reported that as many as 1,063 neighborhood meetings with an average attendance of 20 at each were held in one night in Los Angeles homes. Membership estimates run as high as 750,000; a half million is a more accurate figure.[52]

A June 23, 1934, "Utopian Night at the Hollywood Bowl" had 30,000 people present with at least twenty thousand reported outside the gates, stretched on the hillsides, and listening to loud speakers. The audience, described as mainly white collar middle class, also had "a goodly number of colored folks [as] Utopian doctrine draws no color line." The meeting had an American flag on the stage "kept spread by a synthetic breeze from a mechanized blower." Only word of mouth, with no radio or press announcement, brought the throng. The speaker was actor Jonathan F. Glendon, whose theme was the end of the "system" and the society's mission to create a new order. They sang the song of Utopia and called for abandoning the capitalist system.[53]

A month later the Utopians, denied the Memorial Coliseum, had 7,000 at a Gilmore Field rally. In August, a crisis in the organization's growth caused a deep drop in revenues which brought the discharge of many of the office employees in the headquarters at 831 S. La Brea. How many still remained on the payroll is unknown. A decline in membership was on, even though an August 1 audit showed that $96,939 had been collected in initiation fees, membership dues and collections at the recent meetings.[54]

The Utopians befuddled their opponents. The American Legion, the Better America Federation, and the police sought vainly to red bait them and finally gave up. The left scorned the society. On occasion, the society's power could be felt. A large area bank reportedly cancelled a decision to fire all Hermits on its payroll when it was met with withdrawals, in protest, of $900,000 in two days! The message of the Society was presented on radio station KMTR at 7:45 pm on Monday, Wednesday and Friday for a period, and members could buy a USA pin at a jewelry store advertising in the Utopian News.[55]

In general the Utopian Society kept to its mission; on occasion it spoke out on other issues, such as a labor dispute on the side of railwaymen in the city. It successfully cast its weight in the 1934 battle around an attempt to disenfranchise thousands of voters; backed liberal Judge Ben Lindsey's fight to keep his newly won judicial post; attacked UCLA suspensions of five student activists; played a part in electing Augustus F. Hawkins, a black man, to the State legislature. ("Former Soda-Jerker Age 28, Leads Negroes to Political Freedom"), and blasted the American Liberty League when John J. Raskob came to Los Angeles as its spokesman.[56]

By 1935 the USA was in serious decline. Its effective life span had been, at most 18 months. A year, 1934, was the length of its most effective period. Why had the Utopians fallen so quickly? Like the Technocrats, their program was to be realized in some future time; they also suffered from vast, unsolved organizational problems based on explosive growth; new attractions drained off members. John G. Wenk, USA president in this declining period, may have been more perceptive than he realized, when he wrote in a November 18, 1935, edition of the Utopian News:

> The Society has been in existence scarcely two years. At the first hundreds of thousands

> of people affiliated themselves with it, doubtless many of whom sought relief from intolerable conditions. When the dole system came into existence many of them lost interest.[57]

The 1934 campaign of EPIC, with its strong appeal to USA members who also shared Sinclair's belief in "production for use," obviously drew many of the Society's members into its ranks. When EPIC failed at the ballot box, it sounded, likewise, a death knell for the Utopian Society. In its way the stirring campaign of the End Poverty In California in 1934 represented the best that the USA memberships could hope for. Surely it was a high water mark in the battle for "production for use."

Perhaps the direct entrance into politics and political action was the logic of these spirited and wide movements. The changes occurring in American life due to the politics of the New Deal opened new vistas for the possibilities of political action.

FOOTNOTES

1. See Robert V. Hine, California's Utopian Colonies (San Marino, 1953) for background.

2. Luther Whiteman and Samuel L. Lewis, Glory Roads: The Psychological State of California (New York, 1936) p. 5. Hereinafter cited as Glory Roads.

3. No one can write about this area without acknowledging the perceptive insights of Carey McWilliam's fine studies: Southern California Country (New York, 1946) and California: The Great Exception (New York, 1949).

4. Carey McWilliams, Southern California Country, p. 293.

5. Louis B. Perry and Richard S. Perry, A History of the Los Angeles Labor Movement, 1911-1941 (Berkeley - Los Angeles, 1963), p. 227.

6. Only recently the Los Angeles Times (May 11, 1971) had an interview with a Mrs. Rita Salazar who recalled her part in those days: She found someone "with an old dilapidated truck" who drove her to Buena Park where she asked ranchers for the vegetables they were unable to sell. She was told she and her friends could have all they could pick. "I took the initiative. The others were ashamed to beg. I wasn't," recalls Mrs. Salazar, who distributed the vegetables along with giveaway entrails from a Buena Park slaughterhouse on tables in her front yard. Next Mrs. Salazar successfully added turkey and chicken farmers to her solicitation list, then a bakery and a dairy. "From there I started getting ideas. I went to the owner of the Brown Derby. I told him, 'Mind you, I don't want leftovers from the pots and pans. The food the health inspectors won't allow you to keep.'"

7. Clark Kerr,"Productive Enterprises of the Unemployed. 1931-1938," unpublished dissertation, Berkeley, California 1938, Volume 1, pp. iv, v. This exhaustive, four volume study is rich in material on the California experience (the fourth volume is on non-California experiences) and is a must for study of self-help. Hereinafter referred to as Kerr. The carrot jingle is on page 111 of Volume I.

8. Ibid., p. 86.

9. Ibid., chapter 1, p. 4, p. 37. On page 176 Kerr writes that private bakeries "opposed this development. First they stopped

donations to the units, but this only encouraged cooperative production. Then they greatly increased their donations, a more effective policy.

10. Ibid., p. 5, p. 20. It was followed by 40 others in California in the next seven years - p. 40.

11. Ibid., pp. 43-44.

12. Henry G. Alsberg, America Fights the Depression: A Photographic Record of the Civil Works Administration, (New York, 1934), p. 133; Kerr, passim chapter 1; Kerr differs on this, stating that as New Deal relief programs unfolded, self-help operations were weakened by members getting project jobs (CWA) and federal agencies (AAA, NRA) moved to reduce unmarketable agricultural surpluses, (the FSRC, Federal Surplus Relief Corporation's aim was to garner excess surplus.),p. 12.

13. Ibid., p. 183 "Negroes had more difficulty in securing food and making contacts than did the others, partly because they were in the city of Los Angeles" - Kerr, p. 179. He notes that when Negroes and Mexicans were in the same group the Negroes provided the leadership. One Negro group traded "vaudeville talent." As a pertinent item it is worth quoting this on racial attitudes: "In several units the Mexican or Negro members were given the most unpleasant tasks, which they and other members conceived the natural order of things.", p. 389.

14. Glory Roads, pp. 146-150.

15. Kerr, pp. 606-643.

16. Ibid., pp. 76, 77.

17. Perry and Perry, op. cit., p. 269.

18. Kerr, p. 229.

19. City Council resolution adopted June 2, 1933, found in Borough's collection, Box 4, UCLA Special Collections.

20. Letter to City Council, May 1, 1933, quoted in Kerr, p. 131.

21. Ibid., p. 70, p. 131.

22. Ibid., p. 58, p. 60. Kerr notes that in the two years, July 1934 through June 1936 it was estimated that the State of California saved $800,000 in relief due to the self-help organizations. p. 60.

23. Bernstein, op. cit., p. 421; Kerr, pp. 505-506. As late as March 19, 1940 though, the Los Angeles Times reported a self-help group in a picket line for relief. Kerr, 505-506, has two tables of interest detailing the host of problems and inadequacies of the self-help program, 1934-1936, under seven categories: membership, government policy, organization, operations, distribution to members, inter-unit exchange and the cash market. Benefits to both members and the community are in separate listings. There were many side benefits for members as a 75 percent reduction in the cost of natural gas in which all three major companies (Los Angeles Gas & Electric Corporation, Southern California Gas Company and Southern Counties Gas Company of California) joined. This arrangement lasted longer than three years until April 1937 winning good will for the company with the partial payments covering costs and the loss aiding their tax status as charity contributions. (See Kerr for fuller details, pp. 214-215.

24. Kerr, pp. 461-462.

25. Quoted in ibid., p. 490. Statement by Prof. Paul S. Taylor, Dept. of Economics, U.C. before a California Commission hearing.

26. Ibid., p. 482.

27. Technocracy in Plain Terms: A Challenge and a Warning (New York, 1944), p. 81.

28. Glory Roads, p. 5.

29. Ibid., p. 21.

30. Ibid., p. 33.

31. Ibid., pp. 18-19.

32. Ibid., p. 8.

33. Illustrated Daily News, January 26, 27, 28, 1933.

34. Ibid., January 28, 1933.

35. Ibid., December 10, 1932.

36. Ibid., January 24, 1933.

37. Glory Roads, pp. 12-15.

38. Ibid., p. 7. As late as 1938 Technocracy, Inc. listed five California based magazines. The Technocrat, a monthly, was published at 1007 S. Grand Ave., Los Angeles. As recently as November 9, 1969, the author was given Technocracy material outside a meeting at Los Angeles High!

39. Technocracy in Plain Terms: A Challenge and a Warning (New York, 1944), p. 16.

40. John Franklin Carter, American Messiahs (New York, 1935), p. 59.

41. Kerr, op. cit., wrote: "Virtually all self-help members were Utopians and a large majority were pro-Epic", p. 464; Personal interviews with old timers revealed that activists of those days belonged to two and more of the organizations. On May 17, 1971 I met a woman who went to Utopian Society and Young Communist League meetings in the same period. Glendon rejoined Technocracy, Inc., when he left the USA.

42. Carter, op. cit., p. 65.

43. Carey McWilliams, ed., The California Revolution (New York, 1968), p. 4.

44. 44th Annual Report, Los Angeles Public Library, 1933-34, p. 14.

45. Carter, op. cit., pp. 63-64.

46. Newton Van Dalsem, Evolution of a Radical (Los Angeles, 1955), p. 162.

47. Carter, op. cit., p. 64.

48. Glory Roads, p. 33-34; Rousseau had written a playlet called "Miss Technocracy" which amateurs had produced in the city (Carter, op. cit., p. 61); Reed, in later years became active in the left-oriented American League Against War and Fascism (Glory Roads, p. 43).

49. Material on the "cycles" can be found in Glory Roads, pp. 36-41; the same volume, p. 48 is the source of the characterization on USA members' age levels; deaf mute class, Los Angeles Examiner, August 16, 1934; Utopian News, Volume 1, No. 21, November 22, 1934, found at the Huntington Library, is the source of the insurance salesman's dilemma.

50. Val Dalsem, op. cit., pp. 120-121.

51. *Ibid.*, p. 122.

52. *Glory Roads*, pp. 33-35; Caughey's text, California: A Remarkable State's Life History (New York, 1970) offers the half million figure, p. 459.

53. *Glory Roads*, pp. 23-25; Los Angeles *Times*, June 24, 1934. By 1936, and waning, new leaders were in charge: Hugh MacBeth, Negro attorney of Los Angeles, Harvard graduate and grandson of slave, and John G. Wenk, small manufacturer in the city as president.

54. Los Angeles *Times*, July 20, 1934 (Coliseum account); September 3, 1934 (Gilmore Field); August 12, 1934 (EPIC); September 11, 1934 (audit); Los Angeles *Examiner*, June 20, 1934 (membership claim).

55. *Glory Roads*, p. 55 source of bank item; *Utopian News*, Volume No. 21, November 22, 1934 for radio.

56. *Glory Roads*, pp. 51-56; *Utopian News*, Volume 1, No. 20, November 15, 1932.

57. Quoted in *Glory Roads*, p. 60 from *Utopian News*, November 18, 1935.

CHAPTER 7.

A TIME FOR SHOVING

Self-help cooperatives, Technocracy and Utopianism, movements with a long view, withered as pressures rose for more immediate and greater aid. Thus tens of thousands moved to support new platforms, specific plans, and entered the realm of political action. The New Deal had opened up the federal coffers and new perspectives, and many, in the word of Upton Sinclair of EPIC, saw it as a time for "shoving."

Sinclair's startling movement to "End Poverty in California," which captured the Democratic Party's nomination for governor, had wide support in Los Angeles. John Carter, journalist, characterized Sinclair as a "Tarzan of the EPIC", and "agile ex-Socialist," who "frightened the Native Son prehistoric capitalists into Fascism and put the New Dealers on the Spot in California."[1] Epic News, the publication of the movement, hit attacks as:

> ...obviously the products of nitwits, psychopathics with a persecution complex, disgruntled racketeers, low-grade crooks, third-rate Hessians, deflated megalomaniacs.[2]

Before the campaign was over the city of Los Angeles was knee deep in vituperative material. Faked news films were shown in theatres, and millions of angry words came across the radio waves.

Those passions were aroused when Sinclair upset the political apple cart with his 1933 decision to register as a Democrat and seek the party's 1934 nomination as Governor. Sinclair was not new to California politics, having run as a Socialist, candidate twice for Governor (1926 and 1930), and once for Senator (1922)--never polling more than 60,000 votes on a statewide basis.[3]

Sinclair won the Democratic nomination handily in a field of four. His nearest rival, George Creel, moaned that it was Southern California, mainly Los Angeles, which had defeated him. In his memoirs he recalled that

> Northern California offered no problem, for hardheaded working native sons and daughters were in a majority, but when I crossed the Tehachapi into Southern California, it was like plunging into darkest Africa without gun bearers.[4]

Creel's memory served him well; the primary vote was:

	Los Angeles County	State as Whole
Creel	83,157	288,106
Sinclair	238,308	436,220

It was in Los Angeles, where Sinclair nearly tripled his vote, that Creel lost the race badly, along with seven other Democratic hopefuls.[5]

"Return of the unemployed to the land" was a key to the EPIC plan; land colonies with machinery and expert supervision would lay the basis for the "end to poverty." A transplanted native, Sinclair stressed that EPIC could join the 25,000 useful and beautiful plants that can be grown in California.[6] The EPIC movement was, in EPIC *News* Editor Reuben Borough's words, "a movement back-to-the-land...to place idle men at work in idle factories, and also on the idle land." Borough had been "back-to-the-land Editor" of the Los Angeles Record. It was a time, he though, in which taking over fallow factories and fallow land seemed the natural thing to do.[7] EPIC was in harmony with the thinking and aspirations of the self-help movement according to the candidate who wrote the "cooperatives had sprung up all over the state, and of course that was 'production for use', and those people automatically became EPIC's."[8]

The EPIC program was written with Sinclair's "eye on the state's unemployed cooperatives" and called for three implementing agencies: "the California Authority for Land (CAL) which would place idle workers in colonies on idle farm land; the California Authority for Production (CAP), which would put idle workers in idle factories; and the California Authority for Money (CAM), which would issue the scrip necessary for the exchange of goods with the new side economy."[9] A state scrip would facilitate the entire operation. Tax reforms would end the state sales tax. He called for steeply graduated income taxes, an increase in inheritance and public utility and corporation taxes. Tax exemptions were favored for the small property owners. A Henry George type plank called for a 10 percent tax on fallow agricultural land and empty building lots. In step with the times, there was also provision for a pension to needy aged, incapacitated, and widows with dependent children.

The EPIC cause had a strong base in Los Angeles. The movement listed 36 addresses as local EPIC headquarters. Some 600 of the largest clubs, of the estimated 2,000 in the state, were located in the city. Each Assembly District in California had a secretary and a busy membership. Borough recalled that the clubs were full of unemployed people who "had a lot of time on their hands." This movement, like the others, gave idle people things to do. Going to meetings was an important activity for thousands of individuals during the depression.[10]

One of the large EPIC meetings held in a Los Angeles boxing arena was financed by a $10,000 contribution from Aline Barnsdall (donor of Barnsdall Park), described by Sinclair as a "multi-millionairess." Speaking from the ring, the candidate "distributed [his] time and spoke to each fourth in turn," as loudspeakers carried the talk and "the audience enjoyed the novelty." At a Hollywood meeting a skit written by Sinclair, "Depression Island" with an EPIC motif, served as a rallying point with Charles Chaplin scheduled as a speaker; a July 4th picnic featured Stitt Wilson, once a Socialist Mayor of Berkeley, as a speaker.[11]

Sinclair was at his best in question and answer periods which followed his campaign talk. On one occasion he read aloud a critical Communist leaflet, which had been thrown en-masse from the balcony, and answered it point by point; years later he recalled another meeting on the afternoon before the election:

> A marvelous noon meeting that packed the opera house in Los Angeles. Our enemies had made much of the fact that the unemployed, otherwise known as "bums," were coming to the city on freight trains looking for free handouts. This had been featured in motion pictures all over the state and had front-page prominence in the Los Angeles Times. I told the audience that Harry Chandler, owner of the Times, had himself come into Los Angeles on a freight train in his youth. I shouted, "Harry, give the other bums a chance!" I think the roar from the audience must have been audible as far as the Times building.[12]

Because of their size and enthusiasm, Sinclair rallies amazed veteran politicians with their paid admissions and collections. EPIC orators, such as Borough, hit the basic themes, even making a pitch for conservative support:

> If the real conservatives of this hour only understood, they would not try to thwart your EPIC program--your plan to let people stand on their own legs and be self-supporting and self-respecting.[13]

But the conservatives reacted differently. A minor state official wrote that factory owners were among those "so frightened [that] they have almost lost their minds [and that were] telling their employees they must vote for Merriam or the factory will be closed down."[14]

A special Los Angeles gambit against Sinclair was the threat of Hollywood motion picture moguls to move their studies, staffs and payrolls to Florida if EPIC won. The direct production of movies was utilized to propagandize against Sinclair. In one film sequence, a bearded, disheveled actor asked:

> "Who are you voting for?"
> "Vy, I'm foting for Seenclair"

"Why are you voting for Mr. Sinclair?"
"Vell, his system vorked yell in Russia -
vy can't it work here?"[15]

The Los Angeles Times called the EPIC drive a "threat to sovietize California," and "equivalent to "the appearance of a hostile fleet off our coast." Sinclair's victory, the editorial continued, would give him the "power to turn California into a Communistic laboratory."[16] Though attacked in this manner as "socialistic" and "red," Sinclair's plan was not favored by either the Socialist or Communist parties. Norman Thomas called it "tin-can economy," and denounced Sinclair as a "renegade to the socialist movement," while the Communists labeled it "one more rotten egg from the blue buzzard's nest," linking it to the National Recovery Act blue eagle symbol.[17] Both Marxian parties ran separate gubernatorial candidates and, jointly, hit a low of 3,000 votes in Los Angeles and 9,000 in the state.[18]

An offhand statement by Sinclair, expressing the belief that the unemployed would pour into California if he was elected, was widely publicized. The California Real Estate Association resolved:

> that no man who boasts that he never has owned any real estate and does not believe in owning real estate as a matter of principle should ever be elected Governor of this state.[19]

There was widespread support for Sinclair's EPIC in the city. The pastor of the Rosewood Methodist Episcopal Church called on Protestant ministers and church members to back "Fundamental reform, through the election as Governor of Upton Sinclair, a genuine industrial democrat."[20] Special Assembly District editions of EPIC News were printed in the basement of the Pacific Electric Building, Sixth and Main streets. The presses, recalled the editor," poured out torrents of EPIC protest--which had risen during the primary campaign from a few thousand to a half million copies of EPIC News."[21] State headquarters were in downtown Los Angeles.

The forgotten man in the campaign was Raymond Haight, a Los Angeles lawyer who was the candidate of the Progressive-Commonwealth Party. In the sharp clash between Sinclair and Merriam, the only flurry made by Haight involved an abortive attempt to have Sinclair step down and support Haight.[22] His support in Los Angeles was minor.

Election day in Los Angeles, as well as throughout the state, saw feverish get-out-the-vote actions and a special EPIC poster for displaying near voting booths:

> I'm No Coward
> The Lying
> Special Interest
> Are Not Fooling Me.[23]

Sinclair did not win in Los Angeles County.

The tally was:

Merriam	457,755
Sinclair	405,331
Haight	98,348

The Los Angeles vote was some 46 percent of Sinclair's statewide total. In the County he had taken nearly 43 percent as compared to nearly 40 percent in San Francisco and 38 percent statewide. Thus EPIC had run some 5 percent better in Los Angeles than in the state.[24]

Though Sinclair did not carry Los Angeles County, Culbert Olson, backed by EPIC, went to the State Senate from Los Angeles County. (It was a major step toward his winning the governorship in 1938.) A Sinclair supporter, attorney Orfa Jean Shontz, was elected to the State Board of Equalization from Southern California. EPIC supported candidates won in 18 of the 30 Los Angeles County races for State Assembly. EPIC spokesmen claimed they had been decisive in the election of Judge Ben B. Lindsey, founder of Denver's juvenile court, to the Los Angeles County Superior Court; as well as in the election of three members of the county's five-man Board of Supervisors: John Anson Ford, Herbert Legg, and Gordon McDonough.[25]

For the first time Democratic registration in the county passed the Republican figure (as it did in the state). The Los Angeles County registration figures, 1928-1940, were:

	Democrats	Republicans
1928	217,050	600,636
1930	166,216	603,574
1932	505,620	636,089
1934	680,032	533,422
1936	822,201	498,468
1938	920,034	501,577
1940	1,041,191	578,729

The Democrats, in the lead from 1934 on, nearly quintupled their 1940 registration; the Republicans in that year did not even achieve their 1929 registration.[26]

Though defeated statewide, EPIC backed candidates took enough State Assembly seats to carry out one pledge - repealing the sales tax on food. After the defeat, the EPIC movement disintegrated as

EPIC

WHAT DOES IT MEAN?

<u>E</u>nd <u>P</u>overty <u>I</u>n <u>C</u>alifornia

UPTON SINCLAIR

Democratic Candidate for Governor proposes to the people of California that THEY make EPIC a reality

RUBE BOROUGH

PROMINENT NEWSPAPER MAN AND EDITOR

TELLS HOW

Tuesday, March 6, 7:30 p. m.

Labor Temple Auditorium

FREE 42 E. Walnut St. FREE

Auspices of the Epic Democratic Club, 51 E. Colorado St., Wa. 7567

REGISTER DEMOCRATIC---VOTE FOR THE EPIC CANDIDATES

a result of internal dissension, resignations, a battle about Communist penetration, and a drifting away of supporters. A Production for Use Congress, with more than 1,000 delegates from all parts of the state came to Santa Monica in mid-July 1935. It had been created four months earlier in Los Angeles by a gathering of "Co-operative Units, Utopian Groups, EPIC Clubs, Technocrats, Democratic Clubs."[27] Robert Burke summed it up well when he noted that "almost as soon as he [Sinclair] had boasted 'We are the Democratic Party of California and we are going to stay that,' the EPIC clubs began to vanish and by 1936 there was almost nothing left of his once vigorous organization." In that year EPIC delegates were defeated almost eight to one by the Democratic regulars in a presidential preference primary.[28]

EPIC's vote was a statement that "almost a million American citizens were willing to go a long way beyond the New Deal."[29] Many of them lived in the city of Los Angeles, where the EPIC endorsement would still linger on as a minor force for a period of time.

Sinclair's unwillingness to support the Townsend pension plan was estimated as one of the factors in his defeat. He did not consider it a major rallying point, though his program had a pension proposal. He told the aged that as "self-respecting Americans, you do not want to be dependent upon charity, whether of your relatives, or of the State, or of the Federal Government."[30] Governor Merriam made a direct effort to win the Townsendites. The appeal of the Townsend Plan was simple: each person over 60 years of age would receive $200 a month, to be spent within the month, and financed by a two percent transactions tax. Prosperity would result for all - old and young:

> Two hundred dollars a month,
> Youth for work, age for leisure,
> Two Hundred for the oldster,
> To be spent in ceaseless pleasure [31]

Dr. Francis E. Townsend was a doctor of limited financial means who had come to Long Beach from South Dakota. Though in his sixties, he tried to develop a "dry ice" factory with little success; he served in Long Beach's Health Department until his job was abolished; and then, like countless others, tried to work at real estate. Townsend later claimed that the sight of three old women rummaging for food in a garbage pail outside his window triggered his famous plan. Its roots have been traced to Stewart McCord, a man familiar with the ideas of the technocrats, who had written a paper calling for the retirement of "oldsters upon a monthly annuity, the spending of which was compulsory."[32]

Early in 1934 the plan was launched with a partner, Earl Clements, and the good doctor's brother Walter Townsend, a porter in the Hollywood Hotel. Established as the OARP, Ltd., the Old Age Revolving Pensions, Ltd., the three, as directors, sent a flood of materials. Petitions were circulated in the Spring of 1934 and soon the signatures poured in unchecked and uncontrolled, as "the number was estimated in Amos and Andy fashion at six million, seven million, ten million." Out of this torrent came the clubs with dues set at 12¢ a year, later to rise to 25¢, and a newspaper, Modern Crusader, soon to become Townsend Weekly, a source of rising advertising income. Merchants found it profitable to advertise in the weekly; sometimes boycotts nudged them. Safeway Stores was described as "by far their largest advertiser."[33]

John Steven McCroarty, California's poet laureate, was an early supporter and congressman who later sponsored a similar plan.[34] A mood of a band wagon developed and the inevitable song appeared:

> The Townsend Plan is marching-
> It will never know defeat-
> It will vanish want and sorrow
> And will make our years more sweet;
> Heal the dreads of our tomorrows-
> It will make our lives complete-
> God's plan is marching on![35]

Studies indicate that Los Angeles had accumulated a larger percentage of oldsters than the general average of the nation's metropolitan districts. In the over 65 category Los Angeles had a higher percentage than California. The study's figures for the year 1930 indicated:

Age	Los Angeles Metropolitan District	Calif.	All U.S. Metropolitan Districts	Continental U.S.
45-64	21.0	21.0	18.0	17.5
65 and over	6.8	6.4	4.8	5.4
TOTAL	27.8	27.4	22.8	22.9 [36]

In the prior decade, 1920-1930, when the nation's population of persons 65, or over, increased 14 percent, California's increased 80 percent and the Los Angeles-Long Beach area over-65 group increased

100 percent. The state's population had increased only 37 percent in the same decade. Thus the oldsters had increased at a rate better than twice the California growth rate; in Los Angeles the rate was nearly three fold.[37]

This large amount of old people in the area became a good recruiting ground for the growing Townsend clubs movement. The number of clubs increased as the members found that the meetings offered not only the vision of the plan, but also "furnished the warmth, friendship and color that no longer existed for many old people." As a result many weddings occurred.[38] Los Angeles soon became a pivot for the movement and national headquarters was established in the downtown Spring Arcade Building. Among major rallies in the city which Townsend addressed was one of 50,000 in Tujunga Canyon. By the Spring of 1935 some 175 local delegates went to the movement's national convention in Chicago. The Third National Convention with more than 6,000 delegates took place in Shrine Auditorium.[39] A Hollywood Bowl rally in late September, 1934, heard Governor Merriam's telegram "heartily in favor of old-age pensions," and publisher Manchester Boddy introduce Townsend.[40] An insight into the movement's local strength came in a court suit in which a minor official claimed to have sold 500,000 OARP pamphlets at 25 cents a piece in his district, described as Highland Park to Willowbrook, between Broadway and Santa Fe Avenue.[41]

In mid-May 1936 a Los Angeles caravan set out for Washington, D.C., with 10,581,000 claimed signatures on petitions. A meeting of the Los Angeles Council endorsed the plan with only three nay votes;

the Times said the council was pressured by the 300 assembled Towsendites.[42]

The plan began to exert an influence in the political arena. Journalist Bruce Bliven observed it "far outdistanced the rest. One hears little of the Utopians; and the Epic plan is chiefly valuable, at least for the moment, in enabling various small politicians to get their heads above water in their own district."[43] In 1936 Sinclair proposed an alliance with the Townsendites as an electoral ploy seeking delegates to the Democratic National Convention. He had learned how effective Merriam's 1934 endorsement of the Townsend Plan had been. Merriam had encouraged a memorialization by the Republican controlled legislature to Congress to study and pass a bill with its features.[44] Sheridan Downey, the EPIC candidate for Lt. Governor, who had run some 200,000 ahead of Sinclair, also felt that opposition to the Townsend cause had brought defeat. Within weeks after the election, Downey came out for OARP; in the words of one study: "as soon as he discovered that the Townsend organization was growing by leaps and bounds, Downey also leaped and bounded."[45]

Townsend tried to lead his aged army in different political directions on many occasions in Los Angeles. In the Olympic Auditorium he addressed a 1936 rally for third party candidate William Lemke; two months later at a July Rose Bowl rally he presented preacher Gerald L.K. Smith.[46] By 1938 Townsend's endorsement of Merriam failed to win for the Governor and there was only a four percent vote for the Townsend backed candidate for Lt. Governor in

Los Angeles. The 1938 ballot had a formal Townsend Party of California; its failure ended all plans to establish other state Townsend parties.[47]

Townsend's political coat tails were not long enough to bring victories for the politicians; it was obvious that the New Deal's Social Security scissors had shortened them appreciably. The Plan was a victim, not only of the start of Social Security and the depression's waning, but also its own inflexibility, its fading and mortal membership, its organizational weakness and splits (growing too fast was an ever present danger for these movements), competitive organizations and an inability to get a respectable national figure to support the movement.[48]

By 1937, with Social Security the law of the land, Harry Hopkins could say, with generosity "I don't care what you think of Townsend, but you've got to admit he did some job. He dramatized the situation of the aged."[49] This dramatization moved many in the city of Los Angeles, and though interest and activities slackened on behalf of the Townsend Plan, the pension idea did not die.[50] Townsend clubs were part of the Los Angeles scene for many years after the late Thirties. No doubt part of the immediate Townsend steam went into a new sensational scheme for aid to the oldsters, popularly known as Hame and Eggs.

Of all the scrambled movements to shatter the Los Angeles calm the Ham and Eggs, $30 every Thursday one was the most flamboyant and closest to state-wide legislative success. Its story, climaxing in

1939, sums up a depression decade of causes and crusaders, for in its ranks and leadership were those who came the whole way from technocracy, utopianism, EPIC, Townsend, cooperative and unemployed movements. It rang all the right bells - pension, quick money, easy financing, great slogan (spontaneously cried out at a rally: "we want our ham and eggs!") big rallies, massive petition and election drive, the sweet smell of near success and a tremendous vote cast twice on a state scale - once past a million, and near victory, and once 7,000 short of a million.[51]

A disappointed EPIC supporter and a former real estate salesman, Robert Noble, launched the plan in 1938 on Los Angeles radio station KMTR by calling for a $25 payment every Monday to everyone over 50. The state was to finance the plan with warrants backed by affixed weekly stamp taxes of 2 percent. Noble had many of the qualities and experiences useful to a crusader. He had been unemployed, applied for relief, been a salesman, had a good speaking voice and it was alleged that as a teenager he had studied so hard for the ministry that it took a stay in a sanitarium to disabuse him of the idea that he was Jesus Christ. He had followed Father Coughlin in his time, and made a well publicized grief stricken trip to Huey Long's funeral. Impressed with the power of Dr. Townsend's plan, Noble had made the pensioners' cause his, believing that "$25 every Monday morning would do until two hundred came along."[52] The California Pension Plan, spurred by Noble's radio talks, soon boasted of more than a third of a million members, most located in Los Angeles, who paid a penny a day dues in monthly installments, and carried membership cards to show their status.

Noble lost control of the movement when he was outmaneuvered by Willis and Lawrence Allen, owners of the Cinema Advertising which handled Noble's account, and were promoters of a hair tonic named Grey-Gone. The duo raised the ante to "30 dollars every Thursday" (more money and a different day of the week) and pushed Noble out.

A powerful movement was developed by the Allen brothers who could impress a politician with 25,000 to 30,000 letters organized by their followers in 48 hours. Their greatest challenge took the form of a petition of 789,000 which put Ham and Eggs on the November 1938 state ballot and almost made it law. The vote was 1,398,000 opposed and 1,143,000 in favor. But the defeat by a mere 255,000 votes was a spur to a more threatening drive in 1939. The failure on that year's ballot came despite the 1,103,000 signatures on the vote petitions and an alliance with the labor movement. The joint campaign called for a no vote on an anti-labor proposal coupled with a yes vote on the payment plan. (The labor movement won its vote.)[53]

How powerful was the movement in Los Angeles? The origin, core and main strength was in this city. The leadership included Angelenos who had been active in local movements. Orator Sherman J. Bainbridge, once a member of the Utopian Society, had conceived a dramatic re-burial of a San Diego suicide by the name of Archie Price as an explosive and successful promotion. Orator Captain

Charles M. Hawks, who was a "good radio man," was a "turncoat of the Townsend movement."[54]

The average Ham and Egger was busy listening to the radio talks, attending the meetings and rallies, circulating the petitions, agitating people in the streets and parks about the cause, selling the pamphlets, displaying their membership cards with pride because it had all the extra stamps (devised by the crafty Allens) such as roll call, birthday, gold seal--"you see it has everything on it." Sound trucks toured the streets, one decked out like a locomotive; another in a candy shape. A Liberty Bell "newly cast from virgin metal" was planned with names inscribed for one dollar apiece. The bell was to highlight ceremonies when the expected ballot victory came on November 8, 1939. Neither was ballot won nor bell created, but even in defeat a Shrine Rally had 7,500 in the hall and on stage and some 5,000 outside listened to loud speakers."[55]

The audiences and the activists were there, and in its heyday Culbert Olson and Sheridan Downey, eager for victory, endorsed the plan. Opposition was constant and vigorous in the pages of the Times, and politicians denouncing it included Merriam, Haight and Sinclair. Dr. Townsend as well as Los Angeles' Mayor Fletcher Bowron called for opposition to the plan.

The strong opposition to the Ham and Eggs movement was only one factor in its demise. The plan had come too late in the decade when times were better, the effects of the New Deal were widespread, and war loomed on the horizon. After the defeat on the ballot, the remnants of the movement drifted into anti-Semitism (Gerald L.K. Smith spoke at one of their last rallies) and oblivion. Ham and Eggs closed out the decade of schemes, proposals and movements.

The banners of the "shoving" causes of EPIC, Townsend and Ham and Eggs fell forgotten on the wayside. What remained, allied itself with larger and more stable elements in the city. There had been a transition from the joiners to the shovers--it was the transition from wishful clamor to political clout. Sinclair, Townsend and the Allen brothers understood this. Dr. Townsend wrote in his autobiography that "no man can change the course of things--not in a democracy; he has to have a pile of votes behind him."[56] Eventually these movements did just that--combined their legitimate grievances and their "pile of votes," bringing, in 1938, political change to both Los Angeles and California. In this city there were other changes at work which would accelerate its economic and political stability. The resolution of the ancient struggle between labor and capital and the building of an effective labor movement on the defeat of the open shop was part of that process.

FOOTNOTES

1. John Franklin Carter, American Messiahs (New York, 1935), p. v.

2. Ibid., quoted on page 67. Editorial shows style of Reuben Borough, editor of EPIC News, who often used the terms Hessians and Tories for opponents.

3. Sinclair, a California resident from 1915 on, was called both "an Anarchist writer" and a "Bolshevist writer" by the Los Angeles Times as far back as June 21, 1918; In his association with the American Civil Liberties Union the organization was described incorrectly as the "defensive branch of the I.W.W.," Los Angeles Times, May 24, 1923; On March 28, 1927 the Times modestly noted that the novel Oil had a Los Angeles theme.

4. George Creel, Rebel at Large (New York, 1947), pp. 285-286.

5. Statement of Vote at Primary Election held on August 28, 1934 in the State of California (Sacramento, 1934) pp. 6-7. Sinclair had seven other primary rivals in the race. His vote was greater than the sum of all eight who amassed only 114,587 in Los Angeles County, not half his vote there, and on a state basis they accumulated 405,980, some 35,000 less than Sinclair who had prophesized that he would carry the primary by 25,000! (I Candidate for Governor - p. 36).

6. Glory Roads, p. 213.

7. Reuben Borough and the California Reform Movements, Oral History completed under the auspices of the Oral History Program, UCLA, 1968, pp. 109-117.

8. Upton Sinclair, The Autobiography of Upton Sinclair (New York, 1962), p. 271.

9. Reuben Borough, Jubilant Crusader, unpublished mss. in possession of Madeline Borough.

10. Listing in Upton Sinclair, The Epic Plan for California, (n.p. 1934), pp. 62-64; Boroughs' oral history volume cited, p. 126; estimate of clubs in Glory Roads, p. 213.

11. Sinclair, Autobiography, pp. 273, 275, 281.

12. Ibid., p. 260

13. Borough's papers, box 6.

14. Frederic A. Chase to Lorena Hickok, October 19, 1934 in Harry Hopkins papers, FDR Library.

15. Glory Roads, p. 226; film sequence from Gladwin Hill, Dancing Bear - An Inside Look at California Politics (Cleveland and New York, 1968), p. 77.

16. Los Angeles Times, October 5, 1934.

17. Sinclair, Autobiography, p. 266, p. 271.

18. Statement of Vote at the General Election Held on November 4, 1934 in the State of California. p. 5, Los Angeles County: Sam Darcy (Communist) 2,238 Miles C. Dempster (Socialist) 822 State vote; Communist 5,826; Socialist 2,947. One is led to believe that both groups did not try very hard to hurt Sinclair's chances.

19. Los Angeles Times, September 28, 1934.

20. Upton Sinclair, EPIC Answers (Pasadena, 1934), p. 25.

21. Reuben Borough, Jubilant Crusader, unpublished manuscript. Charles E. Larsen, "The EPIC Movement in California Politics, 1933-34," unpublished M.A. Thesis, University of California at Berkeley, 1945, p. 24.

22. Los Angeles Daily News, October 26, 1934 and Charles E. Larsen, "The EPIC Campaign of 1934," Pacific Historical Review, Volume 27, No. 2, May 1958, p. 144 are sources for Haight attempt to replace Sinclair.

23. Borough's papers, box 6.

24. Statement of the Vote at the General Election held on November 6, 1934 in the State of California, p. 5.

25. Jubilant Crusader; Utopian Society of America also claimed these victories.

26. Statement of Votes, 1928,1930,1932,1934,1936,1938,1940.

27. Borough's papers, box 8.

28. Robert E. Burke, op. cit., p. 5.

29. Glory Roads, p. 229.

30. Upton Sinclair, Instant Epic, (Pasadena, 1934), p. 26.

31. Glory Roads, p. 75.

32. Ibid., pp. 63-64; also "Eight Letters to the Editor: The Genesis of the Townsend National Recovery Plan", edited by J.D. Gaydowski, Southern California Quarterly, Volume LII, No. 4, December 1970, pp. 365-382; also see J.D. Gaydowski, "Dr. Townsend and His Plan, 1867-1934," unpublished M.A. Thesis, UCLA, 1970.

33. Glory Roads, pp. 66-67; the Safeway item on page 94.

34. Ibid., p. 69 (Bill was HR3977 introduced in 1935).

35. Abraham Holtzman, The Townsend Movement: A Political Study (New York, 1963) p. 57. This is the most informative of the studies of the movement.

36. George W. Robbins and L. Deming Tilton, ed., Los Angeles, Preface To A Master Plan (Los Angeles, 1940), p. 32.

37. Holtzman, op. cit., pp. 25-26. California 1920 population-3,427,000; 1930 population - 5,677,000.

38. Ibid., p. 48-56. The first club was organized in Huntington Park, California on Augsut 23, 1934.

39. Glory Roads, pp. 102-104; Los Angeles Times, March 20, 1935; June 21, 1938. The national headquarters was moved from Los Angeles to Washington in mid-1935 (Los Angeles Times, July 12, 1935).

40. Los Angeles Times, September 29, 1936 gave the Bowl attendance as 9,000.

41. Ibid., August 14, 1936.

42. Ibid., May 6, 1936, May 8, 1936, April 25, 1936.

43. Bruce Bliven, "Roses in January; Morons in June," New Republic, Volume 85 No. 1098, December 18, 1935, pp. 161-168.

44. Glory Roads, p. 248; Holtzman, op. cit., p. 189.

45. Glory Roads, p. 230.

46. Los Angeles Times, May 20, 1936; July 6, 1936.

47. Holtzman, op. cit., pp. 184-186; party lost its official existence in California in 1942 when it failed to get 1 percent of the vote.

48. Ibid., pp. 199-200.

49. Ibid., p. 222 (Hopkins speech reported New York Times, May 16, 1937), Secretary of Labor Perkins wrote that FDR "always regarded the Social Security Act as the cornerstone of his administration, and I think took greater satisfaction from it than from anything else he achieved on the domestic front."

50. See Carey McWilliams, "Pension Politics in California," Nation, October 1, 1949, pp. 320-322 for later discussion of the whole impact.

51. Winston and Marian Moore, Out of the Frying Pan (Los Angeles, 1939), p. 62; I find myself in disagreement with Carey McWilliams who does not see this movement as "a product of the depression" as it dates from 1938. (Southern California Country, p. 308). Like the Townsend movement, Ham and Eggs has the depression as a catalytic agent.

52. Moores, op. cit., is a source of much of this. See p. 25ff.

53. Perry and Perry, op. cit., p. 422. They note the "alliance seemed realistic because the opponents of the pension plan were the same persons who favored the State initiative." p. 437.

54. Ibid., p. 48; Carey McWilliams, Southern California Country, pp. 303-308.

55. Ibid., p. 73-74; p. 95, 101, 133.

56. Quoted in J.D. Gaydowski, "Dr. Townsend and His Plan, 1867-1934," unpublished M.A. Thesis, UCLA, 1970, p. 140.

CHAPTER 8

THE COMING OF UNIONISM

Los Angeles was a crucible for many bizarre movements during the depression. Unlike the cities of San Francisco, Chicago, Detroit and New York, this city had developed forms of frenzied organizations unknown to the other urban centers. Much of the local development is part of the California story of political parties weakened by cross filing, nonpartisanship and the tradition of political independence. Yet San Francisco, in the same state, did not duplicate the Los Angeles syndrome. Climate, population,uneven and different industrial and economic development,all are parts of the explanation. But a central gap in the structure of the southern city was the lack of a strong labor movement--a force to give direction and leadership. In the thirties, San Francisco's labor movement captured the national spotlight, and produced major upheavals on the labor front; it was there that Jack London's "Dream of Debs," the General Strike, paralyzed a city. The San Francisco labor movement came into the decade with a long and influential tradition; Los Angeles' labor had little to match it.[1]

On the contrary, the city's labor movement, not too strong to begin with, entered the depression decade with the open shop as the dominant system of industrial relations. A 1929 organizing drive made no appreciable dent for unionism. The AFL was weakened by company unionism and welfare and paternalistic plans. It was also affected by the aggressive anti-union stance of the city's economic powers, and inner union problems. Louis B. and Richard S. Perry, historians of the local labor movement, record a lack of activity, and the disappearance of many unions as the depression affected the city. Rentals for the Labor Temple, where the local unions met, fell to such a low point that extra financing was required.

The general picture was one of a steady decline in membership, impotence, weak contracts and little organizational activity. (See Table 12.) By the end of 1932 at least half of the workers in the building trades were unemployed in spite of the lowering of union wage scales in the depression. As restaurants failed, jobs were lost and union locals were weakened; "canned," the new pre-recorded music, caused a loss of jobs for members of the musicians union; longshoremen and seamen suffered under the continuing practice of open shop hiring and the drop in sea traffic. New York clothing manufacturers, seeking a more profitable, less unionized atmosphere, posed a special threat to local clothing unions. In February, 1932, declining rail traffic brought wage cuts to the railroad workers. A weakened union resulted from a bitter lockout against dairy drivers; taxi cab drivers failed in their attempts to organize two of the city's four companies.

Not all strikes and organizational drives led to defeat of the unions. A ladies garment local won a strike in the fall of 1930; the makers of caps won in early 1932; the printers union held fast despite severe loss of jobs and wage cuts when mergers occurred

TABLE 12--Union Wage Rates Negotiated in Some Principal Trades in Los Angeles - 1929 and 1933.

Occupation	Rate per hour (in cents)	
	1929	1933
Bricklayers	137.5	100.0
Building laborers	62.5	62.5
Carpenters	100.0	100.0
Cement finishers	125.0	100.0
Compositors		
Book and job	106.8	106.8
Newspaper (day work)	117.8	109.6
Electrotypers		
Molders	113.6	104.2
Finishers	113.6	104.2
Granite cutters, inside	112.5	106.3
Inside wiremen	100.0	100.0
Painters	100.0	100.0
Plasterers	150.0	112.5
Plumbers	112.5	112.5
Sheet metal workers	112.5	112.5
Structural ironworkers		
Typesetting		
Book and job, mach.	120.5	120.5
Newspaper, mach.	117.8	109.6

Louis B. Perry and Richard S. Perry, A History of the Los Angeles Labor Movement, 1911-1941, p. 246.

at the Herald and Express and the Hollywood News and Hollywood Citizen. In the main, the local labor movement, with a membership of no more than 20,000, closed out 1932 in poor shape. The city's long anti-labor tradition, the weakness of labor in the political arena and the special harassment by the Los Angeles Police Department's special intelligence squad led by Capt. William F. Hynes, all adding to labor's dim outlook.[2]

It was only with the coming of the New Deal that the local labor movement became part of the national labor's optimism about new organizational possibilities. The National Industrial Recovery Act (NIRA) sparked local demands for a five-day week, six-hour day and a more adequate union wage scale. The AFL, determined to have representation on the NRA code bodies in the city, contacted the Chamber of Commerce, which received a Merchants' and Manufacturers' Association opinion that NRA did not require dealings with organized labor.

The C. of C. later did not deny the right of organization and collective bargaining. The M and M went further, noting in its bulletin:

> There is less necessity for an employee to join American Federation of Labor ranks than ever before, because the administration has guaranteed them decent living wages and shortened working hours....[3]

Company unionism, organized under management direction, was the M and M hope. Among the first to establish such representation in Los Angeles was the Goodyear Tire and Rubber Company on July 1, 1933.

But the NIRA's famed clause 7A giving the right to organize, stimulated independent unionism. The Perrys' estimate that 6,000 joined Los Angeles unions in the first weeks of July, 1933. The organizing drive brought meetings and bookings for the once idle rooms in the Labor Temple. By the fall, nearly 30 new locals were organized, or were in the process of organizing, with an estimated 15,000 new members. Opposition came from the expected triumvirate: the Chamber, the M and M, and the Times, which stood fast for the "pioneer open chop city of America, as it has always been the chief stronghold and outstanding beneficiary of that system of industrial relations."[4] Strikes became more frequent in the city as labor realized that NIRA was only a door to unionism. The key lay only in the organizations' economic clout.

The International Ladies Garment Workers Union led the way with an organizing drive including a special appeal to Mexican-Americans. Rose Pesotta's stirring account of the garment union campaigns, Bread Upon the Waters, charged that in the industry "an appallingly large labor turnover was deliberately fostered by the employers for their own benefit. Workers who showed any inclination to organize for self-protection were promptly fired; and the blacklist operated relentlessly against those who dared protest."[5] The garment workers union shut down a large segment of the industry in a general strike. After nearly three weeks of bitter battles with nonstrikers and police, both sides agreed to arbitration which led to a period of peace to the industry.[6]

Other unions which followed the ILGWU in organizing campaigns were the Amalgamated Clothing Workers, Hotel and Restaurant Employees, Cleaners and Dyers, Building and Construction Trades Council, Meat Cutters and Butchers, Upholsterers and Teamsters. The first firm to lose its NRA emblem or "blue eagle" for noncompliance was a Jewish rye bakery.

By the end of 1933 Los Angeles labor leaders boasted of 60,000 members; labor historians estimate 30,000 as a more accurate figure, add that "labor leaders could hardly be blamed for indulging in some exaggerations." The open shop was thus under severe attack, but not defeated. As the depression unfolded it became a most tense issue, for it was not only part of the city's stormy past, it had now entered into a relationship with new factors of city growth and industrialization, the coming of new mass industries from the east with union agreements, and the general expansion of the labor movement in Los Angeles. Years back the city had developed an open shop policy, cradled in a partial separation from the national economy, developed as a lure to industry seeking lower wage scales, and receiving ideological blessing from the non-union Los Angeles _Times_.

The open shop policy was inadequate for the city's stormy Thirties. Labor saw it as its major hurdle for growth and influence here. The M and M interpretation that the open shop was legal under the NRA, was bitterly attacked by labor. Though the M and M blacklists and pressures became stronger, labor leaders organized a counter-offensive highlighted by an individual pledge by unionists at a March 1, 1934, rally:

> . . . I will help to put over the program of the Labor movement in this city, and I will not cease my efforts until Los Angeles becomes a union city. . . .

There was no significant advance in the size of the Los Angeles labor movement as a result of the pledges. It was not until 1937 and 1938 that local labor leaders were able to initiate as successful an organizing campaign as that of the first few months under the NRA.[7]

Labor fought on many fronts--union rates were won for skilled workmen on WPA projects in county areas but not in the city; the garment workers kept organizing and growing; the famed Brown Derby restaurant saw a partially successful three-month strike conducted by its waiters; a major struggle against the open shop developed in the cabinet and store fixture industry; strikes involved meat cutters and rubber workers.[8]

A labor struggle which had an impact on the city was that of the street and inter-urban railway workers in 1934 and 1935. The NIRA forced the Pacific Electric Railway to desert its long held anti-union policy, and though the first result was a company union including all craft locals, settlements followed with federal mediation playing a key role. At the Los Angeles Railway company matters took a different turn. Though an election indicated, as at the Pacific Electric Railway, that a majority of the workers favored the outside union over the company union, management rejected the result of the vote. A strike followed, with violence, strike-breakers, petty sabotage, stoning of cars, police tear gas assaults and numerous arrests. Strikers' ranks thinned and the Central Labor Council tried to rally the city and the labor movement. An Olympic Auditorium mass meeting involved the EPIC League, the Municipal League, and the Workmen's Circle. Despite government decisions against the company, development of a boycott movement and attempts to develop a competitive transportation system, the Los Angeles Railway Company defiantly continued operations. The strikers' cause became hopeless, and the union disappeared with the strike's defeat.[9]

There were victories for Los Angeles labor unions during the NRA period, and though the act was declared unconstitutional, this was not a serious setback to the local movement. Weaknesses in enforcing decisions, problems of company dominated unions, suspicion of too close relationships between the Chamber of Commerce and Local NRA offices, all played their part in local unionists unsympathetic attitudes to the blue eagle. When Franklin D. Roosevelt signed the National Labor Relations Act (Wagner Act), unionism was given still stronger legal backing. Los Angeles employers resisted the NLRA, and company unions continued to grow until the 1937 Supreme Court decision upholding the NLRA's constitutionality. The open shop was to receive major blows in the next years; unionists in the city continued to organize under the advantages of the NLRA, as the open shop forces regrouped to forestall organization by labor.[10]

One such battle ground was the movie industry. Possibilities of union victory flowed from the Eastern control of film production, and the actual separation of the facilities from the city itself. For the unionists, organization of Hollywood offered particular prestige and influence. The history of unionism in the industry dates back to an 1893 local of stagehands. By the time of the depression, union recognition had been won by various craft locals, though there was no provision for the closed shop. Hard times were complicated by the transition from silent to sound movies, with the musicians as a new labor factor. Negotiations took place, for the most part, in New York, away from the influence of either the Los Angeles Times or the M and M. A basic agreement covering the industry was signed, and it ran, with an extension, to November 1933.

Economic difficulties cut film jobs, wages (for the unorganized), and resulted in a shorter work week and work day as part of a share-the-work effort. By 1933 severe problems had bankrupted Paramount, and forced Fox and RKO to the brink; smaller studios went under. A major management assault on wages was forced back; the industry and its employees were in trouble. Some form of strong labor organization became an object of many in the industry. The NRA period saw unionism emerge and, as Bernstein wrote, "leadership came from the stars, probably the highest-paid employees in the nation."[11] The Actors' Equity ties of many performers from Broadway, coupled with the worsening economic conditions, aided union development. An NRA wage survey indicated that nearly half the actors made less than

$2000 in 1933. The average extra worked 11.7 days and earned $105.63 in 1936.

The Academy of Motion Picture Arts and Sciences, now known for its "Oscars," lost its original purpose as an employee-representation organization when it became the spokesmen for wage and salary cuts in March, 1933. The new union, the Screen Actors Guild, had top stars as members; Eddie Cantor was the first president. Its first victory was in modifying the NRA code so that organizing actors was facilitated; then it worked out an agreement on jurisdiction and rights with Equity, and laid the base for an eventual guild shop contract in May, 1937. By the end of the decade, when nearly 90 percent of all film production workers had located in Los Angeles, unionization was almost complete in the industry.[12]

On another front, the maritime workers of Los Angeles reflected general West coast labor history of intense battles, instability, union factionalism--a tale told more fully elsewhere. Maritime labor successes frightened employers in the city as they feared the spread of unionism inland.[13]

The years 1935 and 1936 were pivotal years for labor organization in the city as well as in the nation. Growing federal attention to depression problems aided the effort to continue the New Deal. The birth of the Committee for Industrial Organization (CIO), accelerated union growth. In Los Angeles unionism was extended to local WPA workers. The CIO-sponsored Labor's Non-Partisan League entered politics, and first reports came in of the CIO in Los Angeles trying to organize rubber and oil workers. The AFL's candidate for district attorney, and a labor leader running for president of the city Board of Education, were both elected. The 1936 Labor Day parade was another small triumph as 142 Los Angeles unions marched up Broadway, some 35,000 in the parade. By the end of the year labor claimed more than 65,000 members in the city. For a short time the illusion was prevalent that the M and M was in decline, but a renewal of interest in the open-shop cause and a new, more aggressive M and M leadership dispelled that unionist hope.

The M and M launched a coordinated drive backed by widespread advertising, management espionage, and a pro-company union propaganda. All was aimed at "maintaining somewhat of an equality with labor and to prevent the domination of labor through the obtainment by organization of this monopoly by the closed shop."[14] To the M and M's dismay that year, 1936, saw 50 strikes involving 10,502 workers in Los Angeles.

The CIO unions expelled from the AFL formed a California State federation in 1938, to which local Los Angeles CIO groups affiliated. The head of the Los Angeles chapter of the American Newspaper Guild became the first state CIO president. The year before, 22 unions had established a Los Angeles Industrial Union Council, and set a goal of organizing workers in the local automobile, aviation, rubber and steel industries of the city. In early 1938, the CIO in the city was claiming a membership of 50,000. The AFL also launched an organizing drive in the area and claimed nearly 35,000 members.

By 1938 it was estimated that approximately 150,000 workers were organized in the city and county in the AFL, CIO and the railroad brotherhoods.[15]

These new union gains increased the anger of the open-shop forces. Labor spokesmen "claimed that open-shop advocates even attempted to influence bank officers to refuse loans to employers who had agreed to recognize outside unions as collective bargaining agents for their employees."[16] The M and M and the Los Angeles Chamber of Commerce joined in the formation of The Neutral Thousands, a supposedly objective women's organization against labor's "encroachments." The TNT claimed a membership of thousands. The group was exposed as neither "neutral" nor "thousands." A similar organization, Southern Californians, Incorporated, was developed at the end of 1937 to coordinate the fight for the survival of "industrial freedom," the Times code for the open shop. Likewise unsuccessful was a short-lived group called Women of the Pacific with a similar purpose.[17]

The year 1938 saw a major confrontation on the open-shop issue. The Times in an editorial heralded Armageddon:

> Not since the Times Building was dynamited by the closed shop union terrorists twenty-eight years ago and twenty-one employees murdered, have the people of Southern California been in such danger as confronts them now.[18]

Unions became involved in many court cases concerning injunctions, boycotts and counter-appeals. An anti-picketing ordinance of some severity, passed by the City Council in the closing days of 1937, was vetoed by Mayor Shaw as unenforceable and unconstitutional. Among its provisions were prohibitions that

> . . . pickets may not, by either voice or banner, attempt to persuade anyone from entering a place of business from working there or seeking work or from buying or selling at the establishment.[19]

It left no mission for the picket!

In the 1938 mayoralty recall election, Los Angeles voters backed an open shop measure by a vote of 198,507 to 152,065, and elected Fletcher Bowron as the new mayor. Bowron, who had opposed the measure, said he would enforce the ordinance. The defeated mayor, Shaw, had taken no position; it seems that the good government issue was the overriding issue in the voters' minds. A year later the ordinance was invalidated by the courts. For labor, Bowron's victory brought an end to the work of policeman Hynes and his squad, a special thorn in the side of the unionists.

Labor's road to the end of the open shop was encumbered with internal strife, before labor boards and on picket lines. The split into AFL and CIO affected labor's political arm, Labor's Non Partisan League. There were also other problems of communist influence and factionalism. By 1938 the Labor Day parade in the city had 75,000 marchers; no CIO unions participated. Again the number of jobless increased in the 1937-38 recession, and the CIO enlisted their unemployed as organizers in an attempt to win new members among the employed.

Union ranks multiplied all over the city and county as organization came to aircraft workers[20] and the cry of outrage rose still higher from the open shop crusaders. The Times called David Beck, of the teamsters, who was organizing milk drivers; "The man who tried to kill Santa Claus." The following month the Times wrote that "Housewives have reported that they have been told they may find poison in their milk if they take milk from men who are not members of the Beck union."[21]

But the union successes continued, and there were bitter struggles involving the May Company, Pacific Freight Lines, Gallenkamp Stores and Blake, Moffett and Towne Paper Company. One strike at the Hollywood Citizen-News involved the American Newspaper Guild which had won agreements by the end of 1937 with the Evening Herald and Express, the Daily News, and the Evening News. The Citizen-News strike was one of the few instances of AFL and CIO unity in the area. It was a strike supported by Hollywood stars and writers; author Frank Scully hosted a curbstone cocktail party for the pickets before a compromise agreement was finally signed.[22]

As 1939 dawned, labor's position in the city, as well as the state, had improved tremendously.[23] For the first time in the Twentieth century a Democrat, Culbert Olson, was governor; he had started his administration with a pardon for Tom Mooney, labor leader who had become an international cause celebre. Mayor Bowron's victory had brought a friendlier atmosphere for labor with the clean up of the police department. The Mayor, faced with the problems of increasing stoppages and labor-capital conflicts, proposed a city board of labor leaders and employers to mediate disputes. But local AFL leaders refused to sit alongside CIO delegates, and some employers saw a permanent mediation board as the death knell of the open shop. The Court invalidation of parts of the 1938 anti-picketing ordinance accelerated the demise of the open shop, but the M and M was not ready to give up, though others on management's side retreated. There was an absolute increase in manufacturing in the city. By 1940 eight Los Angeles firms were so large that they employed 75 percent of all in manufacturing. The firms were, in order of importance: transportation equipment (automobiles not included), food products, machinery, iron and steel and their products, petroleum; printing and publishing, furniture and wood products, and apparel. To the city early in the decade came such firms as General Motors, Armour, Chrysler, Dow Chemical, Studebaker, Sherwin-Williams, General Cable, Canada Dry, Firestone, and General Foods. They were soon unionized. By the end of the decade the aircraft industry was on the way to predominance in the area. The coming of national industries whose plants in the East were unionized; new and more varied economic endeavors, the national market and the pressures of World War II finally buried the open shop.[24] It was then that Los Angeles went from a small industry town to a big industry city.

Mayor Bowron dramatized this new and changing Los Angeles in a mid-1939 address to a CIO conference:

> Even the most conservative manufacturers have come to realize that workers must organize, that bargaining cannot be with individuals, and that the effort to maintain the open shop is a lost cause.[25]

Los Angeles had become a union city.

FOOTNOTES

1. The Dream of Debs, short story by Jack London, can be found in Philip S. Foner, ed., Jack London American Rebel (New York, 1947), pp. 240-257; for early (1875-1912) history of local labor movement consult Grace H. Stimson, Rise of the Labor Movement in Los Angeles (Berkeley and Los Angeles, 1955).

2. Louis B. Perry and Richard S. Perry, A History of the Los Angeles Labor Movement, 1911-1941 (Berkeley and Los Angeles, 1963) is the main source for this chapter. Though not an intriguing volume, it is invaluable. p. 214, pp. 221-239; Hannah Bloom, "The Passing of 'Red' Hynes," The Nation, Volume 175 No. 5. August 2, 1952, pp. 91-92.

3. Perry and Perry, op. cit., pp. 247-248.

4. Ibid., pp. 249-250.

5. Rose Pesotta, Bread Upon the Waters (New York, 1945).

6. Perry and Perry, op. cit., pp. 251-267.

7. Ibid., pp. 270-275; pledge, p. 274.

8. Ibid., pp. 275-296.

9. Ibid., pp. 298-311; Utopian Society support referred to in chapter 6 of the work.

10. Ibid., pp. 315-317.

11. Irving Bernstein, The Turbulent Years (Boston: 1969), p. 137 ff. The section in this book on Hollywood, pp. 137-142, is very informative on film unionization; also see Perry and Perry, op. cit., chapter IX: "Union Success in the Movie Industry."

12. Perry and Perry, op. cit., p. 359.

13. Ibid., Chapter X, "Revival at Harbor," pp. 362-397, 403.

14. Ibid., pp. 398 ff; quotation against open shop, p. 402.

15. Ibid., pp. 420-425.

16. Ibid., pp. 426.

17. Ibid., pp. 426-430.

18. Ibid., p. 429. Quote from Los Angeles Times, February 21, 1938.

19. Ibid., p. 434.

20. Ibid., pp. 435-444; court invalidation, p. 498.

21. Ibid., p. 468, quote of Los Angeles Times, January 2, 1938, and Los Angeles Times, February 22, 1938.

22. Ibid., pp. 476-477.

23. Ibid., p. 522; see Irving Bernstein, The New Deal Collective Bargaining Policy (Berkeley: 1950) for good basic presentation of national setting. Hines' squad was abolished in November and the famed policeman was assigned to a post in West Los Angeles (Los Angeles Times, December 1, 1938). His career of 22 years with the L.A.P.D. began in 1922; he seemed to have found his direction the next year as an undercover man in an IWW strike in which he became secretary of the strike committee and editor of its strike bulletin (Los Angeles Times, May 18, 1952).

24. Perry and Perry, op. cit., pp. 526-536. Bernstein indicated that M and M gave up in 1937: see p. 19, Irving Bernstein, Labor Relations in Los Angeles (Los Angeles, 1965).

25. Perry and Perry, op. cit., Bowron statement, p. 521.

CHAPTER 9

PAGE ONE PROBLEM

Very early in the depression, spokesman for the organized unemployed began to appear before the Los Angeles City Council. In May of 1930, a Committee of the Unemployed League asked permission to use Pershing Square for a meeting. The Council referred the request to the Board of Park Commissioners. The referral of all unemployed meeting and parade permit requests to various committees became standard Council procedure. Almost a year later when the Unemployment Conference requested a permit for a parade on February 6, 1931, the matter was sent to both the Police and Fire Commissions. The Los Angeles Conference for Unemployed Insurance request for a permit was also denied. They planned

> . . .Unemployed Demonstration and Mass Meeting, Tuesday, February 10, 11:30 a.m. at City Hall. . . for the purpose of presenting demands for immediate cash relief for the unemployed.

This organization was characterized as "a branch of the Communist group." The Council's vote for rejection was unanimous. The next day a request of William W. Busick, chairman of the Unemployed Conference, to present their program to the Council was shunted to committee. A year later the same council policy prevailed when the city committee of the Unemployed Council sought permission for a 5th and Towne Avenue rally or provision of a hall.[1]

In the streets, with permits denied, a different drama was being acted out. There were violent confrontations between police and demonstrators involving 20 arrests, tear gas, and police use of their clubs in the Plaza area on February 26, 1930. A Los Angeles Communist-led demonstration on March 6, part of a national unemployment protest day, ended in a melee and 26 arrests. Hynes' men were very active in rounding up leaders of the demonstrators. Hynes raided a headquarters at 3rd and Spring Streets, arrested all present, oblivious to whether they had been involved in a nearby demonstration. (Arrested on both February 27 and March 6 was Francis Waldron, in his twenties, later known as Eugene Dennis, head of the American Communists.) Charges of police brutality were dismissed by the County Grand Jury which described witness as "generally unworthy of credence," with the implication that "the Communists have organized 'defense squads' in Los Angeles, whose duty [it] is to attack the police." The American Civil Liberties Union was disparaged as "sponsors and sympathizers" of the Communists.[2]

On February 16, 1932, the floor of the City Council was given to George H. McLain of the Los Angeles Unemployed Voters Association, who proposed power bond funds for immediate relief.[3] Communications from unemployed organizations decreased as the depression continued; at best the groups considered the Council a forum as they were receiving no permits or support. In the beginning of 1933 a communication from the State Hunger March Conference of Los Angeles called for improvement in relief allocations and insisted "that evictions and the shutting off of water, gas and lights be discontinued."[4]

A typical demonstration in 1933 of 100 women of the self-help movement protested a threat to cut free milk. According to the report they declared: "You dare not refuse us milk for our children. We mothers won't stand by and see our children starve."[5] An EPIC News story described a group of 300 led by the Unemployed Workers League routing the Board of Supervisors in late March 1935.[6]

The City Council considered most petitioners Communists, or Communist backed, an opinion held by the police and other authorities. When demonstrations held without permits ended in violence and arrests, this opinion was confirmed, and the press headlines were of "reds" and "rioters."[7] The Socialists fared little better before the City Council. The Council denied a permit for a parade of the unemployed requested by William Busick, Socialist Party secretary. The action was taken on the report of Captain Hynes, as one Councilman

> . . .concluded with an attack on Busick terming him a troublemaker and agitator, with a total lack of any sincere intention to reduce unemployment.[8]

It was basically only the Communists and the Socialists who tried to organize the unemployed. In Bernstein's opinion:

> [For] the two Marxist parties in the United States, the Socialists and the Communists, economic collapse was an unrivaled opportunity and they viewed the capture of the jobless as a great prize.

The labor historian indicated that the Socialists first urged "the creation of unemployed councils in every city to agitate for relief and public works" in May 1929. Little success followed the proposal. Bernstein noted that "the Socialists, in effect, defaulted to the Communists, who alone were ready to get out on the streets to organize the jobless for revolution."[9] Perhaps this complete rejection of the system was the key to the Communist approach. Confrontation exposed the State and the police as "tools" of the capitalists (read, they said, State and Revolution by Lenin); cadres were hardened and tested in the physical battle with the police; the unemployed would see who was fighting hardest for them, and the Communists would win leadership and members. The Communists, alienated from the political process, saw no need to compromise with it (this in the pre-popular front days); the struggle in the streets also exposed the Socialists (Socialists in words, Fascists in deeds) who were absent when the struggle was difficult; this alienation was also the mood of sections of the unemployed. Work among the unemployed was a high party responsibility, for the jobless were the most oppressed victims of the system (the German Communists had built a powerful movement of the unemployed and they were hailed as models).[10]

A classic expression of this Communist approach was presented at a state hearing in 1932 by a representative of the Youth Committee of the Unemployed Council:

> We don't expect to gain anything through this hearing. What we do want to do is to have before your minds that we are presenting before this Commission the true facts of the unemployed youth,

> and then if nothing is done, we will deal with them as our class enemy--a commission who represents the big interests and refuses to give the unemployed any relief.[11]

The Communist presence among the unemployed was stressed by Police Chief Davis in pressing for his 1934-35 department budget. After noting that rising crime was "a direct result of economic unrest and organized lawlessness," he added that he was also faced with "Communistically inspired social unrest."[12] The enemies of the Communists often over stated the party's power,surpassing the Communist claims. A speaker before a Los Angeles City Employees Association meeting in 1932 charged that the C.P. had six million members in the country, and some three million subscribers to the Communist press. He, at least, wisely concluded that "restoration of employment was the only way to portect Americanism."[13]

Communist activity among the unemployed of Los Angeles was constant; the December 1931 national Hunger March organized by the Communist Party and the Trade Union Unity League, its labor arm, had a Los Angeles contingent.[14] Typical was a local publication, The Hunger Fighter, with headlines: BREAD! NOT POLICE CLUBS!, and an article stating that

> . . . Nowhere else in the U.S. does such a relic of barbarism exist, as the Los Angeles POLICE TERROR. The Red Squad is the pampered pet of the Merchants and Manufacturer's Association, of the Chamber of Commerce, of the local charity organizations, of the City Council and of the County politicians.[15]

Police harassment was a continuing problem for the Communists. When Herbert Benjamin, national leader of the Unemployed Councils, came to Los Angeles in October 1932, he was stopped by the police from speaking on "Unemployment Insurance" at the ACLU's Open Forum. Both Communist national candidates in the 1932 campaign, William Z. Foster and James W. Ford, were arrested in a Los Angeles hotel. The ACLU protested a police attack on persons assembled at the John Reed Club, a party cultural group.[16]

An ACLU spokesman recorded the remarks of a member of the Los Angeles Police Commission, Mark Pierce, whose attitude on the rights of the Communists was: "The more the police beat them and wreck their headquarters, the better. Communists have no constitutional rights and I won't listen to anybody who defends them."[17]

Communist led unemployed organizations were not popular with most members of the self-help cooperative movement. Bill Downing, one of their spokesmen, said:

> Communists, hunger marchers, bonus marchers, the single floater and other forms of dissenters are not welcome on these units. This is no place for radical expression against duly authorized American law and order.[18]

Kerr indicates that six of the early self-help cooperatives were sponsored by the Unemployed Aid Society, "an innocents' society of one branch of the Communists." These six formed the nucleus of the Unemployed Cooperative Relief Association described as a body "which exerted a great influence during the winter of 1932-33."

Basically the Communist-led unemployed groups failed in the self-help movement. As they were routed, they turned elsewhere. The UCRA became more political, desiring to "unite the unemployed, not of Los Angeles County, not of California, but of the whole world." At one time the Communists boasted "at least three members in every (self-help) unit in the City of Los Angeles." Kerr identified two Communists as leaders in UCRA.[19]

A rare exposition of the Communist approach to organizing the unemployed is captured in Kerr's transcript of part of a speech he heard:

> It has been possible to organize the workers around a turnip as they have never been organized before. Though we knew this would lighten the burden of the taxpayer, we looked to a time when units would be thick and commissaries empty. Then the workers would be organized workers, today asking what they are going to do and tomorrow making demands.
>
> Vegetables have become scarcer and scarcer and the unemployed more and more. Units now for a month have been unable to feed themselves. The situation has suddenly gone to the left and the units are beginning to take on militant action by turning on utilities.
>
> The average mass of unemployed are only receptive to ideas when the facts of hunger stare them in the face. We can never go farther than the working class understands and knows and wants to go. This movement started as a carrot proposition but it's now becoming a working class movement. We must lead them along the lines of what they think they need, not what we know they need.[20]

Slight and temporary were the Communist successes in the cooperatives.

For a time the self-help movement "as the largest organization of the jobless in the county, sought to represent all the unemployed" and presented a program against relief cuts and for better work relief conditions. In the early part of 1933 they led forceful opposition to eviction of members from their homes, and against the shutting off of utility meters. Stickers of the group to be pasted on utility meters, car windshields and in house windows read:

PROTEST AGAINST CLOSING
OF GAS, WATER AND ELECTRIC
OF OUR PEOPLE
DON'T TURN THIS WATER OFF
by order of the
Unemployed Cooperative Relief Association

Communist suggestions to forcibly resist evictions were rejected, and vain attempts were made to get state tax benefits for landlords providing building space for unemployment relief purposes. Communist direct action tactics often became the order of the day. Cooperatives on the south side of Los Angeles elected "home guards" and "huskies" to oppose evictions. Kerr claims at least 14 units were represented on one "committee" which moved an evicted family back into its home. It was estimated that possibly 40 to 50 families were aided. Water and gas was turned on for more than 200 families. That the tactics were popular for a time was evidenced by the

> . . . action of 37 members who signed an 'honor roll' at a meeting of the City Council of the UCRA in February declaring their willingness to go to jail, if need be, to keep the unemployed in their houses with full utility service.[21]

Kerr offers one "eviction case" in early March as illustrative:

> [It] started when a woman called the Unit 14 headquarters on the telephone, asked for Manager Haddon, and told him she had been "set out on the street by the sheriff." Haddon got together a "committee" of about 30 persons and drove to the scene of the ejection. There they found an expectant mother, with an eleven months old baby which had just come down with the measles, huddled in old blankets on the sidewalk amid some miscellaneous furniture. The husband was away from home looking for work. The family had been living in a one-room shack, with no utilities, one table, one chair, one bed and almost no food. The house was owned by a Los Angeles mortgage company.
>
> After an unsuccessful attempt to secure assurance of assistance from the County Welfare Department, the "committee" elected Mr. Haddon as chairman and then passed a resolution to move the mother and child back into the house. It was carried out in an orderly manner.[22]

A class consciousness developed in the ranks of these unemployed and ironically undermined the barter-for-surplus ideology. Expressed by one, was the idea that they "actually found something fundamentally wrong with society [and that] the economic structure was not being operated for human need, but for individual greed."23 Yet the spring months of 1933 saw a decline of radical strength resulting from the success of several demonstration which won continuation of gasoline grants and free milk. A bitter inner struggle connected with a berry workers strike in which some scabbed, and some picketed, accelerated the UCRA's demise. A purge of the left completed their defeat and several of the "red" cooperative units changed into locals of the Relief Workers' Protective Union.[24]

A mixed marriage of unemployed and unionism developed in the federal work project years as organization came to WPA workers who, short months before, had been only concerned with problems of evictions and denial of relief. A Los Angeles publication, <u>Unemployed Leader</u>, "official organ of the Public Works and Unemployed Union State Federation Unemployed and Allied Organization," listed 65 meeting places in the County, and devoted nearly two of its eight pages to Spanish language material. Left or Communist influence was present, judging by the paper's approach, electoral support for C.P. backed Leo Gallagher for Superior Judge, and various advertisements. A call for a Second convention, July 17-19, 1936, would indicate it lasted at least a year. The organization supported the National Unity Convention of the Workers Alliance of America, held that spring in Washington, D.C. It was then that the Unemployed Councils and the Workers Alliance united into one organization bearing the latter name.[25]

The grievances of countless unemployed were expressed in these movements and support was larger than the many thousands directly involved. No doubt, inaction on the part of the majority was due to many factors. How does one measure apathy, fear of possible violence, rejection of association with causes branded as unpatriotic or "red," and the general psychic handicap of being unemployed--a condition possibly reflecting one's own deficiencies? Opprobrium extended to all on relief. One letter to the <u>Times</u> in 1936 suggested that "no person on relief should have the right to vote [to] prevent those on relief from putting pressure on politicians." A few days later another letter writer attacked the idea.[26] In 1933 a contrary proposal from the Los Angeles Unemployed Voters Association called for striking from the relief rolls all unemployed who did not exercise their franchise![27]

A special campaign was instituted against Mexican nationals, unemployed, on relief, or suspected of unorthodox political views. Abraham Hoffman's recent study on repatriation of this group during the Great Depression highlights the role of Charles P. Visel, head of a Los Angeles job program, who saw as his main effort the necessity of aiding a national deportation campaign against Mexican nationals. (Los Angeles contained the largest number of Mexicans outside of Mexico city.)

Raids, roundups, searchs and interrogations aimed at deportations and frighte.ing the local Mexicans to depart voluntarily were widespread. Even prisoners in jail on other charges were questioned. One coordinated raid saw a police encirclement of 400 in the central Plaza, and the taking into custody of 11 Mexicans, 5 Chinese and a Japanese. By April 22, 1931, some 389 Mexican aliens left voluntarily and involuntarily due to roundups and raids involving nearly 4,000 persons. The local Mexican community objected to the raids as harassment, and a cause of worsening economic conditions in the eastside. By mid-April, 1934, it was estimated 13,332 persons had left on 16 County sponsored trips costing

$194,501. County appropriations for the deportations were justified as saving the potentially much larger relief costs. Unrecorded thousands left in the wake of the general anti-Mexican alien atmosphere.

Reaction was mixed in the city, with the Times fearful of a farm labor shortage; others were upset at bad publicity while the city was preparing to celebrate its 150th birthday in 1931 with the theme "La Fiesta de Los Angeles" (City Hall telephone operators answered with a "Buenos Dias" greeting); hopes were also expressed that the deportation drive would not hurt the international good will for the city's role as host for the 1932 Olympics. Local Mexican-Americans were resentful of the general opprobium that was cast over all of Mexican descent.[28]

One group of unemployed, completely immune to deportation threats, were the veterans of World War I. They became involved in a major national movement of the unemployed of the Great Depression, the Bonus March of 1932.[29] Los Angeles had pre-March rumblings more than a year earlier when some 30,000 veterans applied for loans against the bonus. Congress had promised payment of the bonus in 1945 to veterans of the Great War.[30] The national movement had started in Portland, Oregon, where the first contingents of what was to become known as the Bonus Expeditionary Force, or B.E.F., commandeered freight cars and began the long trek to the national capital. The Los Angeles contingent[31] began with an encampment by 13 World War I veterans from Bakersfield on the corner of Washington and Hill

Streets. Royal W. Robertson, a Navy veteran, standing rigidly tall in a permanent neck brace due to a service injury, became the contingent's leader. Robertson's band grew; he warned Communists to keep out. By early June about 5,000 attended a rally and some 2,500 pledged to make the trip. Donations of food and supplies were received from Angelenos. Contributions included two ambulances and a hearse, the latter was assigned to the transport of commissary and medical supplies.[32]

On June 10 the veterans, 1400 according to the Times, marched up Broadway to Main Street and then to the east. A group in the parade carried a large canvas into whihc coins and dollars were thrown. "It was a good natured crowd, however, without trace of Communistic activities or demonstrations" opined a reported who also noted:

> Dilapidated automobiles, trucks of an early vintage and tires about ready for the junk heap seemed to be largely the equipment on which the marchers pinned their hopes of locomotion.[33]

The flag bearers leading the march were members of "a chiefly colored" post of the Veterans of the Foreign Wars who also supplied most of the 36-piece band which followed.[34] An estimated 350 vehicles were in the line of march and Mayor Shaw called upon them not to do anything that "would disgrace the name of Los Angeles." Like a Los Angeles contingent of Coxey's Army nearly forty years earlier, they headed out to San Bernardino; they had perhaps $2,500 in their treasury and a "red patrol" in their ranks to watch for signs of radicalism.

Passing through Phoenix, Arizona, their strength was estimated at nearly 2,300 (including 20 women and children) in 40 trucks and autos. By car and by freight the group crossed Texas, Arkansas, Tennessee, West Virginia; the first contingent of 250 arrived at the capitol on July 9, six weeks after leaving Los Angeles. In Washington, Robertson's contingent refused to go to the outlying camps at Anacostia, Virginia, believing they would be more effective in the city proper. They presented a petition to the Vice President and the Speaker of the House asking relief for all unemployed veterans. The Angeleno contingent was a high point in the March, parading in a single file "death vigil" in front of the capitol and opposing the general leadership for not pressing for a reconsideration of the bonus bill after Congress had voted it down. When Robertson left for home, the remaining Angelenos named Arthur Scott their leader. Shortly thereafter the entire Bonus Expeditionary Force was burned out of Anacostia, and dispersed.

Some of the Los Angeles delegation came back to the veteran's facility at Sawtelle; others tried to keep a camp going near Maywood, but it folded by October. Robertson spoke at local veteran's organizations, attended the Portland parley of the American Legion in November, called for a new Bonus March in 1935, and after working at his trade as a roofer, died in Los Angeles in 1938. Los Angeles had not been found wanting in the Bonus March, it had provided marchers, some leadership, certainly high drama and was part of a movement of a sector of the unemployed who won their demands in 1936 when Congress passed the payment of the bonus over President Roosevelt's veto.[35]

The demonstrations, the marches, the riots, the special police actions, the organizations of the unemployed--all became history only as the depression waned with the coming of federal aid, federal work programs, and the full employment years of the war. Of those earlier days Bernstein's estimate that the Communists, though they "failed to produce the revolution in America" with the demonstrations of the unemployed, did however aid non-Communist elements seeking relief and jobs, for the demonstrators' "bleeding heads converted unemployment from a little-noticed to a page-one problem in every important city in the United States."[36]

Los Angeles was not an exception; the City Council, the city police and the Communists put the problem of unemployment on the city's front pages. The demonstrations by its jobless, perhaps not as frequent and violent as those in New York, Chicago or Detroit, had their own intensities flowing, in good part, from the local police hysteria. Capt. Hynes' police squad was a special provocative Los Angeles aspect. That his work was part of the normal local police arrogance was seen nationally when the police department organized a special blockade in the month of February, 1936. That peculiar operation to cope with thousands of unemployed is a memorable part of Los Angeles and the Great Depression.

FOOTNOTES

1. City Council Minutes, Volume 232, February 1, 1932, p. 281. A youth group of the Unemployment Council protested the City Council's refusal to give a permit for the County Hunger March (City Council Minutes, Volume 236, September 29, 1932), p. 585.

2. Los Angeles Times, June 10, 1932.

3. Council Minutes, Volume 232, February 16, 1932, p. 509.

4. Ibid., Volume 238, January 4, 1933, p. 104.

5. Los Angeles Illustrated Daily News, May 30, 1933, quoted in Kerr, op. cit., p. 123.

6. Borough's papers, UCLA Special Collections, Box 8.

7. Los Angeles Times, March 5, 1930, has a pre-demonstration story headlined: POLICE READY FOR RED RIOT.

8. Ibid., February 5, 1931; Perry and Perry, op. cit., p. 229.

9. Bernstein, The Lean Years, pp. 425-426.

10. Later the official party analysis of the Hitler victory in Germany criticized the German C.P. for concentration on the unemployed instead of the working section of society.

11. Abstract of Hearings on Unemployment before the California State Unemployment Commission, April and May 1932 (San Francisco: 1932); testimony of Max Olson, Unemployed Youth, representing the Youth Committee of the Unemployed Council, San Francisco, p. 169; See Nation, July 26, 1933, p. 86 for sober and unlistened to advice offered the American Communists.

12. Davis to Board of Police Commissioners, March 15, 1934. Letter in Los Angeles Times morgue envelope marked Davis, J.E.

13. Los Angeles City Employee, June 1932, p. 4.

14. Perry and Perry, op. cit., p. 229.

15. Copy of front page, The Hunger Fighter, Volume 1, No. 1, October 15, 1932, Los Angeles, in Robert Bendiner, Just Around the Corner (New York: 1967), p. 10.

16. Clinton J. Taft, Fifteen Years on Freedom's Front (Los Angeles, 1939), p. 8, 22, 14.

17. Ibid., p. 14.

18. Kerr, op. cit., p. 96.

19. Ibid., pp. 104-121.

20. Ibid., p. 115.

21. Ibid., p. 119. Kerr's chapter VII: "The Radical Period" is rich in material on the unemployed struggles and the radicals.

22. Ibid., p. 119.

23. Ibid., p. 122.

24. Ibid., pp. 122-124.

25. Unemployed Leader, July 1, 1936, found in Borough's papers, UCLA, Box 6.

26. Los Angeles Times, March 18, 1936; rejoinder, March 27, 1936.

27. Council Minutes, Volume 238, February 6, 1933, p. 524.

28. Abraham Hoffman, "The Repatriation of Mexican Nationals from the United States During the Great Depression," unpublished Doctoral Dissertation, UCLA, 1970, is my source here. See especially pp. 69, 78, 87, 90, 96 and 148.

29. The first full-length study to appear is Roger Daniels, The Bonus March: An Episode of the Great Depression (Westport, Conn. 1971).

30. Los Angeles Times, March 3, 1931; 23,000 applied by mail, 7,000 came down in person.

31. Source for much of these are Los Angeles Times files and an unpublished paper by David Disco, "The California Contingent and the Bonus March of 1932," written for a History 199 Senior History course with Roger Daniels at UCLA. Paper in my possession. A third source is my own recollection of 14 days, July 8 through 22, 1932, which I spent as a teenager at the Bonus Encampment and Environs.

32. Los Angeles Times, June 9, 1932.

33. Ibid., June 11, 1932.

34. California Eagle, June 17, 1932, p. 4. This item asserts that nearly 250 of the marchers were colored.

35. The Bonus March image lasted into myth and nostalgia. See last chapter of Daniels' study. The Boroughs papers at UCLA contain a 1933 letter endorsing him for City Council on the stationery of "The Independent Voters League and the Bonus Army of Los Angeles and California," Box 5, folder 6.

36. Bernstein, The Lean Years, p. 427.

CHAPTER 10

"BUM BLOCKADE"[1]

Los Angeles, beset by its own thousands of unemployed, came up with a plan in 1936 to cope with the countless unwanted and unemployed invaders at its gates. Relying only on its own police force, the city sent a short-lived "foreign legion" hundreds of miles to the borders of California to bar destitute migrants. A magazine writer described the state's mood as that of a "brooding San Francisco and her big blond sister, Los Angeles, [where] the authorities were fretting themselves sick about all this migration of the unemployed."[2]

The depression years had put a new slant on the westward movement to California, turning what was once the great desideratum to the great fear. The state, once proud of John Sutter and his New Helvetia with his pioneer program of aiding American immigrants with relief trains, shelter, clothing and food, turned its back on that tradition in the hard times. The fear of the transient migrant was not only a depression phenomenon, for even in good times it was only the productive and economically solvent migrant who was sought; the depression troubles flowed from the fact that the unwanted portion of the migrants had increased much too much.

The idea that the unemployed were overwhelmingly out-of-staters is an old California theme going at least as far back as Governor Henry Markham (1891-95), who told the legislature of those depression years that three-fourths of the unemployed had come from elsewhere. He inferred that Coxey's Army of 1894 had difficult recruiting problems in Los Angeles because the jobless were unwilling "to leave the salubrious climate of California for the uncertainties of a winter trip across the continent."[3] Part of the early myth was the belief that the local unemployment problem became impossible only because of the influx of alien jobless. "If the rest of the country will let California alone, she will dig herself out," wrote correspondent Chapin Hall at the end of 1932.[4]

According to a social worker's 1933 report the transient or migratory family was "not a type new to American life." Pre-depression migrants were categorized as chronic wanderers, the family following seasonal crops, those lured to booms or new industries, the rural-urban migrants, seekers of more healthful climes, those spurred by social disasters or restlessness (e.g. automobile gypsies) and runaway children and youths. All these were augmented by the coming of the Great Depression as trickles turned into human flood-waters. Communities faced with their own depression created problems were unable to extend even the minor help they had once offered. What once were manageable local problems had become an overwhelming national dilemma.

"This transient thing is funny," wrote an aide to Harry Hopkins. "Men unable to get work in California and enroute to the Kansas wheatfields, actually meet up in Denver with men unable to get work in the Kansas wheatfields and on their way to California."[5] A Senate committee was told that as many as 20 to 25 percent were boys under

21, many with good educations, coming

> as a rule from a higher type of family with a more stable social background than the transients of predepression days. Social workers, police, and railroad men state that the overwhelming majority of young transients are boys who would be at school or at work under normal conditions.

Sons of unemployed and destitute familes, these young men were joined by married men on the freight cars and as hitch-hikers in search of work. On the road they were subject to disease, starvation and physical hazards (especially "riding the freights").[6] There were also the dangers of demoralization, incomplete education, degeneracy, and criminal activity. General Pelham D. Glassford, Superintendent of the District of Columbia's police during the 1932 Bonus March, told a Congressional Committee that the "most critical human product of the depression and unemployment is the transient situation. It is a menace to the manhood of America, and unless something is done about it, I am sure it will have a very deteriorating influence on our coming generation."[7]

Throughout the decade there were endless proposals to cope with the destitute migrants. The classic approach was "One night in jail, breakfast, and on your way." Some 39 states had residence requirements for relief ranging up to ten years; several states lengthened their requirements in response to the new crisis.[8]

The transient jobless problem was national, but it posed a special problem for communities in warm areas such as Los Angeles. A recent study noted that Florida, Arizona and New Mexico had similar situations as "more and more of the unemployed despaired of finding work in their own communities. One estimate, believed to be conservative, placed the number at 1,250,000."[9]

Los Angeles became the sunny Mecca for many tens of thousands of destitute migrants. Mayor Porter, in his first annual message in 1930, warned that the "attractiveness of our climate creates a winter unemployment situation in our city, which is never easy to meet."[10] The delegates to a city conference on unemployment held as early as December, 1929, agreed that the All Year Club's usual advertisements for the area be changed to discourage people from coming to the area.[11]

Propaganda and civic-minded hopes were no deterrents to the transients. How many were there, who were they, and from where did they come? The answer can not be found in the population increment figures for the depression decade, for transients, by nature, are an in-and-out group, often impervious to decennial censuses. Very little of the migrant story is contained in the fact that the city's increase was only 266,229 in the 1930's as contrasted with prior decade's leap of 661,375. It is more a measure of those who stayed, and bears witness to the conclusion of social researcher Jacqueline R. Kasun that the "myth that people came to Los Angeles chiefly during depressions has by now been pretty well exploded; indeed during at least one year of the 1930's there appears to have been a net out-movement and for the decade as a whole in-migration to Los Angeles County was markedly less than during either the 'twenties or the 'forties." Though her figures refer to the county, there is no reason to doubt their application to the city.[12]

At the end of 1931 it was estimated that California had "100,000 nonresidents, jobless, homeless and peniless men with perhaps 70,000 in Los Angeles alone." The same source reported more than 1,200 new arrivals each day.[13] By the end of 1933 the Los Angeles Municipal Service Bureau reported a transient registration for that year of 97,140.[14] Border patrol points of the state's Department of Agriculture, with a record of incoming transients incidental to their plant quarantine mission, counted 71,047 from mid-1935 to mid-1936; 16,315 were listed as Californians who were returning home from vain job hunts.[15]

Who were these transients and from where did they come? A Federal Transient Service official in Los Angeles reported that 10,000 youths between the ages of 16 through 20, registered between December 12, 1933, and November 12, 1934, came from every state of the union, Alaska, Hawaii, Puerto Rico, Phillipines, Brazil, Canada, China, England, Ireland, Italy and Mexico![16] Information about nearly 100,000 transient men and boys is offered by the 1933 Municipal Service Bureau report noted earlier. What did they want?

Meals and lodging	87,933
Medical care (688 were afflicted with veneral diseases)	5,430
Clothing	4,226
Transportation	298

The Bureau listed 90,056 in good medical condition. Some 34,000 of the men and boys filled out a questionnaire of the Bureau. The majority (17,102) were out of work for one year or more, unskilled (30,539), single (28,240), citizens (32,448), from other states (20,202), a short time in the city (23,831) and with only a grammar school education (19,399). Most were counted as "American" (29,027)--other classifications were Negroes (1,008), Mexicans (856) and aliens (2,038). Some 1,449 had gone to college, 12,711 to high school, and 255 listing no schooling. Only 4,815 claimed long time Los Angeles residence.[17]

Men and boys were not the only transients. Girls were also reported in the hegira. A Travelers' Aid Society executive noted:

> a change in the type of girl heading west. Before the depression many youngsters were eager to break into motion pictures. They'd steal a bit of money from their parents, then take a train for Hollywood. That's changed today. We find many boys and girls hitch-hiking or "riding the rods"[18]

Families, as well as single men, boys and girls, were in the migration. The plight of one such incoming family is caught in Paul S. Taylor's California border vignette:

> ...At worst these people lack money even for a California auto license. Asked for the $3 fee, a mother with six children and only $3.40 replied "That's food for my babies!" She was allowed to proceed without a license.[19]

California and the city pondered a difficult situation. "The state's agricultural sentries, stationed at her many gates to repel the Japanese beetle, the Mexican bean bug, the boll weevil, the gypsy moth, the European peach pest and kindred perils"[20] were perhaps the envy of those who wished the human invasion could be handled in the same way.

Prior to the organization of the formal border blockade, there were "a number of disconcerted Californians there, official and otherwise, engaged in the wholly futile business of shooing them off." One such premature border guard was described by the magazine writer Walter Davenport as a man

> dressed in nicely fitting khaki, long trousers, a stiff-brim campaign hat and a Sam Browne. Very erect and primly severe, he addressed the slumped driver of a rolling wreck that screamed from every hinge, bearing and coupling. "California's relief rolls are overcrowded now. No use to come farther," he cried. The half collapsed wanderer ignored him.[21]

The wanderers who ignored the warnings caused a rising tension in the city and the state; in 1935, Los Angeles members of the state legislature spoke up for the enactment of powers authorizing the Governor to exclude "all paupers, vagrants, indigents and persons likely to become public charges."[22] The problem of the unwanted migrant was called "the gravest problem before the United States" by a Los Angeles Times columnist, The Lancer, who went as far to question the value of good roads:

> The Chinese, wiser than we, have delayed building a great system of highways for that very reason - to head off these dangerous migrations - indigent people stampeding from farms into cities to live on charity. Incidentally, that was one of the reasons why Rome crashed.[23]

Tension on the question of transients climaxed at the end of 1935 when the federal government closed its Transient Camps as part of the temporary Roosevelt decision to "take the federal government out of the general relief business" and to give the responsibility back to the state and local governments. With that approach, the federal government established WPA projects to provide useful work with a high proportion of the monies going into direct wages for those formerly on relief rolls.[24] Thus, transients had become a local problem again. Relief official Aubrey Williams characterized the transient camps as failures, for "instead of alleviating a sorry situation proved to be the focal point for thousands of wand s"; they had become "Federal poorhouses."[25]

As the program closed in September of 1935, the Los Angeles Times lamented that "indigents are pouring into the State at the rate of 2,000 a week [and that the] situation is one which threatens to break the financial back of California.

The paper also hit at Upton Sinclair and Dr. Townsend as "partly to blame." Only a hope that a federal plan was in the works to pay the costs of transporting indigents back to their original states brought Times approval.[26]

Reports from the border fed the growing anxiety. Economist Paul S. Taylor reported in January, 1936, that 37,331 men, women and children had entered California in the five months ending November 15, 1935.[27] Moderating estimates that "approximately the same number goes back home, drops into private employ or finds temporary occupation on the works relief programs" did not abate the fears. Mrs. Dorothy Wysor Smith, director of the Los Angeles County transient aid department, tempered that statement with the opinion that if federal aid ended, there would "indeed be a serious problem."[28] The aid ended a month later.

All roads seemed to lead to the blackade as 1936 dawned. The city's police chief, James E. Davis, called the situation "alarming, if not desperate, to the residents of this community," and hit out at "the indifference of the Federal Government [which] left California wide open and helpless to protect herself."[29] He was determined to close the doors. Out of the melange of mounting relief costs, local mass joblessness, talk of rising migrant crime, possible health and degeneracy dangers, the endless human stream at the borders and a general xenophobia came the chief's forced exclusion policy.

Davis, the organizer of the police border operation, first came to the post of police chief in 1926, at the age of 37, "the youngest Police Chief in Los Angeles history." He served till 1930, returning to the post in 1933 under Mayor Frank Shaw. Local historian Remi Nadeau described him as "the police chief who had served through much of the crime-marked twenties." Davis was an adroit man winning, unquely, both the right-handed and left-handed pistol championship of the United States in 1932. As far back as 1929 he had been criticized by the Los Angeles Record for "his retention and defense of brutal third degree." Davis earned little love from civil libertarians at any point in his career. His defense and support of the activities of Police Captain William Hynes of the infamous Red Squad, earned him a special renown during the depression years. When the Shaw administration was recalled in 1938, both Davis and Hynes were swept out with the Mayor.[30]

But that was in the future, and Davis was high in the saddle as a preliminary conference was held with executives of the Los Angeles Chamber of Commerce and the City Prosecutor's office. They decided to fingerprint "all hoboes and beggars 21 years of age, with the chief adding "the fingerprinting of all adult vagrants and men arrested as residents of various hobo jungles." He announced that he had three new fingerprint men on his staff.[31] It is clear that Davis was thinking of fingerprinting and its use at the borders. He was not put off by the County's deputy counsel's opinion given to the Board of Supervisors that there was no legal way to fingerprint transients entering Los Angeles County, as suggested by the Chamber of Commerce.[32]

Chief Davis claimed that the general plan for the patrol was worked out in a series of meetings held in November, 1935. Representatives of the Los Angeles Police Department, he said, had obtained promises of cooperation from the police authorities in the various border counties affected. He boasted that the blockade plan was the product of a series of meetings which involved the Sheriff's office, railroads, the County Department of Charities and state relief agencies.[33]

On February 3 Chief Davis deployed 136 Los Angeles police officers on California's borders adjoining Oregon, Nevada and Arizona.[34] Police organization of the border patrol called for three divisions - northern, central and southern, all under acting Captain Jack Horrall, later a Chief under Mayor Fletcher Bowron. The northern are included Del Norte, Siskiyou and Modoc counties; central included Plumas, Nevada, Mono and Inyo counties; and the southern division was San Bernardino, Riverside and Imperial counties. Yreka, Truckee and San Bernardino were the respective area command posts.

Blockade procedure called for halting, at sixteen major entry points on the California borders, all would-be railroad fare evaders, hitch-hikers and, in the Times' words "all other persons who have no definite purpose in coming into the State." Families in automobiles, paying passengers on the railroad, "anyone who can show he or she has a good reason for entrance" and, naturally sea and air arrivals, were not to be bothered. Procedures involved the cooperation of the railroad companies in halting freight trains at points advantageous to the police. The companies also pledged to return undesirable itinerants to other states.[35] When it was determined that the new arrival had neither "visible means of support" and "no definite purpose" in entering the State they were to be taken into custody. Under the plan the transient was offered a simple choice: either leave the state or serve a 30 to 80 day term at hard labor on charges of evasion of railroad fare or vagrancy.

Parallel to the border patrol activities, Chief Davis launched a drive within the city against indigents. Backed by a County relief appropriation to finance return trips, he began a round up of "indigent families, single women, juveniles and men unable to work because of illness or infirmities.[36]

The state borders were still in the spotlight as the major police effort. Some insight into the conditions at the border near Blythe was given in a letter to The Nation. The Chamber of Commerce of Blythe

> had entertained a speaker from the Los Angeles Chamber, under whose influence they had sent a letter endorsing Chief of Police Davis of Los Angeles for protecting their town from those criminals who are trying to enter California.

The letter writer described two migrants, young men, 22 and 23, both with high school educations, one with two years of college:

> both staunch Republicans, well mannered and evidently from good homes...believed that the NRA was a great infringement on peoples rights. On their arrival at the state line they were met with the questions, "Any money? Any work? Well, this is as far west as you go.

An LAPD officer claimed he was "only finger-printing the ones who looked like criminals."[37]

Los Angeles policemen operating far from their city did not have clear authority or complete cooperation in all counties. Davis, alert to some of the complexities, claimed that his men needed no special authority for their new roles, "any officer has the authority to enforce state law."[38] Nevertheless, he asked the sheriffs of the border counties to deputize his men in their areas, without remuneration. Modoc County refused to continue its cooperation with the LAPD when local residents were halted by the policemen. The Modoc Sheriff ordered the police out of the county, threatening to "use means" to see that they left, adding that he had "stood for a lot and tried to be fair, but you have violated all the rules of decency." The Los Angeles police contingent withdrew and the Sheriff announced that

> with the evacuation by the Los Angeles police of their Modoc outposts quiet agair prevails here and the citizens of this county hope that the Angelenos are gone to stay.

A later report told of the Modoc LAPD unit transferring to Siskiyou County, where they were deputized. Modoc County's Attorney challenged the legality of the blockade. In response to some of the local resistance, Davis made a blustering threat to act against local police officers not cooperating.

At Truckee, permission to use the California Highway Patrol's station was denied to Davis' men. Refusal also came from the State's quarantine station there,"until legal aspects of the matter had been settled." The LAPD sergeant in charge notified Los Angeles headwuarters he was unable to carry out his assignment until, "arrangements could be made to provide them shelter against the snow and the cold." The officer claimed 25 less hoboes a day entered the Truckee area.[39]

Despite the difficulties, in the main the border patrol functioned and in Los Angeles the acclaim for the blockade was widespread. Public approval of the border blockade took many forms. A Los Angeles Municipal Judge in sentencing vagrants praised the police drive, and added: "I will be doing the taxpayers a favor if arrangements are made for you to leave town."[40]

Loud and enthusiastic plaudits came from Harry Chandler's Times. In answer to critical cries that the blockade was an outrage, the editorial writer answered:

"LET'S HAVE MORE OUTRAGES"

> ...it is the kind of outrage that ought to have been perpetrated in California several years ago. If it had, we would have been saved a good many millions of the hard-got tax money that has since gone to the support of the indigent from other states. If it had, we would not now be struggling with a $70,000,000 deficit. If it had, our citizens would have been spared many of the depredations of our present army of imported criminals. If it had, California would not now be the paradise for radicals and trouble-makers that it is.[41]

Times editorials hailed the news that "Los Angeles has stopped being a national Santa Claus;" praised Florida's blockade by the state authorities, since "it does not leave the task for any one city to do;" and defended the patrol's legality. A learned article in the paper's Sunday Magazine compared Chief Davis to Queen Elizabeth who had "launched the first war on bums." The editors assured all that Davis was "getting results." A special editorial asserted that the blockade would not cause a labor shortage of needed seasonal help.[42]

Besides the approbation of the Chamber of Commerce, other groups, such as the Apartment House Association of Los Angeles County, Inc., passed a resolution commending the patrol as an "important step in reducing the burden on taxpayers." The Pomona Chamber of Commerce endorsed the patrol; from Bakersfield the Police Chief sent quick congratulations. Federal attorney John Hall "tentatively upheld the police program" finding a fine precedent during the World War "when Arizona citizens picked up 196 so called 'wobblies', took them to the New Mexico border and shoved them across."[43]

There was also wide criticism of the blockade which erupted in the City Council. Councilman Parley Parker Christensen who had won his seat with EPIC support, introduced a resolution asking Davis to state his authority for the patrol. A heated exchange followed as another councilman attacked "this continual hammering at the Chief of Police." It was charged that local unemployed "cannot get aid, but floaters and box car tourists coming into town can get on the dole in a minute." It was resolved to ask the City Attorney's legal opinion on the border patrol, and the jurisdiction the Council might have over the police.[44]

The Los Angeles Evening News struck out strongly:

> Considered purely from the philosophical point of view, the program violates every principle that Americans hold dear. On the face of it, it is un-American to question the right of any citizen

> to go where he pleases. The urge to travel back and forth between the cold Eastern States and the sunny warmth of Southern California is not peculiar to those who are still rich. As a matter of fact, some of these wanderers may have been here before, and in happier circumstances.[45]

Sacramento reactions were guarded. The Governor made no comment; the Deputy Attorney General, Jess Hession, states: "Los Angeles police will soon find they have no right to control the border stations of the State" and he attacked the patrol as an "illegal proposition"; Senator Thomas Scolland of Sacramento who led the successful fight at the State legislature to kill a bill denying entry to the state to destitute itinerants, called Davis' plan "damnable, and outrage and absurd." He warned "Los Angeles will find it can't take the whole state into its city limits."[46] The State Comptroller proposed an exclusion plan in which "any kind of disease would be sufficient excuse to prevent their entrance."

An American Civil Liberties Union spokesman said: "If Jesus Christ were on earth today, he couldn't get into California--he would be stopped by Chief Davis' border patrol!" Ernest Besig, Los Angeles ACLU director, denounced the blockade as "conspiring to take away the civil rights of United States citizens, a punishable offense under the code." Besig also charged that use of funds by the LAPD on this mission was a violation of the city charter and the state and federal constitutions. An immediate end to the "so called 'foreign legion'" was also asked by the Municipal League.[47]

The national, state and local debate increased. In his weekly dispatch to the New York Times, Chapin Hall of the Los Angeles Times wrote.

> The Los Angeles Police Department has undertaken an interesting experiment involving an original interpretation of the Constitution of the United States which has aroused this State as have few other matters.[48]

From Lincoln Steffens' Pacific Weekly in Carmel, came the acid comment that the blockade "is the clearest Nazi and lawless act yet perpetrated by law officials in California."[49] The San Francisco Chronicle, though trying to be sympathetic, said the problem "can not be solved by the arbitrary action of one city Chief of Police. It is a national problem."

The Los Angeles Times, perhaps because it suspected its support for the blockade was on shaky grounds, gave its readers a reprint of some of the antagonistic out of town editorials. The St. Louis Post Dispatch noted that Upton Sinclair was not responsible for the migrants. Failure for the blockade was predicted by the Portland Oregonian. What would be the effect on tourism asked the Kansas City Times. The Boston Transcript called the operation one "of such high-handed nature that it would seem destined soon to be brought to an end."[50]

In Washington Senator Hiram W. Johnson received an informative letter from his constant correspondent attorney Frank P. Doherty who suggested the patrol

> be called the Liberty League Police, because their acts are in line with the construction of the Constitution of the Liberty League. This Constitution of ours is like the Bible, it can be used to justify the cause of all sides or, in fact any side that wishes to put its own construction upon it. The logical effect of the attitude of Los Angeles is to have California partially secede from the Union. They have to set up their own immigration department between states. They arrest those in charge of vagrants who refuse to be turned back. It is a most unusual world in which we live.[51]

California's neighbors, the states along her borders, had unfriendly reactions. The Literary Digest called Nevada "unworried, but alert; Oregon "angry"; and Arizona "given to gibes." Reno's Nevada State Journal editorialized:

> If the Constitution doesn't guarantee citizens the right to breathe the air, walk on the earth, view the sunset and hunt for a job without a mounted policeman's approval, then we've no Constitution. How many Forty-Niners would've been able to show "visible means of support" on entering California?

Grant's Pass, Oregon's Daily Courier worried about "having California's thousands of wandering vagrants pile up [and] create a relief and crime problem, unknown here now." In Phoenix The Arizona Republic said Arizona will suffer most from California's exclusion policy.[52] Governor Merriam charged that Arizona Chambers of Commerce furnished "gasoline to itinerants to help them along to California."[53] He offered no proof for the assertion.

Chief Davis reported success on many fronts. In the first week of operations, he reported that 1,000 "penniless winter visitors" were stopped: 662 at the Arizona border; 51 at the Nevada border and

312 at the Oregon border.[54] Great victories were claimed in the war against crime. "POLICE TRAP SUSPECT IN BORDER WAR" was the headline on the capture of "Negro Jesse A. Gains, 27" who was wanted for murder in Imperial County![55] In the first days of the blockade, the chief announced a 25 percent decline in robberies, burglaries and purse snatching in the city. Davis prophesized in a speech to the Breakfast Club that $1,500,000 would be saved "from the thieves and thugs" and that $3,000,000 "in relief money will be salvaged" due to the patrol.[56]

The LAPD reported that vagrancy and panhandling were at a new low; the number seeking aid from local relief agencies had dropped; juvenile delinquency was on the wane; new registrations at the Central Employment Bureau for Veterans were reported the "lowest since last July." Said the Times in agreement - "local agitation against transients has borne fruit" and "vagrants are now as hard to find as the proverbial hens' teeth." Police reports spoke of the daily vagrancy arrests, at 150 a day when the drive began, dropping to less than ten a day five weeks later. Capt. Warren L. Justin boasted that vagrants, given the choice of leaving the city and state or hard labor in the stone quarry chose exit 75 to 1![57]

The Chief told the Garvanza Congregational Church that the border patrol "is not a stroke in the dark but a movement directed by intelligent consideration of the facts." He asserted that "the campaign will aid rather than retard the growth of the city...a cleaner city, free from crime, will entice better-class citizens to come to Los Angeles." Davis used the occasion to note that the Police Department had 83 men less than in 1926, "notwithstanding the fact that our population has increased nearly 500,000, with 200,000 additional automobiles on our streets and highways."

The pressures against the blockade kept mounting. From the beginning, the spectre of its unconstitutionality haunted its proponents. In the first days of the blockade State Attorney General Ulysses S. Webb attacked the blockade as illegal. In a message to the Los Angeles Chamber of Commerce, he stressed that interfering with the ingress and egress of citizens of the United States into California was illegal. In answer to the claim of the city and a Federal Judge that the general welfare required this emergency action, Webb wrote:

> Government -- State, county and Municipal -- should protect and preserve and defend the general welfare, but this ultimate object would be accomplished through lawful methods. Governments, no more than individuals, can justify the reaching of even proper ends through unlawful means.[58]

In a lengthy letter, City Attorney, Ray L. Chesebro, avoided the constitutional issue and kept to such questions as whether the Los Angeles police could be deputized as sheriffs at the borders, problems of vagrants, the complete observance of the legal process by the officers ("the motto 'they shall not pass' has not been substituted") and the pressing crime and charity problems the city was trying to cope with. No one, at any time, publicly asserted that people could legally be prevented from crossing the border.[59]

The Los Angeles Times position on the legality or illegality of the patrol was not as subtle:

> The Attorney-General may succeed in proving Chief Davis legally in the wrong. It was up to somebody to do something and Chief Davis did it. He may get licked but it will take some time to do it. In that interval a lot of undesirables can be turned back and a lot more discouraged from even starting in this direction. If it is proven illegal to use city policemen to do work the State ought to be doing, the results may at least point the way to accomplishing the same thing in accordance with Hoyle.[60]

The patrol's continuance was at stake in a suit in the Federal Court by the American Civil Liberties Union on behalf of John Langan, a Los Angeles resident who had been halted at the border by the LAPD. Langan, returning from a mine he was working in Arizona, dressed in work clothes, was prevented from entering California at the Blythe blockade point. The city attorney sought the aid of two prominent local attorneys, Judge Benjamin Bledsoe and Joseph Scott, to fight the suit. Suddenly Langan withdrew his suit. His counsellors intimated that he had been pressured by the police, that police Lt. Earl Kynette "used all his arts on Langan before he got control of him; he cajoled him, promised him a job in the movies, and finally terrorized him." Langan, in a letter to Chief Davis denied all this, praising Kynette as "most pleasant and cordial," stating that he "was in error in maintaining a law suit" and was now convinced of "the effectiveness for the common welfare of the Border Patrol." In closing his letter he suggested "the promotion to a higher office of Kynette." The ending of the patrol soon after the close of this case gives credence to the ACLU view that Langan's suit was decisive and "a moral victory."[61]

Only with an examination of police records can one obtain a full explanation of the patrol's end. It would seem that a combination of pressures, not the least of which was its dubious legality and constitutionality, brought the patrol to an end.

How long did the patrol last? On April 7, 1936, about two months after its start, Davis was reported as planning to recall the patrol. It is clear that barely more than a score of officers were then on the patrol, and these in southern county areas only.[62] Originally, the Chief had spoken of a one or two month's campaign.[63] The cutting of the size of the contingent was attributed "to milder climactic conditions in the East."[64] Confusion was compounded by his statement that the "patrol will continue in effect until such time as other arrangements for the halting of undesirable itinerants are made by the State authorities."[65] At most, the patrol lasted, in waning strength, for approximately two months.

The blockade was not revived, though there were further plans and hopes that the State or County Sheriffs would re-establish it. There was continuing, nostalgic reference to the blockade's effectiveness, and unrealized ideas of establishing a health blockade against the ill, and even the possibility was voiced that the city of Los Angeles could establish a blockade around its own limits.[66]

How effective was the patrol? As it came to its end, Davis claimed that 11,000 had been turned back from February 6 through March 31, and that the "exodus was directly responsible for the absence of a seasonal crime wave in Los Angeles for the first time in many years." There were words of praise from a patrol inspector of the U.S. Immigration and Naturalization Service at El Centro. Eight aliens had been apprehended! A Southern Pacific Railroad agent hailed the drop in accidental deaths and injuries of transients and trainmen.[67] The Los Angeles Rotary Club president saw the patrol as saving money for the taxpayers, ridding the area of persons with criminal records, cutting job competition for local citizens, discouraging migratory tendencies of the nation's unemployed. They also expressed praise for Davis' publicizing to the transients that they were eligible for WPA jobs in their home states, but not in California.[68] By June, Davis was asserting that seven to eight million dollars could be saved annually if the patrol was maintained. But none of this seemed to make a case for the effectiveness of the patrol in cutting the flow of destitute migrants into California and the city of Los Angeles.

A Monthly Labor Review study noted the blockade's effect "was to 'back up' the refugees and delay them temporarily in states surrounding California." Noting that "repercussions of this situation were felt as far east as El Paso," the study concluded that it "is illogical to assume that turning back these migrants from the borders of any State affords a solution to the fundamental problems involved or that lasting benefit accrues to the State invoking such action." (It was true that March 1935 showed the lowest number of migrants in a six month period).[69]

In the first days of the border effort the secretary of the Florida Transient Committee, who was quick to congratulate the LAPD had added these prophetic words: "California will find, as Florida, found, that [the] border patrol doesn't work,...is too expensive... and brings an avalanche of criticism."[70]

The question of the exclusion of citizens of one state from another was finally decided by the United States Supreme Court in a unanimous decision rendered on November 24, 1941. Known as Edwards vs. California the case involved Fred F. Edwards of Marysville, California. He had been convicted for violating California law when he transported his indigent brother-in law, a citizen of the United States, from his residence in Spur, Texas, to Edwards' California home in Marysville. Some 27 similar State laws fell with the Supreme Court decision asserting that such a law "imposes an unconstitutional burden upon interstate commerce." Justice William O. Douglas' concurring statement was blunter:

> It would permit those who are stigmatized by a State as indigents, paupers or vagabonds to be relegated to an inferior class of citizenship. It would prevent a person because he was poor from seeking new horizons in other states.[71]

The Los Angeles "Foreign Legion" remains a dramatic and symptomatic splash in the city of Los Angeles' depression history.

Though touted as an attempt to lessen crime and criminals, there was never absent from the minds of the organizers the belief that it would drastically cut charity and relief problems and guarantee to the city residents whatever job opportunities that were available. The border patrol was to accomplish these tasks immediately, and in the long run, lighten tax burdens and make for a better and purer city and state. The patrol was a unique city answer coming from a Los Angeles which had built itself on luring migrants. It seemed as if the city aimed to reverse its past, but perhaps the border legion supported by a wide climate of opinion also reflected another aspect the city's history - the slice known as xenopobia - the fear and hatred of outsiders. Once it had struck out at Chinese and Japanese (in the war years it would strike harder yet); in this case it struck at those who lived just across the border - the enemy came from the other 47 states. Not all were aliens and enemies - only the poor - but there were, it seemed, too many of them.

FOOTNOTES

1. Term used by John Anson Ford in Thirty Explosive Years (San Marino, 1961), p. 13.

2. Walter Davenport, "California, Here We Come," Colliers, August 10, 1935, p. 10.

3. A.A. Gray, History of California From 1542 (Boston, 1934), pp. 512-513. A $2 per day rate on public works in Los Angeles in that time was cut to $1 per day to lessen the city's appeal to the jobless.

4. New York Times, December 25, 1932, IV 6:7. This dispatch "Jobless 'Floaters' Worry California" is full of details backing the belief that the "state could care for its own but destitute outsiders made the situation look hopeless."

5. Lorena Hickock to Harry Hopkins, June 25, 1934, Hopkins file, F.D. Roosevelt papers, Hyde Park, N.Y.

6. U.S. Senate, Subcommittee of the Committee on Manufactures, Hearings on S. 5125, Unemployment Relief, 72nd Congress, 2nd Session 1933 p. 33 Source for this material is a report given by a social workers' committee headed by Katherine F. Lenroot.

7. U.S. Senate, Committee on Banking and Currency, Further Unemployment Relief through R.F.C., S.5336, February 203, 1933 Washington, D.C., 1933).

8. Lester V. Chandler, America's Greatest Depression, 1929-1941 (New York, 1970), p. 47.

9. Ibid., p. 46; See also Hannah op. cit., pp. 120-123.

10. John C. Porter, Annual Message, January 2, 1930. The full text is in an envelope under the Mayor's name in the Los Angeles Times morgue.

11. Los Angeles Citizen, December 13, 1929.

12. Kasun, op. cit., p. 10-11. Her figures, though given for the county, are relevant.

Period	Estimated in-migration
1920-1924	285,577
1925-1929	377,979
1930-1934	268,030
1935-1939	331,888
1940-1944	485,899
1945-1949	422,846

13. Chandler, _op_. _cit_., p. 46.

14. This was found in Reuben Borough's papers, UCLA Special Collections, Box 8, Folder 3. It was submitted by Anna B. Smith, General Manager, Dept. of Social Service to Lt. Joseph E. Shaw at his request.

15. Edward J. Rowell, "Drought Refugee and Labor Migration to California in 1936", _Monthly Labor Review_, Volume 243, No. 5, December, 1936, p. 1355 Seasonal farm work factors have to be considered.

16. George E. Outland, "Sources of Transient Boys," _Sociology and Social Research_, Volume 19, pp. 428-34. June 1935, The chart of the 10,000 is on p. 434. Outland was Supervisor of Boys Welfare in Southern California's Federal Transient Service, Los Angeles. A report of the Community Boys' Lodge in Los Angeles listed 623 applying for shelter in the five months ending March 31, 1932 as coming from 45 states and the District of Columbia (New York led the list with 76). A. Wayne McMillen, "An Army of Boys on the Loose," _The Survey_, Volume LXVIII, No. 11, September 1, 1932, p. 391.

17. See footnote 14.

18. Los Angeles _Times_, September 21, 1935.

19. Paul S. Taylor, "Again The Covered Wagon," _Survey Graphic_, Volume XXIV, No. 7, July 1935, pp. 348-349.

20. Davenport, _op_. _cit_., p. 10.

21. _Ibid_., p. 11.

22. Quoted in Zelma E. Parker, "A History of the Destitute Migrant in California, 1849-1930" unpublished M.A. thesis, U.C.Berkeley 1940, p. 96.

23. Quoted in Taylor, _op_. _cit_., p. 350.

24. Chandler, _op_. _cit_., p. 203.

25. Los Angeles Times, July 24, 1937. In the same dispatch Williams made a stirring plea for the transients: "These out-of-staters aren't stumblebums! They are your potential settlers who opened Minnesota and Wisconsin and then the Dakotas. Now they are coming here. Given half a chance they will become useful citizens. All they need are jobs, sanitation and good food."

26. Ibid., September 12, 1935, November 1935. For earlier warnings see issues of June 12 and August 2, 1935.

27. Ibid., January 8, 1936.

28. Ibid., August 3, 1935.

29. Ibid., February 5, 1936; New York Times, February 9, 1936 (Section IV)

30. Source for some of the biographical material on Davis Los Angeles Times, June 21, 1949 (obituary); Los Angeles Record, November 16, 29, 1929 noted that with four exceptions, Davis being one of them, police chiefs in Los Angeles averaged 11 months in office. Also see Remi Nadeau, Los Angeles - From Mission to Modern City (New York, 1960), p. 259.

31. Los Angeles Times, January 9, 1936.

32. Ibid., January 22, 1936.

33. Ibid., February 16, 1936. An attempt to consult the obviously much involved Los Angeles Chamber of Commerce files was rebuffed by that organization in the fall of 1970; Los Angeles Times, February 16, 1936: The Times found a 1923 precedent for the blockade in a combined action of the Bakersfield Chief of Police and the Southern Pacific Railway. Los Angeles Times, February 17, 1936.

34. The Los Angeles Herald, February 4, 1936, gave the figure as 126 officers. Whether this was a journalistic or typographical error, or just part of the general confusion is not clear.

35. Los Angeles Times, February 4, 1936.

36. Ibid., February 7, 8, 1936. Sadly and ironically, the County Board of Supervisors was considering the burial in Potter's Field of the ashes of dead indigents who had been cremated before February 12, 1933. The County Superintendent of Charities explained to the Board that "the county cemetery has limited facilities for storing unclaimed ashes of persons cremated at county expense." Ibid., February 17, 1936.

37. The Nation, Volume 142, No. 10, March 4, 1936, p. 295.

38. Los Angeles Times, February 4, 1936.

39. Ibid., February 6, 7, 8, 11, 12, 16, 1936.

40. Ibid., February 10, 1936.

41. Ibid., February 5, 1936.

42. Ibid., February 7, 13, 20; March 13, 23, 1936, March 1, 1936; The Portland Oregonian picked the theme, quoted the Times noting that: Perhaps the Los Angeles police could get some ideas from the law of 1536. This provided that a beggar should be whipped and sent to his own village. He should be provided with a testimonial to the effect that he had been whipped, which would entitle him to food and lodging every ten miles. If he loitered, part of the right ear was to be cut off; if he loitered a second time, he was to be put to death.

43. Los Angeles Times, April 15, March 26, February 7, 9, 1936. See John H. Lindquist and James Fraser, "A Sociological Interpretation of the Bisbee Deportation," Pacific Historical Review, Volume XXXVII, No. 4, November 1968, pp. 401-422, for interesting insights on the 1917 event.

44. Ibid., February 5, 1936.

45. Literary Digest, Volume 121, No. 7, February 15, 1936, p. 9.

46. Los Angeles Times, February 14, 1936.

47. Ibid., February 9, 1936; Municipal League Bulletin, Volume 10, No. 12, March 15, 1936, Borough papers, Box 8, UCLA Special Collections; Los Angeles Times, February 7, 1936, Clinton J. Taft, Fifteen Years on Freedom's Front (Los Angeles, 1939), p. 43.

48. New York Times, February 9, 1936, section IV.

49. Literary Digest, Volume 121, No. 7, February 15, 1936, p. 9.

50. Editorials reprinted in Los Angeles Times, February 13, 1936.

51. Frank P. Doherty to Hiram W. Johnson, February 8, 1936 in Johnson papers, Bancroft Library.

52. The Literary Digest, Volume 121, No. 7, February 15, 1936, p. 9, is the source of the border state reactions.

53. New York *Times*, February 5, 1936.

54. Los Angeles *Times*, February 15, 1936.

55. *Ibid.*, February 8, 1936.

56. *Ibid.*, February 13, 1936.

57. *Ibid.*, February 15, March 15, 1936.

58. *Ibid.*, March 18, 1936.

59. Chesebro letter reprinted in full, Los Angeles *Times*, March 24, 1936; Deputy Chief of Police of Los Angeles Homer B. Cross stated months later that "No person can be legally prevented from crossing the border" while trying to organize a ten county plan. Los Angeles *Times*, November 8, 1936.

60. Los Angeles *Times*, February 5, 1936.

61. On the Langan case, sources are Los Angeles *Times*, February 20, March 11, 18, 31; a copy of Langan's letter to Davis under his name in the *Times* morgue and C.J. Taft, *op. cit.*, pp. 43-44.

62. Los Angeles *Times*, April 7, 1936.

63. *Ibid.*, February 13, 1936; Los Angeles *Herald*, February 4, 1936, carried the 30 day statement.

64. *Ibid.*, April 3, 1936.

65. *Ibid.*, March 22, 1936.

66. This particular city blockade was claimed by Police Captain Warren L. Justin in *The Guardian*, publication of the Los Angeles Police Revolver and Athletic Club, Inc (Los Angeles, 1937), p. 163.

67. Los Angeles *Times*, April 7, 1936, April 3, 1936; The El Centro report, *ibid.*, March 26, 1936.

68. *Ibid.*, March 21, 1936.

69. Rowell, *op. cit.*, pp. 1359-1360; migrant figures for 1935 were: month ending January 15, 5,435; February 15, 6,137; March 15, 2,522; April 15, 4,012; May 15, 4,685; June 15, 5,076. (page 1357).

70. "California: The Golden State Insists on Golden Passports," _Newsweek_, February 15, 1936, p. 15.

71. Edwards v. California, 314 U.S. 160 (1941); Los Angeles _Times_, November 25, 1941.

CHAPTER 11

FEDERAL IMPACT

The federal government's aid to the American city in the Great Depression was an act born of crisis. It was one of those unplanned points in history--a product of a grinding necessity which neither the city nor the nation could avoid. Hoover, when he reluctantly signed the first federal grants, really loans, bemoaned that "this expenditure has been forced upon the Government by the Democratic leaders."[1] His view was too limited, for behind the Democrats, stood the shadow of the coming election and the mounting problems of the cities.

Philosopher John Dewey headed a committee which warned Congress in 1933, that "throughout the country the cities are bankrupt and have exhausted sources open to them through their taxing power." A year earlier Donald R. Richberg, labor attorney, had asserted "that the Federal Government alone has the capacity to tap the resources which are available." He described local government as "entirely impotent to meet the needs of the present situation."[2]

Old time economists would bemoan the process as the "pitful sight of some important local governments holding mendicant palms toward the state and Federal governments,"[3] but the pressures were irresistible. Attorney Doherty, alert to the rising clamor, wrote Senator Johnson in September, 1931:

> I have no faith whatever in relieving unemployment by Governmental public improvement. It takes too long for the mechanics and routine to get functioning to give the relief that is needed. After all is said and done, the dole is the most practical and immediate method of relief. It has its abuses and, of course, is quite a come-down for a nation with such vaunted prosperity and resources. It, however, relieves distress immediately.[4]

As a result of the inadequacies of the five-million-dollar-bond appropriations for jobs, the Los Angeles City Council pressed for national aid, a resolution calling the situation "a major emergency in the history of the United States" was introduced by the Council President Charles Randall. The President of the United States was asked "to call Congress to meet in extra session as early as possible, to formulate plans and enact legislation by which the Federal Government with its unlimited credit and command of money at low interest rates shall take the leadership." Proposed actions stressed five billion in bonds for federal construction projects, and the allocation of loans to the states. Only two of the 15 councilman voted against the resolution.[5]

The first act of federal aid, passed in 1932 known as the Emergency Relief and Construction Act, authorized the lending of $300 million to state and local governments for emergency relief and work relief. The bill required repayments to be made out of future federal funds for highways and postal roads (in the Roosevelt years the repayment provision was cancelled). Before funds were issued states had to certify both necessity and financial inability. The

Reconstruction Finance Corporation was authorized to make the loans which were issued slowly under the stresses of these severe standards of "need" and state bureaucratic tangles. (Only $30 million, ten percent of the federal funds, were released by the end of 1932.) California, under Republican governors unhappy with the philosophy of federal aid, "held cooperation to a minimum," according to John Caughey, who noted that "not until the very end of the Public Works program were the regents of the University of California willing to accept federal money for much needed University buildings."[6]

Under this first federal grant of RFC funds (see Table 13) to which were added local monies, it was reported that 15,062 work relief jobs (based on a 91 1/2 hour work month) were provided in the one year period ending November 1933.[7] Nearly 30 percent was applied to the Department of Public Works' highway projects. Two thirds of the money went into wages for the 3,300 men employed. The largest projects involved Vermont Avenue, Adams Blvd., Western Ave. and Arroyo Seco Drive. The Park Department received $3,238,760 for major work in Griffith Park, employing 8,725 men; this sum included city funds besides the RFC allotment. Work was undertaken for improvement of playgrounds and fire prevention patrols.[8]

The Roosevelt administration enacted the Federal Emergency Relief Act of 1933. It set up a Federal Emergency Relief Administration (FERA) headed by Harry Hopkins, the social work executive from Iowa, who had served under Governor FDR in New York State's relief

TABLE 14--Federal Aid to the City of Los Angeles During the Great Depression, November 1932-July 1938.

RELIEF AGENCY	Source of Funds	Duration of Relief Agency	PERSONNEL: Number of Projects	PERSONNEL: Est. Av. No. Emply.	PERSONNEL: Total Man Hours Worked	EXPENDITURES: Labor	EXPENDITURES: Other Costs	EXPENDITURES: Total
Projects Completed or Closed								
Reconstruction Finance Corp. and Bureau of County Welfare	RFC	Nov. 1932 to Nov. 1933	98	15,062	12,651,712	$ 5,144,725	$	$ 5,144,725
	City					204,055	899,163	1,103,218
	Total					$ 5,348,780	$ 899,163	$ 6,247,943
Civil Works Administration	CWA	Dec. 1933 to March 1934	98	25,798	9,900,283	$ 4,840,301	$ 624,210	$ 5,464,511
	City					250,975	67,288	318,363
	Total					$ 5,091,276	$ 691,598	$ 5,782,874
State Emergency Relief Administration and Los Angeles County Relief Administration	SERA	April 1934 to Aug. 1935	97	8,910	10,068,773	$ 5,604,328	$ 499,275	$ 6,103,603
	City					684,979	595,452	1,280,431
	Total					$ 6,289,307	$ 1,094,727	$ 7,384,034
Public Works Administration	PWA	July 1, 1934 to June 30, 1938				$ 566,638	$ 902,446	$ 1,469,084
	City					937,571	1,517,906	2,435,477
	Total		54	273	2,323,563	$ 1,504,209	$ 2,450,352	$ 3,951,561
Works Progress Administration	WPA	Aug. 22, 1935 to June 30, 1938	59		21,616,566	$12,023,878	$ 3,533,392	$15,557,270
	City					1,122,011	298,339	1,120,350
	Total					$13,145,889	$ 3,831,731	$16,977,620
Projects Operating								
Works Progress Administration	WPA	June 30, 1938	38		18,430,876	$10,568,746	$ 2,026,860	$12,595,606
	City					640,382	384,806	1,025,180
	Total					$11,209,128	$ 2,111,666	$13,620,794
Total	WPA		97	10,614	40,047,442	$22,592,624	$ 5,560,252	$28,152,876
Total	City					1,762,393	683,145	2,445,538
Total Combined						$24,355,017	$ 6,243,397	$30,598,414
All Projects, Completed, Closed, and Operating								
Grand Total, Relief Agencies						$28,748,616	$ 7,586,183	$46,334,799
Grand Total, City of Los Angeles						3,839,973	3,793,054	7,633,027
GRAND TOTAL			444	12,077†	73,997,773	$42,588,589	$11,379,237	$53,967,826

†Represents the average number given employment throughout all Relief activities to June 30, 1938, based on a weighted average of a 91½ hour work month

Source: Survey of Unemployment Relief Activities in the City of Los Angeles, California, 1932-1938 (Los Angeles, 1938), p. 4.

administration. With a half billion dollars appropriation from Congress, FERA was authorized to give money on a grant-in-aid basis to states. Every FERA dollar had to be matched by three local dollars. (Hopkins was authorized to use up to half of the federal money without requiring matching dollars from localities unable to carry their share.) The program was beset by a host of troubles, and five months later was supplanted by CWA.[9]

The Civil Works Administration, in part, was an answer to the difficulties encountered by FERA. Established by an executive order on November 9, 1933, CWA was also placed under Hopkins' direction. The first major federal job project program, it undertook to give work for 4 million unemployed during the winter of 1933. (Nationally, it employed 4,311,000 at its January 1934 peak, spending $950 million by spring; 75 percent on wages.) CWA was a federal program of work administered by federal officials in Washington, D.C. It was run by local offices manned by persons who were sworn in as federal employees. Project decisions of CWA were influenced by local and state governments.[10] In California the State Emergency Relief Administration became the local administrative arm of CWA. Los Angeles named its City Engineer to head the CWA operations in the city. He made a comprehensive survey and analysis of needed projects which the City Council approved and forwarded to the CWA.[11]

The City Engineer estimated that CWA funds (see Table 13), plus city matching sums, helped develop 98 projects which spent 90 percent in wages paid to 25,798 individuals in the period December 1933 to

March 1934. In its four months operation, the bulk of the monies went to the Department of Public Works, Bureau of Engineering. The major allocations of the funds were:

Department of Public Works (Bureau of Engineering)	$3,152,151
Park Department	1,171,541
Playground and Recreation Department	161,034
Fire Department	491,538

Major efforts included "drainage in gutters on streets in entire city of Los Angeles," Griffith Park care and improvement, pruning and trimming of street trees, playground maintenance, and fire department firebreak operations. Sums also were allotted the city planning commission, rodent control, clerical help in the library, school crossing guards, a juvenile delinquency project and a county sewing project.[12]

When CWA ended, the California State Emergency Relief Administration, (SERA) no more the arm of CWA, was reorganized to continue new work relief programs with State and Federal funds. These SERA projects in Los Angeles were put under the City Engineer again who proposed the city projects.[13] In the 17 months of SERA projects (see Table 13) in the city, SERA and the County Relief Administration handled 97 work and service projects involving an average of 8,910 employed (using 72 hours as a work month). The sum of $6,289,307 went for wages, of the $7,384,034 spent. City funds of the amount were $1,280,431. Some $700 was the average income for the 17 months (a resultant $41 per month is arrived at).[14]

As on other city projects, the bulk ($3,390,470 of the $7,384,034) went for Department of Public Works, Bureau of Engineering Projects. Jefferson Boulevard and Slauson Avenue drainage systems received the largest sums. Sewers, culverts, grading, surfacing, and storm drains were developed elsewhere in the city. The old city halls in Van Nuys and Wilmington were demolished.[15]

Monies went to playground and recreation improvement, sorely needed painting of some library branches,[16] and even to relief workers who erased notes in library books made by careless readers.[17] More than one million dollars went into four Department of Water and Power projects.[18] Not neglected were the Harbor and Fire departments (for always needed fire breaks). Park Department maintenance and improvements were aided as well as the Airport Department. The City Attorney received funds to codify ordinances. A sum of $54,593 was given to the Library Department for additional help; $155,458 went for Police Department school crossing guards. Some $989 went for Christmas baskets distributed by the Social Service Commission for the 1934 holiday season.[19] The SERA ended its work projects program on August 22, 1935, continuing only as a direct relief investigative operation and as a certification agency for Works Progress Administration employment.[20]

The longest and most effective work relief program was the one known as the WPA (the Works Progress Administration) born on May 6, 1935. Announced by the President in a fireside chat on April 28,

1935, it aimed "to take the federal government out of the general relief business," leaving direct aid to state and local governments. Roosevelt outlined a works program slated to put a high proportion of the monies into wages. Usefulness to society and persons was a major perspective, with hopes that the projects would result in quick spending of the funds. The huge program called for major construction, conservation and service projects directed to education, libraries, museums, writers, musicians, artists, theater, research and records and miscellaneous welfare operations.[21]

WPA, like earlier plans, was placed by the City Council under the City Engineer who proposed projects they approved.[22] To the City of Los Angeles, WPA came with an impact that brought an average payroll of 10,614 persons. Total sums, city and federal (see Table 13) came to more than $30,500,000 over a period of some three years.[23] The men involved earned an average of $84 a 91 1/2 hour month. The labor unions waged bitter and uneven battles against the WPA wage scales which they considered below standard.[24]

Los Angeles' WPA projects included the usual Department of Public Works efforts in drainage, street improvements and sewerage which took a major portion of all funds (money still poured into the Slauson drain system). The Arroyo Seco storm drain cost $3,760,691. A new Griffith Park nine-hole golf course was built as over $3 million was spent in the park. Work was done in other parks, playground and recreation facilities--the Rancho Cienega Playground was allotted nearly a quarter of a million dollars, and the Police Department's

Elysian Park training center was given nearly $300,000. Police officials spent nearly $300,000 for school guards at crossings; again, the library was a beneficiary as $234,302 (only $9 of it for other costs) went to pay library workers; and $478,413 added playground and recreation workers (only $850 of this for non-wage costs)[25] A special Federal government program improved flood control channels throughout the County with $14,042,700 expended on this work within the City under the U.S. Army's Corps of Engineers. It resulted in hundreds of direct jobs.[26]

The City also participated in the PWA (See Table 13) FERA public works built by the normal construction procedures. It ran alongside of the Hopkins WPA machinery. Headed by Harold L. Ickes, the Public Works Administration, emphasized the economic soundness of projects, and did not worry about slowness of operation, inability to hire those inexperienced or unable to work in construction lines, or that a large proportion of the government dollars went into materials and equipment, and not wage earners' pockets. (Hopkins had a peak of 4,855,000 working in 1934 for WPA and the like, with 2,000,000 plus as a minimum during the period; Ickes' peak rolls involved 741,000 in 1936 and then declined.)[27] By June 30, 1938, the city had developed 54 PWA projects, involving nearly $4 million in joint funds. (Federal grants or loans were 30 percent of the costs by law, with 70 percent coming from the local sponsors.)[28]

A special Los Angeles PWA effort was made in the school-building crisis, complicated by the March 1933 earthquake. New

State requirements necessitated new schools at a very inappropriate time. In the words of the official report:

> For nearly three years the sound of hammers could be heard in every section of Los Angeles County as workmen tore down buildings marked unsafe and as others went up in their places. Architects and engineers busied themselves with thousands of blueprints and drawings. On project sites the sign "Skilled Workmen Wanted" went up. Contractors ordered additional equipment. Solidly built schools rapidly began to replace the tents, bungalows, and temporary shelters that were set aside for the children.

It was described as "the largest school building and rehabilitation program ever undertaken" and resulted in 536 buildings rehabilitated or newly constructed at a cost of $34,144,000 of which loans and grants totalling $18,424,727 were of PWA origin. The project, considered one of the key national efforts, lasted from August 7, 1934, to completion on April 27, 1938, giving more than 15 million man hours of work, and $10,547,198 going into wages.[29]

Not to be neglected for its impact on the city during the depression was the culmination of nearly 20 years of effort to get federal support for the Boulder Dam project which began to be a reality in 1930 and 1931 with appropriations for construction of the dam and powerhouse. By the decade's and depression's close in 1941, the Dam was completed. Los Angeles, and 44 neighboring communities, invested in a joint Metropolitan Water District to facilitate the Dam's operation. Jobs, contracts, electricity and water all came to the city, in part PWA funded.[30]

In that hectic spring which followed FDR's inauguration, the Civilian Conservation Corps was established by executive order. Within three months of its birth on April 5, 1933, there were 1,600 camps established nationally; by October there were 220,000 youths in the camps. (The August 1935 peak was 480,000.) Prior to 1941 there were not less than 233,000 in the CCC. In Los Angeles the CCC did important conservation jobs in major park areas. The CCC constructed a drainage channel to take care of the storm waters from Burbank in Griffith Park, and built a series of pools and cascades in the Fern Dell at Griffith Park which were lined with artificial rock.[31] By the spring of 1936 some 2,375 youths of Los Angeles County, single, unemployed in the 17-28 age bracket, from families on relief were eligible for CCC jobs.[32] From its start there was general community approval of the CCC and in its first year it was reported that fire losses were at their lowest and that "credit goes to the conservation camps scattered through the mountains." Some 37,000, not all Angelenos, were reported at work removing fire hazards from 60,930 acreas. They had built 925 miles of truck trails, 593 miles of telephone lines, 212 miles of firebreaks, and 976 miles of road fireproofing.[33]

Another Federal youth program was the National Youth Administration, established by the President in June 1935 and headed by Aubrey Williams. Geared to aid youth, in-school and out-of-school, it involved, during its lifetime, some 1.8 million youths not in school and nearly 2 million in high school, college and graduate school. It served to keep many in school who might have become "dropouts."[34] Local jobs included work in schools and even construction and design work at Lincoln Park.

Another and vital aspect of federal work in the area was that accomplished in the field of arts. A Los Angeles guide published in 1941 represented a major Writers' Project effort, and was officially sponsored by the County Board of Supervisors[35]. The idea of federally subsidizing artists, sculptors, and actors became a reality in the depression. There were local antecedents for this in the self-help cooperatives. An organization of "unemployed painters, actors, artists and would-be artists" tried to trade with others and "found an unappreciative market." Some of them issued a publication, Clarion, as the organ of the self-help movement. Kerr describes one group composed of Hollywood motion picture extras and a benefit they organized which was supported by prominent actors and actresses.[36] WPA sculpture and art remains in Los Angeles as continuing reminders of the Arts Projects. They include the trio of statues at the entrance to the Hollywood Bowl, Prometheus at the eastern side of MacArthur Park, murals in the County Hall of Records, a wooden mural in the Hollywood post office, the multiple statue in front of the Planetarium and a further list quite long and yet to be assembled.

A major event on the cultural front was the creation of the WPA's Federal Theatre Project. Launched nationally in 1935, it began its Los Angeles career with the interviewing of theater job applicants on October 29.[37] A ten-act vaudeville production at the Wilshire Ebell theater 4401 West 8th Street, on December 31, 1935, only two months after the initial interviews, made Los Angeles' Federal Theatre the first such production in the nation for which admission was paid. It was to break other new paths and soon was presenting performances in leased or rented Los Angeles theaters: Beaux Arts, Belasco, Experimental, Figueroa Playhouse, Greek (a marionette show there in the summer of 1937 attracted more than 100,000 patrons), Magic Strings, Mason, Mayan, Musart and the Playhouse in Hollywood. Backing up the performances were design shops, workshops, a wardrobe department and a research center.

Los Angeles project wage scales, slightly below New York's and therefore irksome, were $55 per month for unskilled, $85 for skilled; and $94 per month for professional or technical employees. Admission prices for the public was within a range of ten cents to a high of $1.10 for "Two-A-Day," a popular musical. Usually the top price was 55 cents, and fellow WPA workers could come in free on certain days. Generally the anti-New Deal press, the Evening Herald and Express and the Times let the players be--even running positive reviews on occasion. Ambitious projects in the Los Angeles Federal Theatre included classical, children's drama, vaudeville, a quiet successful Negro unit, foreign language (Yiddish and French--but no Spanish-speaking group!) and modern drama. Musicals were the top hits in Los Angeles and many toured local schools, camps, hospitals and playgrounds.

> No quite in the touring category, but still in the travel classification, was the constant shifting of plays from one stage to another within the Los Angeles area...whole new audiences could be found by moving a successful play.

This was an adaptation to the city's size and population sprawl.

In the pre-1936 election period attacks developed and the Evening Herald and Express called the theater project "an undisguised propaganda activity."[38] Living Newspapers, a dramatic documentary form, never had the success in Los Angeles it had in Eastern cities. The year 1937 was considered the most successful period, and national director Hallie Flanagan hailed the Los Angeles effort as "probably the most efficient show shop in the country."[39]

The Federal Theatre died in Washington when a more economy-minded and anti-New Deal Congress took office in January 1939. In a slashing of WPA funds Federal Theatre, a special hate of many of the legislators, was soon destroyed in a circus atmosphere. When the Federal Theatre was closed in Los Angeles in mid-1939, 1,150 jobs were lost (600 were actors, 75 musicians and the rest were technicians and skilled workers).

Throughout the depression the cities had hammered at the federal government and its treasury. The pressures took the form of delegations, visiting mayors and endless resolutions and reports. Los Angeles was part of that caravan. The United States Conference of Mayors, itself a depression-born organization, issued a 1937 report pressing for continuation of the WPA work program. Los Angeles' section of the report hailed WPA projects as "useful and needed improvements of a permanent nature for the benefit of the people of this city" and noted that the county had approximately "15,000 cases of employable persons who are receiving direct relief because the Federal Work Program has not absorbed them." Mayor Shaw made a strong plea against reduction in WPA funds.[40] Through the years he was often at the nation's capital in attempts to get federal cash for the city. He was described by the Los Angeles Times as one of the "busy municipal bees" anxious to "get some of the governmental nectar."[41] In mid 1938 Los Angeles was absent from the pleading city volume (as was New York).[42] Times had changed.

How many people were employed on federal relief work projects in Los Angeles from November 1932 to June 30, 1938, from the first funds of the dying Hoover administration to the time when the depression itself was waning? The City Engineer estimated that 12,077 was the average number working on some federal work project at a given time in the nearly six years from November 1932 to the end of June 1938. The number of employees on the major projects in this city were:

RFC	15,062
CWA	25,798
SERA	8,910
PWA	373
WPA	10,614
TOTAL	60,757 [43]

Rough calculations back the City Engineer's average figure. It is difficult to determine how many individual Angelenos were involved in the 60,757 figure. Surely it was quite a bit beyond the 12,077 average--in fact it must be more of the CWA's 25,798 figure. It is therefore possible that nearly 40,000 worked in this city, at one time or another, on federally funded work projects.

The key accomplishment of the federal impact was the human one - that perhaps 40,000 unemployed worked with dignity and wages and human erosion was halted or , at least, slowed. Those years have also left impressive improvements, changes and structures in the city--the downtown Federal Building, the Hollywood post office, Elysian Park's police training academy, a new sub-City Hall in Van Nuys; the greatest school and reconstruction program in the nation, a larger base for a municipal airport, development of the city's water resources, drainage and flood control, a better and more useful Griffith Park and other recreation facilities.[44] The financial assistance to the city's services was also one of the federal aids. Los Angeles in the depression years had been both continued and changed.

FOOTNOTES

1. Lester V. Chandler, America's Greatest Depression, 1929-1941 (New York, 1970), p. 50.

2. U.S. Senate, Subcommittee of the Committee on Manufactures. Hearings on S. 5125, Unemployment Relief, 72nd Cong. 2d Session, 1933, p. 149.

3. Carl H. Chatters and Albert M. Hilhouse, Local Government Debt Administration (New York: 1939), pp. 388-389.

4. Letter, Dougherty to Johnson, September 9, 1931, Johnson papers, Bancroft Library.

5. Council Minutes, Volume 229, September 21, 1931, pp. 629-630.

6. John W. Caughey, California (New Jersey: 1953), 2nd ed. p. 520.

7. Survey of Unemployment Relief Activities in the City of Los Angeles, California (Los Angeles: 1938), p. 4. Hereinafter referred to as Survey.

8. Ibid., pp. 11-16.

9. Chandler, op. cit., pp. 198-199.

10. Ibid., pp. 199-200.

11. Survey, p. 3.

12. Ibid., pp. 17-23. The later listing included CWA projects funded to March 1935.

13. Ibid., p. 3. The Los Angeles Times, March 18, 1936 bitterly noted: "Incidentally, the S.R.A. has dropped a letter. Evidently it no longer considers itself an 'Emergency' organization, relief has become chronic."

14. Survey, p. 32.

15. Ibid., pp. 24-25.

16. Ibid., pp. 26-27.

17. 47th Annual Report, Los Angeles Public Library, 1934-35, p. 17.

18. Survey, p. 29.

19. Ibid., p. 32.

20. Ibid., p. 3.

21. Chandler, op. cit., pp. 203-205.

22. Survey, p. 3.

23. Ibid., p. 4.

24. Los Angeles Times, October 29, 1935.

25. Survey, pp. 33-43.

26. This type of flood control operation had been proposed by the Municipal League in its February 18, 1931 Bulletin as a "Joint Cure for Unemployment and Flood Menace," a cogent piece.

27. Chandler, op. cit., pp. 198-194.

28. Survey, pp. 43-46, p. 3.

29. America Builds, The Record of the PWA (Washington,D.C.:

30. Harold L. Ickes, Back to Work, The Story of PWA (New York: 1935), p. 115.

31. Your City at Work--Los Angeles Year Book--A Report on City Government Operations During 1940 (Los Angeles: 1940).

32. Los Angeles Times, March 19, 1936; The Young Worker, published by the Young Communist League, itemizes a strike of ten CCC boys, one a Negro in La Cienega CC, November 12, 1935.

33. New York Times, November 12, 1933.

34. Chandler, op. cit., pp. 206-207; the author was an NYA worker in Brooklyn College in 1936.

35. Los Angeles, A Guide to the City and Its Environs. Sponsored by the Los Angeles County Board of Supervisors (New York: 1951), 2nd ed. See Los Angeles Times, May 4, 1972 for the most recent attempt to locate existing art.

36. Kerr, op. cit., op. cit., p. 202.

37. Robert Holcomb, "The Federal Theatre in Los Angeles," The California Historical Society Quarterly, Volume XLI, No. 2, June 1962, p. 131. This article, pp. 131-147, is the source for my material on the Los Angeles Federal Theatre.

38. Quoted in Ibid., p. 138.

39. Ibid., p. 139, quotes from Hallie Flanagan, Arena (New York: 1940), pp. 282, 299.

40. U.S. Conference of Mayors, A Report on the Existing Relief Situation Covering 100 Major American Cities with Special Reference to the Continuation of the WPA Work Program Through June 30, 1937 (Washington: 1937), pp. 3, 9, 6.

41. Los Angeles Times, June 6, 1936.

42. United States Conference of Mayors, Do the WPA Projects Which the Cities Have Sponsored Represent Careful and Desirable Works of Public Benefit? (Washington: 1939), Oakland, San Francisco and Long Beach are in the volume. Pueblo, Colorado has a long three page, single space report!

43. Survey, p. 4.

44. John Anson Ford, oral history record UCLA, p. 90. He mentioned a new social hall at Plummer Park. It must have been important in his mind for he recalled it to me in a personal interview, May 31, 1971.

CHAPTER 12

A NEW POLITICAL ESSENCE

Politics is the constant summation of the churning of people and events. The changes which come in society are made most effectively in the political arena. In Los Angeles it was a decade when old issues faded, new issues rose, great agitations seized tens of thousands in many ephemeral causes, parties swayed and faltered and allegiances broke out of ancient ruts. Politics tends to boil down a conflicting mass of demands and interests, with a resultant new residue--perhaps not pleasing to many, but actually containing an acceptable and workable essence for most.

Prohibition, the cause of the "drys," was a political power before the depression. In the decade from 1928 to 1938 Prohibition Party registration fell from 11,556 to 4,046 in Los Angeles County. The vote for an independent Prohibition Party presidential candidate, never impressive, fell from the 1928 county figures of 6,458 to a 1936 figure of 5,827. On one occasion, as late as 1932, a spirited campaigner such as Robert P. Shuler, well-known cleric and firebrand orator, polled an amazing 310,200 votes in the county as the Prohibition Party candidate for U.S. Senator. Nevertheless, he was third, behind the Democratic and Republican candidates; the figure must also be considered in light of the meager vote for the Prohibition Party candidate for the presidency -- 8,713.[1] In that senatorial race, McAdoo, the Democrat, picked up many "dry" votes, as his Republican rival, Tallant Tubbs, was known as a "dripping wet."[2]

Next year Los Angeles "fell off the water wagon" as prohibition was ended, and a host of other bans fell in its wake; horse racing was legalized and puritanical rules about women's bathing suits were voided. This change was hailed by one reporter:

> Ever since the days when wicked San Francisco and the naughty North dominated the State by reason of numbers, the South has been the crepe hanger, so far as liberal interpretation of fussy laws was concerned. Many's the good-time-San Francisco-Charlie we have killed off at the ballot box, but that's all changed now and the South has cocked her hat over one eye, and is off in a cloud of dust.[3]

When the city went "wet," Mayor Porter, described as "even dryer than his speeches," lost his bid for re-election to a reform candidate, Frank L. Shaw, who won with a 30,000 majority. Porter's defeat was not only the result of his pro-prohibition stance; good government forces had opposed him for incompetences in office. The vote was, a reporter wrote, the expression of an electorate "anxious to hurry the new deal promised by the new mayor whose prospectus is along the line made familiar by President Roosevelt."[4]

Traditionally, Los Angeles had always voted Republican; the Great Depression changed that. As urbanism and the immigrant had come of age nationally, the New York Irish Catholic Al Smith's candidacy had swept many cities into the Democratic column. Bernstein has noted that where these forces were focused, as in

Boston, "the Democrats made sweeping gains," but where they were blurred, "as in Los Angeles, the Democrats made only slight advances because urbanism was diluted by trans-planted midwestern farmers who were mainly old stock Protestants and were without a working-class outlook."[5] The truth of this is contained in the opposite side of the coin discussed in earlier chapters--Los Angeles was the breeding ground for non-working class, hot house and utopian movements and the emergence of a post-productive political force--the senior citizen--a revolt of those unable to make a revolution! But alongside of these groups--and sifting through them--Los Angeles turned to the Democrats. (The registration swing is detailed on page 143 of this study).

How did the votes reflect this?

Presidential Votes

Los Angeles County

	Democrats	Republicans
1928	209,945	513,306
1932	553,896	373,738
1936	757,351	347,401
1940	822,718	574,266[6]

From 1928 through 1940 the Democrats moved from 29 percent to better than 58 percent of the major party vote. Los Angeles had become a strong Democratic town--twice the 1928 proportion--and the Republicans had fallen from 71 to less than 42 percent of the vote. In 1928 Los Angeles had been Republican along with 23 other cities in a list of the top three dozen (New York, Boston, St. Louis and San Francisco were Democratic); by 1932 Los Angeles, like 31 others, had become Democratic (only four Eastern cities, and those by small margins, had remained Republican).[7] San Francisco with more than 50 percent over 60 percent in 1940 (in 1932 the percentage was at a 67 percent high).

The state, which had cast nearly 35 percent of its major parties' votes for the Democrats in 1928, had by 1940 increased it to almost 58 percent--about the same as Los Angeles' share. In 1936 Los Angeles was more Democratic than either San Francisco or the state as a whole.[8]

After 1932, Los Angeles' political importance as a Democratic stronghold grew in many ways. The 1932 national Democratic convention had a California delegation with a majority of delegates from the southern part of the state; the first Garner-For-President clubs were organized in Los Angeles.[9] Garner's primary victory over Roosevelt and Smith was in good part due to the Los Angeles vote where he had the backing of the state party chairman, McAdoo; press backing, especially from Hearst; the benefit of the wet vote splitting between his rivals and the sizeable block of ex-Texans in the area.[10]

When Roosevelt became the candidate, Los Angeles made its big turn. "Fervid," was the word used to describe California politics. The Mayor, unhappy with the Democratic candidate, out of touch with the city, added to his long list of blunders by declining to greet candidate Roosevelt.[11] Mayor Porter remained loyal to President Hoover, but Los Angeles had become quite disenchanted.

Hoover's 1932 effort in Los Angeles was desperate; appeals were made to as engineers, with promises of work on the coming Boulder Dam, and stressing that he was "himself an engineer."[12] A special appeal was made, in that bonus army year, to veterans (estimated at 120,000 in the city)[13] There was Republican party anger in the city when Hiram Johnson came out against Hoover; the Los Angeles County chairman of the Republican Party called the Senator "a Benedict Arnold."[14] The demoralized Downtown Republican Club of Los Angeles cancelled a dinner rally when a postcard poll of its 130 members showed 70 percent planning to vote for FDR.[15] The anti-Hoover mood had been brewing in Los Angeles Republican circles long before his second nomination.[16] At the end of 1931, Attorney Doherty wrote Senator Johnson that Hoover would not only be unable to carry California, "it is extremely doubtful if he could carry Los Angeles County."[17] The election results proved him correct; Hoover lost the state by nearly a half million votes, and the county by some 180,000 votes. The Los Angeles opposition to Hoover was slightly heavier than the general state rejection. In both counts, county and state, FDR's vote bested Hoover by 3 to 2.[18]

A Southern Democrat, a Los Angeles matron, living in Brentwood Heights expressed the high hopes and problems of inauguration day:

> ...left the dishes stacked and rushed over to Helen's to listen over her radio to the Inauguration doings in Washington City. It was most interesting.

> Roosevelt's inauguration speech was splendid, we thought. He plans to take immediate steps towards solving the banking problem and is to call a special session of Congress for that purpose. We have just had a three-day Bank Holiday and no cheques could be cashed, but Ralph's and other places gladly honor cheques so we can at least eat. But it is very worrying and Bob is of the opinion that the banks will not do business as usual on Monday either--or possibly for a longer time--and there is talk of "scrip" being used. It surely is worrying...[19]

Los Angeles' independence in the ballot booth, was reflected in the proportion of voters who registered as "declined to state." (See Table 1-.) Compared to San Francisco and the State, Los Angeles voters consistently expressed a refusal to list their political affiliation by a much higher rate.

TABLE 15--Percent of Registrants Who "Declined to State" a Party Choice, Los Angeles, San Francisco and California, 1928-1940.

	Los Angeles County	San Francisco County	State of California
1928	9 1/2	4	7 1/2
1930	8	4	6
1932	6	2	5
1934	6	2	4
1936	4	1	3
1938	4	1 1/2	3
1940	5	1 1/2	3 1/2[20]

John C. Porter soon followed Herbert Hoover in defeat. The new mayor, Frank Shaw, a former Councilman and Supervisor, won on a reform ticket; he benefitted from the earlier recall campaign against Porter, though it had failed. With public pronouncements on unemployment during his years as a County Supervisor, Shaw had created an image of a politician anxious to tackle depression problems in a new way. It was not a mistaken judgment of citizen John Anson Ford (later a supervisor) who congratulated Shaw

> not only on your recent election but also on your announced purpose to tackle in a Roosevelt-like way the great problem of unemployment and business depression.[21]

Shaw, unlike Porter, was sensitive to the angry winds of the depression. Porter may have gloried in such administration highlights as the arrival of the Graf Zeppelin, the 150th celebration of the city's birthday and being host to the Olympic Games, but Shaw knew that depression politics was made of sterner stuff. Of Porter's departure novelist Nathanael West's words about Faye Greener are appropriate--the city "didn't love him and he couldn't further her career." An old time radical called Shaw's victory "a revolt against the moralistic element and the goody, goody prohibition crowd."[22] Porter's election eve statement that the people "applaud the constructive and virile leadership of President Roosevelt" was too little and too late. Years later Porter would still be explaining that he had not, in his official capacity as Mayor, snubbed FDR the candidate.[23]

Frank Shaw understood the politics of the depression--go to Washington often, and get as much as you can.[24] He was described as "an affable man" with "all the salesman's tricks and graces."[25] Indicative of Shaw's keen attention to the problems of the depression was a long letter he wrote to a state FERA official, during his first months in office. He protested Ickes' estimate that Los Angeles' unemployment was 15 percent of its working population. Shaw asserted that it was "quite evident that the total number of unemployed in this city will greatly exceed 20 percent." His interest in the larger percentage figure flowed from his belief that "this is necessary in order to secure proper consideration of the urgency of expediting our public works program so that a humane and sensible relief may be provided."[26]

Shaw looked to the federal treasury for aid; the State was in the grip of the cow counties, and not sensitive to the needs of the car county. "Since 1926," wrote McWilliams, "less than six percent of the voters of California have elected a majority of the State's 40 senators."[27] By the end of 1937, Shaw's endless trips to Washington, D.C., prompted Republican Doherty to write that he "will do more harm than good; in fact, it might be well for him to get turned down." Doherty felt the Mayor had no constructive program and his requests were in conflict with other projects.[28] There was no end to Mayor's visits; on one occasion Mayor Shaw "called at the White House before departing and paid his respects to President Roosevelt."[29] To be aligned with FDR was a special ambition of the Mayor. When FDR came through Los Angeles in mid-July of 1938, he rode in the President's car "on the little jumper seat."[30]

In 1938, Shaw, under the rising cloud of the recall, urged more and more Federal funds.[31] He attacked forty percent as too high a local contribution toward WPA projects, wrangled for housing funds, hit out at threatened cuts and opposed a plan to give transients WPA jobs.[32] The Times was ambivalent on the allocation of federal funds to the city, worrying that "relief costs will go up instead of down," and that "it is impossible for officials to take a judicial attitude on the needs of individual cities. If starvation is going to be the fate of deserving persons because relief is denied, it will have to be granted." The Times concluded that Los Angeles must get "the help to which it is entitled." Shaw succeeded, and the funds came in for work on the municipal airport and WPA expansion.[33] (Many of the projects outlined in the prior chapter of this work were Shaw "victories," real or claimed."

Mayor Shaw symbolized Los Angeles depression politics in the five years he was the city's spokesman. His activities took place in a city with mass movements of the unemployed, the alienated and a rising labor movement described in earlier chapters. Shaw, though he continued the controversial Hynes police squad, winning no particular admiration from picketors or demonstrators, was amenable to delegations of writers to whom he pledged assistance in getting federal funds or winning a sewing project.[34] He was the classic politician, recently described, as more often concerned with "how the unemployed will vote, not how they live."[35] The alert politician listened to EPIC or bent to such pressures as Townsendism to curry favor. Political activity and interest reached new highs in the County. Kerr tells of a 94 percent registration in Los Angeles self-help groups.[36] Porter had sought and received the support of Pay May, leader of the unemployed who spoke at a Philharmonic Rally in 1933. "We don't always tell 'em who to vote for," May said, "but we do tell them who their enemies are."[37] In this instance the appeal had failed. The unemployed as a political force were a constant worry to old time politicians. In December of 1932, a group of conservative Los Angeles County leaders formed a Citizens Committee, "to take the unemployed by the hand," in an attempt to avoid the Seattle "path of radical protest." They took heed of May's advice: "feed 'em and you can lead 'em."[38]

As anxious as the Socialist and Communists were to lead the hungry and the seekers of a better life, it is ironic that these Marxist parties went nowhere in the electoral process in Los Angeles, though EPIC strength had shown that tens of thousands were ready to modify or abandon capitalism--the parties most committed to that goal did very poorly.

The Socialist Party vote, never large after 1912 in Los Angeles, or the state, reached a high point in the County in 1934 with a U.S. senatorial vote of 41,328. By 1938 the Socialist vote for the same post was 9,503, in Los Angeles smaller than the comparative 1928 vote. Thomas' 1932 presidential vote of 27,518 was the highest he received as presidential candidate in Los Angeles.[39] Perhaps most potential supporters of the Socialist Party agreed with Upton

Sinclair's 1934 statement: "I have seen the horror which has come in Germany, and I realize that the American Socialist Party wouldn't make one good-sized bite for American Big Business, when it gets to the biting state."[40] The victories of the Socialist Party came as their basic minimum program became major party programs.[41]

The Communists, stronger and more active in Los Angeles, won small victories on campuses, among the unemployed and in the organizing and leadership of some unions, but had not much more electoral success than the Socialists. (At best the Los Angeles Communist Party achieved 1,500 members in 1937 and always suffered from a "turnover" in which new recruits barely kept up with losses).[42] The Communists described EPIC as a movement of "petty bourgeois. Utopian illusions" at the time of Sinclair's bid for the governorship; some time later the C.P. leaders considered their opposition wrong in that campaign.[43]

Electorally, the Communist high point in Los Angeles came in 1938 with a state-wide vote of 98,791 for Controller, 46,129 of it coming from Los Angeles. In 1934, Anita Whitney, the same candidate, running for the same post, had received state vote of 100,820, but Los Angeles had only provided 36,709. In those four years Los Angeles had increased its Communist vote by some 10,000.[44] Communist backed candidates had done better. Local candidates did very poorly, and there is no doubt that "united front" tactics of backing other candidates, and various harrassments did not make political life easy for the Communists. In 1932 they were not on the California ballot and their presidential candidate, William Z. Foster, was arrested in Los Angeles while addressing a rally.[45]

A "united front" political activity of the Communists in Los Angeles involved them in the 1938 recall movement against Mayor Shaw. Though their leaflets are lost ephemera, we have a description of one leaflet in a C.P. publication of the time it called for "a swamping the united front of Mayor Shaw, Governor Merriam, Chief-of-Police Davis, open shoppers and underworld gangsters."[46] Labor's Non-Partisan League, led by Don Healey, (first husband of Dorothy Healey, later leader of the Los Angeles Communists) played a significant part in that recall movement, offering support to Bowron's nomination and election.

A year before the recall, Frank L. Shaw was opposed for re-election by John Anson Ford, a County Supervisor. Shaw stressed his record of unemployment relief; his getting for Los Angeles "Your Share of the New Deal;"[47] he claimed that he had obtained $51,435,000 in Federal funds which brought work to 40,000 heads of families. The campaign highlighted alleged Communist "endorsement" for Ford,[48] also included charges of pressure on federal project workers by Shaw. A letter writer in the Daily News twitted Shaw who "claims he put an end to the depression, and next he'll be taking credit for our California sunshine."[49] The Times had backed Shaw, the winner, with the comment that he was a "successful businessman before he turned to public office," and Ford was a "press agent and did not make an outstanding success even of that." Shaw, wrote the Times, was "the better man." The paper charged that Ford, "although he holds himself aloof," was receiving support from the Communist party and the C.I.O.[50]

It was a confident Shaw who expected to duplicate his 1937 victory with the same ingredients as in that campaign. He stressed his strong role in meeting depression problems, anti-radicalism, and a general assault on reformers. Shaw had heavy handed Times support. Local community papers, often anonymously edited, blanketed the city with virulent charges against the recall, against Bowron's candidacy. One, the Herald of Decency, in its August 10, 1938, issue depicted Bowron as the "hand-picked candidate of the Communists." Attacks were directed against Clifford Clinton, chairman of the reform Citizens Independent Vice Investigating Committee (CIVIC), lay religious leader and owner of Clifton's Cafeteria. His restaurant's cleanliness and labor conditions were criticized. Insinuations were made that Clinton wanted to become "vice czar" of Los Angeles.

Shaw tried to remain aloof from the gutter level campaign waged in his behalf. He emphasized his 1937 campaign theme that the city had prospered in his regime. He cited statistics to show that the city tax rate had dropped, and that residents were paying a much lower per capita tax as compared with 1933.

As the recall race became more desperate, Shaw stressed his ties to C.D.R., and hammered away at his anti-depression accomplishments. A KFWB broadcast by a supporter hailed the Shaw-FDR friendship:

> Truly it may be said both are great men. Mayor Frank L. Shaw has done for the City of Los Angeles what Franklin D. Roosevelt has done for the nation.[51]

The orator, summing up the relief history of the decade, referred to the city employees who "had voluntarily donated a portion of their salaries to feed and clothe the poor." He also noted that "an apple selling campaign was conducted." These things were necessary before Shaw's regime according to the broadcast, "because, as usual, when a reform administration is in power, more attention is given to the regulation of the morals of the community than to the creation of jobs so that men may feed their families, their children."

The Bowron reform ticket was the target. It was implied that only Shaw had worried about the depression's effects:

> work did not begin, funds were not made available until Mayor Frank L. Shaw saw his friend, Franklin D. Roosevelt, and obtained the money with which to start the job.

Shaw was described as FDR's "close, bosom" friend and "out of this friendship Los Angeles has gained immeasureable." To the president who had just visited the city, the radio orator cried out:

> President Roosevelt, we hope you come again. Our front door is always open to you; when storms beset you, there will be a light in the window to guide you to the shelter of our city.[52]

Charges that Shaw and his lieutenants used the WPA work projects as a political base were often made. A letter to the Mayor's secretary from a Shaw supporter in early 1937 discussed

> A plan suggested by Mr. Bennecke and myself, that the small Frank Shaw cards be distributed amoung [sic] those WPA workers that are favorable to the Mayor and should a discussion arise amoung [sic] any one of the workers favorable to other candidates, these particular WPA workers could tell them that the City administration is responsible for the WPA projects as well as the money received from the government and the Mayor is the one responsible for keeping these projects going. . . .

After discussing other problems and the dangers of politicking on the job, he noted that one of the City foremen

> is doing a wonderful piece of work on behalf of the Mayor on the Arroyo Seco project, and he certainly should receive a great deal of consideration for what he is doing.[53]

Attorney Doherty examined the charge of political activities in the WPA more than a year later, and complained "that is very difficult to get anything authentic." He was trying to determine Democratic manipulation, but concluded that

> there is not enough open and active Democratic politics in the WPA situation in this County to amount to a scandal or to warrant making a scandal.

He did feel that those on federal jobs had a "feeling of gratitude and appreciation [and], they are friendly to the administration."[54]

Shaw's defeat was stunning. Bowron's vote of 233,427 over Shaw's 122,692 showed that neither the good record of an administration in obtaining federal work projects for the city, nor pressures to influence people on those projects, nor the earnest attempt to ride in on FDR's coat tails helped. The entire anti-depression record of Frank Shaw had not been able to overcome the anger and disgust with the widespread corruption in the city. Shaw's defeat came at the hands of a broad reform coalition led by Clinton.

Decisive in the campaign was the exposure of a near successful attempt by Los Angeles police Lieutenant Earl Kynette to kill one of Flinton's investigators with a bomb planted in his car. It was a blast heard round the city. Shaw "fell under a barrage of charges of vice and corruption."[55] His brother and assistant, Joseph Shaw, was indicted and later convicted on 63 counts of selling civil service jobs and promotions, but he never served time.[56]

The campaign of 1938 showed that the pressing issues of the depression did not take priority in the mind of the electorate. There were still people out of work on federal projects and on relief. But in terms of top political interest--those questions had taken second place. Had they been the major questions, it is possible that Shaw's time in office would have been continued beyond the half decade he served. The election had become a choice between a Republican called corrupt, and a Republican called honest. Thus had the politics simmered, and a few weeks later Los Angeles expressed its support for the Democrats in the campaign for governor. The vote was 612,499, Democratic; 446,069, Republican. Los Angeles had given the Democrats 57.8 percent of its major party vote, becoming 3 1/2 percent more Democratic than the State.[58] Within two months the city had expressed its political direction as Democratic, even though its new Mayor was a Republican.

In the depression decade, Los Angeles, as well as California, moved into the Democratic column. Republican "Sunny Jim" Rolph opened the thirties as the continuation of three decades of the party's state rule (the Hiram Johnson years, of course, reflected a different kind of GOP); as 1939 began, Culbert Olson, Democrat, became governor. The EPIC capture of the Democratic standard had perhaps delayed the party's victory until 1938. The decade in Los Angeles opened with the victory of a fundamentalist Republican, John C. Porter, as mayor, and closed with a righteous good government Republican, Fletcher Bowron, as mayor. It did not seem too much of a change compared to the state picture; it was the Los Angeles way of coping with its problems. Depression issues had swirled around Porter and Shaw, and Shaw won in 1933. In 1937, he repeated his victory, backed by his reputed role as a mayor who had accomplished much for the city in the depression. Part of the reason for his victory was his ability to portray his opponent, John Anson Ford, as a radical. When crime and corruption "did him in" in the recall, Shaw was not defeated by a radical; the radicals had been part of the coalition. (They decided not to press for their candidate, the rebel Sam Yorty.)

The coalition that defeated Shaw was composed of those not desirious of his return. He was a symbol of the worst in the past--open shop, oppressive police practices--governmental inefficiency and corruption, and connivance with the worst elements in the city. Bowron represented a repudiation of this; his meeting with New York's Fiorello La Guardia, here for an American Legion convention, symbolized the new day. The city, teeming with radical politics, vast and shaking movements, ended up ironically with the victory of a candidate who had little to say of revolution or depression. Los Angeles was looking in a different direction.

FOOTNOTES

1. Eugene E. Kerrick, Jr., "California and the Presidential Election of 1932," unpublished M.A. thesis, Bancroft Library, Berkeley, 1956, p. 7. See Edmund Wilson's sparkling, if at times, exaggerated essay, "The City of Our Lady The Queen of Angels" in The American Earthquake (New York, 1958), pp. 379-396 wherein he describes Shuler who had become "more and more popular in Texas, but he was so fierce against the saloons and antagonized the liquor interests and the drinkers so that the bishop didn't know what to do with him."

2. Kerrick, op. cit., p. 79.

3. New York Times, June 25, 1933, IV p. 8.

4. Ibid., on Porter's dilemma see New York Times, April 2, 1933, IV p. 6.

5. Bernstein, Lean Years, p. 76. Also see Samuel Lubell, The Future of American Politics (New York, 1956).

6. Statement of Vote, California, 1928, 1932, 1936, 1940. It is interesting that a recent study claims a falling off of the Democratic vote in the 1928 election claiming that comparison to the 1920 election is a wrong one--that the comparison should be made to 1924. In that comparison the Los Angeles figures for its Democratic vote were the following in percentages:

1920	22.4
1924	33.4
1928	28.7

A case is made for 1920 being a "deviant one in which voters were responding to short-term stimuli not present four years earlier and not present four years later." These short-term issues were defined as League of Nations, the Treaty of Versailles and Prohibition. See Michael Paul Rogin and John L. Shover, Political Change in California, Critical Elections and Social Movements, 1890-1966 (Westport, Connecticut, 1970), pp. 92-93, p. 100. Los Angeles' crawl to the Democrats during the twenties--23.8 percent of its major party vote in 1920; 29 percent in 1928--also reflected a poor white migration from the classic Democratic South--how decisive it is hard to estimate.

7. Bernstein, The Lean Years, p. 509.

8. Statement of Vote, California, 1936. In that year Los Angeles was 67.7 percent Democrat compared to San Francisco with 64.8 percent and the state of California with 65.8 percent.

9. Kerrick, op. cit., p. 22, p. 35.

10. Ibid., pp. 77-79; vote was Garner 222,000; FDR 175,000; Smith 141,000.

11. New York Times, October 2, 1932, #7.

12. Kerrick, op. cit., p. 147.

13. Ibid. There was a Hoover Progressive Club organized.

14. Ibid., p. 151.

15. Quoted in Kerrick, op. cit., p. 166 from New York Times, August 29, 1932.

16. Doherty to Johnson, June 25, 1931. Johnson papers, Bancroft Library.

17. Ibid., December 28, 1931.

18. See Chapin Hall, New York Times, October 20, 1932.

19. Ingram Diary, March 4, 1933, Huntington Library.

20. Statement of Vote, California: 1928, 1930, 1932, 1934, 1936, 1938, 1940.

21. John Anson Ford to Frank Shaw, June 15, 1933 in Shaw papers, UCLA special collections.

22. Interview with Reuben Borough, June 4, 1969.

23. Los Angeles Times, May 28, 1933.

24. Ibid., August 13, 1937.

25. Interview with Borough, June 4, 1969.

26. Frank Shaw to Hamilton H. Cotton, Chairman State Advisory Board, FERA of Public Works, September 29, 1933. Letter in Hirim W. Johnson papers, Bancroft Library, Berkeley, California.

27. McWilliams, The Great Exception, p. 209.

28. Doherty to Johnson, November 13, 1937.

29. Los Angeles Times, February 13, 1937.

30. Doherty to Johnson, July 20, 1938.

31. Los Angeles *Times*, June 15, 1938; June 16, 1938.

32. *Ibid.*, June 16, 1937; June 18, 1937; July 19, 1933; September 10, 1937; July 24, 1937.

33. *Ibid.*, November 18, 1937; November 20, 1937.

34. *Ibid.*, April 3, 1937; March 22, 1937.

35. Max Frankel in New York *Times*, May 13, 1971.

36. Kerr, *op. cit.*, p. 388.

37. *Ibid.*, p. 144.

38. *Ibid.*, pp. 20-21.

39. Lee, *op. cit.*, p. 85. In 1912 26,227 voted for Debs in the County.

40. Sinclair, *I Candidate*, p. 20; Norman Thomas wrote Upton Sinclair that he had "turned Democrat at the very hour when the decadence of capitalism and the hopeless inadequacy of capitalist parties was most manifest." Quoted in Arthur Ekiych, *Ideologies and Utopias* (Chicago, 1969) p. 187 from Thomas to Upton Sinclair, September 27, 1933 Thomas papers (New York Public Library).

41. Carter, *op. cit.*, pp. 156-158 for 26 point program.

42. California State Membership Committee, "Building the Party in California," *Party Organizer*, Volume X, No. 3-4 March-April 1937, pp. 19-25.

43. Al Richmond, *Native Daughter, The Story of Anita Whitney* (San Francisco, 1942), pp. 167-168.

44. *Statement of Vote*, California: 1934, 1938.

45. Richmond, *op. cit.*, p. 55; ACLU recorded an incident wherein high school students were denied diplomas due to membership in Communist Youth groups. Taft, *op. cit.*, pp. 36-37.

46. George Morris, "A Review of California Agitational Material," *Party Organizer*, Volume XI, No. 6, June 1938, pp. 30-31.

47. *Daily News*, April 16, 1937, in scrapbook in Joe Shaw papers.

48. *Ibid.*; also interview with Ford, May 31, 1971.

49. *Ibid.*, April 22, 1937.

50. Los Angeles Times, May 2, 1937.

51. Jerry Saul Caplan, "The CIVIC Committee in the Recall of Mayor Frank Shaw," unpublished M.A. Thesis, UCLA, 1947. See pp. 116-127 for campaign details. Address by Edward C. Purpus on KFWB, July 16, 1938, Joseph Shaw papers, Special Collections, UCLA, box 8. In the same box there is a single-spaced one page document, author unknown, summing up the Shaw administration. For recall campaign also see Guy W. Finney, Angel City in Turmoil, (Los Angeles, 1945).

52. Purpus address, cited above.

53. Letter from Bert E. Wood to Charles Welch, Sec'y to Mayor Shaw, March 12, 1937, Shaw papers, Box 8.

54. Doherty to Johnson, March 28, 1938.

55. Caplan, op. cit., pp. 122. The recall vote was 236,525 with 129,245 against recall. Los Angeles Times, Shaw's obituary, January 25, 1958.

56. New York Times, March 25, 1939.

57. Caplan, op. cit., pp. 126-127, makes this point.

58. Statement of Vote, California, 1938.

CHAPTER 13

CONCLUSIONS

As we have seen, the city of Los Angeles and its people came through the Great Depression in better shape than many other American cities. The municipal government avoided the extremes of bankruptcy, defaulting on bonds, payment of city employees with warrants, and insufficiency of cash reserves (though it dipped into other funds). There were severe cuts in the city's services as tax assessments, tax collections, budgets, appropriations and the number of city employees declined. The county bore the public relief burden, an incalculable advantage for the city not shared by some other American cities. The people suffered through unemployment, reductions in salaries and payrolls, hunger, inadequate private and public relief standards and declining health and housing conditions.

Though Los Angeles increased its population in the period by some 250,000, the smallest growth rate in its history (17.7 percent), the greater changes occurred in its people, their political and economic outlook and moods. Angelenos, in a widespread shift of loyalties, moved from the established politics of the Republican Party to the Democratic Party as part of an unprecedented churning by tens of thousands in spasmodic and anti-business oriented movements for which the city served as cradle and hothouse. Townsendism made Los Angeles its national headquarters; no other area had a greater share of participants in the self help movement; opposition to the crusades reached new heights here. This city with its high proportion of the restless and the aged, a population composed of many who had come to seek a sunnier life, was a rich soil for all the ferments. The Los Angeles which entered the depression as one of the last urban bastions of Prohibition, Hoover Republicanism, and the religious righteousness of Mayor John C. Porter was gone forever as the decade waned.

The period also saw the end of the dominance of the open shop, historic escutcheon of the embattled Los Angeles Times and the Merchants and Manufacturers Association. Los Angeles finally joined the main-stream of capital-labor relations, as it turned from its quasi-agricultural past to a major urban industrial center with strong ties to the national economy. From those years on, the labor movement became an economic and political factor of significance in the city. In the Great Depression, as a result of favorable national policies and labor's organizational efforts, Los Angeles became a union city.

It is important to note that Los Angeles,once a most distant and separated city, was brought closer to the nation in this period. The city turned to the New Deal coffers, along with the other cities as her attempts at voluntarism and boot strap community aid failed. As many as 40,000 Angelenos worked on national project payrolls during the depression. The city that once prided itself on its special salvations of tourism, real estate speculation, exotic agricultural products, sudden oil riches, and "Hollywood" had begun to march more in step to the national drum beat.

It would be wrong to conclude that everything changed in those years. The discredited police chief, Davis, became the security head of a growing aviation plant; the Chamber of Commerce asserted that a half million residents attended the city's 540 churches; the reform mayor, Bowron, chided the 1940 census takers for missing 53,208 Angelenos, and called upon the uncounted residents to step forward as their "patriotic duty." Long trends dating back to the expropriation of the Indians and the Californios were underlined by the depression's memorable and unconstitutional Los Angeles city police blockade against indigents at the entrance to California. The mass harassment and deportation of Mexican nationals from this city, in which they were second in number only to Mexico City itself, was of the same cut. The dreary exonophonic tradition continued into the war years when Japanese, nationals and citizens, were placed in camps.

The depression years saw changes in the face of the city as new federal construction (and some federal art) rose; a new Union Terminal for the railroads was opened; cement was poured for the first of the freeways; and strange towers were being erected by a man in Watts. Battered by a serious earthquake in 1933 the city, with massive federal aid, completed its greatest school reconstruction program.

Results of those years are still present in the city. At the University of Southern California there is the depression-born School of Social Work. The Los Angeles Sentinel, dominant weekly publication in the black community , developed in the thirties in an equal employment struggle. To this day the Los Angeles Public Library closes at nine, an hour earlier, due to an economy decision of the hard times.

It is the central contention of this study that Los Angeles' depression years, with its contradictions and changes, were the ones in which the city matured and prepared for its position in the front ranks of American cities. The twenties had only laid the basis for the city's coming of age with its doubling of population (passing the million mark in 1930) and the coming of new industries. Los Angeles needed the ten years to get from the excitement of the visit of the dirigible Graf Zeppelin to the mass production of planes (in 1939 there were 13,300 aircraft workers--by 1944 there were 228,000). The union membership card had to become legal and acceptable before the mass eastern industries could function freely here. The city's rule had to move from a naive and isolated Republicanism, heavily in the grip of a powerful reactionary cabal of the Times and ingrown capitalist entrepreneurs, to a good government coalition backed by wider based popular forces which toppled a corrupt administration and venal police force. The election was a victory of "recall," and perhaps symbolic of all the things that the depression decade had to recall in the city. Only then was the city and her people tempered, so that Los Angeles in the forties became the second largest war production center, behind Detroit, and a fortress for democracy.

The period of the Great Depression was one of change and testing out of which Los Angeles emerged as the leading city of the West, and one of the great American metropolises. The city had come of age.

BIBLIOGRAPHY

Manuscripts and Private Papers

Borough, Reuben, papers, Special Collections Division, University of California, Los Angeles.

____________, "Jubiliant Crusader," in manuscript form in possession of Madeline Borough.

Clinton, Clifford, papers, in possession of Joseph Gerald Woods.

Doherty, Frank P., correspondence, Hiram Johnson papers, Bancroft Library, University of California, Berkeley.

Harper, S.O., papers, University of Wyoming, Laramie, Wyoming.

Ingram, Graham Galt Diary, Henry E. Huntington Library, San Marino, California.

Mayor Frank Shaw - The Executive - The Man, pamphlet, in Joseph Shaw papers, Special Collections Division, University of California, Los Angeles.

Shaw, Joseph, papers, Special Collections Division, University of California, Los Angeles.

Steele, Ernest C. Diary, Henry E. Huntington Library, San Marino, California.

Stimson, Marshall, papers, Henry E. Huntington Library, San Marino, California.

(Unknown last name) Mary Elizabeth, Diary for 1932, in possession of author.

Interviews

Borough, Reuben, June 4, 1969, Los Angeles, California.

Ford, John Anson, May 31, 1971, Los Angeles, California.

Oral History

In Special Collections Division, University of California, Los Angeles: Reuben Borough; John Anson Ford

Public Documents

California, Secretary of State, Statements of Vote, 1928-1940.

California, State Unemployment Commission, Report and Recommendations, San Francisco, November 1932.

California, State Unemployment Commission, Abstract of Hearings on Unemployment, April and May 1932, San Francisco, 1932.

Los Angeles, City Council Minutes, 1928-1937.

Los Angeles, Angeles Community Welfare Federation, Los Angeles City School District School Publication No. 263, Los Angeles, 1934.

Los Angeles, Board of Civil Service Commissioners, Annual Report, 1930-1938, Los Angeles.

Los Angeles, Budget Message, Mayor of the City of the Los Angeles, 1928-1940.

Los Angeles, Controller's Annual Report, 1929-1940, Los Angeles, 1928-1940.

Los Angeles Public Library, Annual Report, 1930-1938, Los Angeles.

United States Bureau of the Census, Fifteenth Census of the United States, 1930, Washington, D.C.

__________, Sixteenth Census of the United States, 1940, Washington, D.C.

__________, Eighteenth Census of the United States, 1960, (Washington, D.C.) Vol. 1.

United States Senate, Committee on Banking and Currency. Hearings on S.4632, S. 4727, etc., Unemployment Relief. 72nd Cong., 1st Sess., 1932.

__________, Subcommittee of the Committee on Commerce. Hearings on S.3059, S. 3060 and S. 3061, Unemployment. 71st Cong., 2d Sess., 1930.

____________, Subcommittee of the Committee on Manufactures. Hearings on S. 4592, Federal Cooperation in Unemployment Relief. 72nd Cong., 1st Sess., 1932.

____________, Subcommittee of the Committee on Manufactures. Hearings on S. 5125, Unemployment Relief. 72nd Cong., 2d Sess., 1933.

Periodicals and Newspapers

California Eagle

EPIC News

Los Angeles Citizen

Los Angeles City Employee

Los Angeles Examiner

Los Angeles Illustrated Daily News

Los Angeles Times

Municipal League Bulletin

The Nation

New Republic

New York Times

Open Forum

Security First National Bank of Los Angeles. Monthly Summary of Business Conditions in Southern California.

Southern California Business

Utopian News

Dissertations and Theses

Burke, Robert Eugene, "Cross Filing in California Elections, 1914-1946." Unpublished M.A. thesis, University of California, Berkeley, 1947.

Caplan, Jerry Saul, "The CIVIC Committee in the Recall of Mayor Shaw." Unpublished M.A. thesis, University of California, Los Angeles, 1947.

Chamberlain, Ernest R., "The CIVIC Committee of Los Angeles," unpublished manuscript in Clifford Clinton papers, 1941.

De Graaf, Lawrence Brooks., "Negro Migration to Los Angeles, 1930-1950." Unpublished Ph.D. dissertation, University of California, Los Angeles, 1962.

Discoe, David, "The California Contingent and the Bonus March of 1932." Written for a History 199 Senior History course with Roger Daniels. University of California, Los Angeles.

Findley, James C., "The Economic Boom of the Twenties in Los Angeles," Unpublished Doctoral Dissertation, Claremont Graduate School, 1958.

Gaydowski, John D., "Dr. Townsend and His Plan, 1867-1934," Unpublished M.A. thesis, University of California, Los Angeles, 1970.

Hannah, James J., "Urban Reaction to the Great Depression, 1929-1933," Unpublished Ph.D. dissertation, University of California, Berkeley, 1956.

Hoffman, Abraham, "The Repatriation of Mexican Nationals from the United States During the Great Depression," Unpublished Ph.D. dissertation, University of California, Los Angeles, 1970.

Kerr, Clark, "Productive Enterprises of the Unemployed, 1931-1938," Unpublished Ph.D. dissertation, University of California, Berkeley, 1938.

Kerrick, Eugene E., Jr., "California and the Presidential Election of 1932," Unpublished M.A. thesis, University of California, Berkeley, 1956.

Larsen, Charles Edward. "The 'Epic' Movement in California Politics, 1933-1934," Unpublished M.A. thesis, University of California, Berkeley, 1945.

Modell, John, "The Japanese in Los Angeles: A Study in Growth and Accommodation, 1900-1946," Unpublished Ph.D. dissertation, Columbia University, 1969.

Parker, Zelma E., "A History of the Destitute Migrant in California, 1849-1930," Unpublished M.A. thesis, University of California, Berkeley, 1940.

Sherman, Jacqueline Gordon, "The Oklahomans in California During the Depression Decade 1931-41," Unpublished Ph.D. dissertation, University of California, Los Angeles, 1970.

Van Valen, Nelson S., "Power Politics: The Struggle for Municipal Ownership of Electric Utilities in Los Angeles, 1905-1937," Unpublished Ph.D. dissertation, Claremont Graduate School, 1964.

Books

Abbott, Grace, From Relief to Social Security - The Development of the New Public Welfare Services and Their Administration, Chicago, 1941.

Alsberg, Henry G., America Fights the Depression - A Photographic Record of the Civil Works Administration, New York, 1934.

Bendiner, Robert, Just Around the Corner, New York, 1967.

Bemis, George and Basche, Nancy, Los Angeles County as an Agency of Municipal Government, Los Angeles, 1946.

Bernstein, Irving, Labor Relations in Los Angeles, Los Angeles, 1965.

____________, The Lean Years, Boston, 1960.

____________, The New Deal Collective Bargaining Policy, Berkeley, 1950.

____________, The Turbulent Years, Boston, 1969.

Bird, Frederick L., The Present Financial Status of 135 Cities in the United States and Canada, New York, 1931.

Brander, J.P., _The Community Chest_, London, 1941.

Brown, Josephine C., _Public Relief, 1929-1939_, New York, 1940.

Burke, Robert E., _Olson's New Deal for California_, Berkeley-Los Angeles, 1952.

Carr, Harry, _Los Angeles, City of Dreams_, New York, 1935.

Carter, John, _American Messiahs_, New York, 1935.

Caughey, John W., _California: A Remarkable State's Life History_, Englewood Cliffs, New Jersey, 1970.

__________, _California_, Englewood Cliffs, New Jersey, 1953.

Chalfant, W.A., _The Story of Inyo_, revised edition, Bishop, California, 1933.

Chandler, Lester V., _America's Greatest Depression, 1929-1941_, New York, 1970.

Chatters, Carl H. and Hillhouse, Albert M., _Local Government Debt Administration_, New York, 1939.

Cleland, Robert Glass and Osgood, Harry, _March of Industry_, Los Angeles, 1929.

Cleland, Robert Glass, _California in Our Time (1900-1940)_ New York, 1947.

Coons, Arthur G. and Miller, Arjay R., _An Economic and Industrial Survey of the Los Angeles and San Diego Areas_, Sacramento, 1941.

Cox, Edwin Burk, _Trends in the Distribution of Stock Ownership_, Philadelphia, 1963.

Creel, George, _Rebel at Large_, New York, 1947.

Crouch, Winston W. and Dinerman, Beatrice, _Southern California Metropolis: A Study in Development of Government for a Metropolitan Area_, Berkeley and Los Angeles, 1964.

Daniels, Roger, _The Bonus March: An Episode of The Great Depression_, Westport, 1971.

Ekirch, Arthur, _Ideologies and Utopias_, Chicago, 1969.

Feder, Leah Hannah, Unemployment Relief in Periods of Depression - A Study of Measures Adopted in Certain American Cities, 1857 through 1922, New York, 1936.

Finney, Guy W., Angel City in Turmoil, Los Angeles, 1945.

Fifty Years in Retrospect, First Swedish Baptist Church of Los Angeles, n.d.

Flanagan, Hallie, Arena, New York, 1940.

Fogelson, Robert M., The Fragmented Metropolis - Los Angeles 1850-1930, Cambridge, Massachusetts, 1967.

Ford, John Anson, Thirty Explosive Years, San Marino, 1961.

Gray, A.A., History of California From 1542, Boston, 1934.

Hamilton, Andrew and Jackson, John B., UCLA On The Move During Fifty Golden Years, 1919-1969, Los Angeles, 1969.

Hill, Gladwin, Dancing Bear - An Inside Look at California Politics, Cleveland and New York, 1968.

Hine, Robert V., California's Utopian Colonies, San Marino, 1953.

Holtzman, Abraham, The Townsend Movement: A Political Study, New York, 1963.

Hoover, Herbert, The Memoirs of Herbert Hoover, The Great Depression, 1929-1941, New York, 1952.

Ickes, Harold L., Back to Work, The Story of PWA, New York, 1935.

Jeter, Helen R., The Administration of Funds for Unemployment Relief by the Los Angeles County Department of Charities Prior to November 24, 1933, Los Angeles, 1933.

Jones, Helen L. and Wilcox, Robert F., Metropolitan Los Angeles, Its Governments, Los Angeles, 1949.

Kasun, Jacqueline, Some Social Aspects of Business Cycles in the Los Angeles Area, 1920-1950, Los Angeles, 1954.

Los Angeles: A Guide to the City and Its Environs, sponsored by the Los Angeles County Board of Supervisors, New York, 1951.

Los Angeles Chamber of Commerce, Southern California and National Defense, Los Angeles, 1940.

Lynd, Robert S. and Helen Merrell, Middletown in Transition: A Study in Cultural Conflicts, New York, 1937.

Martin, Jay, Nathaniel West, The Art of His Life, New York, 1970.

McWilliams, Carey, Southern California Country, An Island on the Land, New York, 1946.

Mitchell, Broadus, Depression Decade - From New Era Through New Deal, 1929-1941, New York, 1947.

Moore, Winston and Marian, Out of the Frying Pan, Los Angeles, 1939.

Nadeau, Remi, Los Angeles - From Mission to Modern City, New York, 1960.

Neff, Philip and Weifenbach, Annett, Business Cycles in Selected Industrial Areas, Berkeley and Los Angeles, 1949.

Ostrander, Gilman M., The Prohibition Movement in California, 1848-1933, Berkeley and Los Angeles, 1957.

Ostrom, Vincent, Water and Politics: A Study of Water Policies and Administration in the Development of Los Angeles, Los Angeles, 1953.

Perry, Louis B., and Perry, Richard S., A History of the Los Angeles Labor Movement, 1911-1941, Berkeley and Los Angeles, 1963.

Pesotta, Rose, Bread Upon the Waters, New York, 1945.

Ridley, Clarence E., and Nolting, Oren F., What the Depression Has Done to Cities, Chicago, 1937.

Richmond, Al, Native Daughter, The Story of Anita Whitney, San Francisco, 1942.

Robinson, W.W., What They Say About the Angels, Pasadena, 1942.

__________, Lawyers of Los Angeles, Los Angeles, 1959.

Rogin, Michael Paul and Shover, John L., Political Change in California, Critical Elections and Social Movements, Westport, Conn., 1970.

Romasco, Albert U., The Poverty of Abundance - Hoover, The Nation, The Depression, New York, 1965.

Schlesinger, Arthur M. Jr., The Crisis of the Old Order, 1919-1933, Boston, 1957.

____________, The Coming of the New Deal, Boston, 1959.

____________, The Politics of Upheaval, Boston, 1960.

Shevsky, Eshref and Williams, Marilyn, The Social Areas of Los Angeles, Berkeley and Los Angeles, 1949.

Sinclair, Upton, The Autobiography of Upton Sinclair, New York, 1962.

____________, Depression Island, Pasadena, 1935.

____________, Epic Answers, Pasadena, 1934.

____________, The Epic Plan for California, Pasadena, 1934.

____________, I Candidate for Governor, Pasadena, 1934.

____________, Instant Epic, Pasadena, 1934.

Soule, George, Prosperity Decade, From War to Depression, 1917-1929, New York, 1947.

Stimson, Grace H., Rise of the Labor Movement in Los Angeles, Berkeley and Los Angeles, 1955.

Taft, Clinton J., Fifteen Years on Freedom's Front - The Story of the Struggle for Civil Liberties in Southern California from 1923-1939, Los Angeles, 1939.

Technocracy in Plain Terms: A Challenge and a Warning, New York, 1944.

Terkel, Studs, Hard Times, New York, 1970.

United States Conference of Mayors, Do the WPA Projects Which the Cities Have Sponsored Represent Careful and Desirable Works of Public Benefit?, Washington, D.C., 1939.

____________, A Report on the Existing Relief Situation Covering 100 Major American Cities With Special Reference to the Continuation of the WPA Work Program Through June 30, 1937, Washington, 1937.

Van Dalsem, Newton, Evolution of a Radical, Los Angeles, 1955.

Vieg, John A., et al., California Local Finance, Stanford, 1960.

Vorspan, Max and Lloyd P. Gartner, History of the Jews of Los Angeles, San Marino, 1970.

Warren, Harris Gaylord, Herbert Hoover and the Great Depression, New York, 1967.

Work Projects Administration, Writers Project, Los Angeles, A Guide To The City and Its Environs, New York, 1951.

West, Nathaniel, The Day of the Locust, New York, 1939.

Whiteman, Luther and Lewis, Samuel L., Glory Roads: The Psychological State of California, New York, 1936.

Wilson, Edmund, The American Earthquake, New York, 1958.

Workman, Boyle, The City That Grew, Los Angeles, 1935.

Young and Koenig, Inc., Los Angeles: Its Economic and Financial Position, Pasadena, 1936.

Articles

Bird, Frederick L., "American Cities and the Business Depression." National Municipal Review, XX:11 (November, 1931), 634.

Bliven, Bruce, "Roses in January; Morons in June," New Republic, (December 18, 1935), 161-168.

California State Membership Committee, (Communist Party) "Building the Party in California," Party Organizer, Vol. X #3-4, (March-April, 1937), 19-25.

"California: The Golden State Insists on Golden Passports." Newsweek, (February 15, 1936), 15.

Canterbury, John B., "Ham and Eggs in California," The Nation, 147 (October 22, 1938), 408-410.

"Causes of the Depression," Fortune, (August, 1931).

Bloom, Hannah, "The Passing of 'Red' Hynes," The Nation (August 2, 1952), 91-92.

"The Cry of the Apple," City Employee, (April, 1931), 13.

Carlson, Oliver, "Los Angeles Grows Up," The Nation, 146 (January 8, 1938), 43-44.

Davenport, Walter, "California, Here We Come," Colliers, (August 10, 1935), 10.

__________, "California Scrip Tease," Colliers, 102 (October 15, 1938), 12-15 et passim.

Ford, Thomas, "Los Angeles Votes Extension of Water Supply System," National Municipal Review, (July, 1930), 457.

Freeman, Harry H., "How American Cities Are Retrenching in Time of Depression," supplement to the National Municipal Review, XXI:4 (April, 1932), 267-281.

Garet, Garrett, "Los Angeles in Fact and Dream," Saturday Evening Post, (October 18, 1929), 6.

Gaydowski, J.D. (ed.), "Eight Letters to the Editor: The Genesis of the Townsend National Recovery Plan," Southern California Quarterly, LII:4 (December, 1970), 365-382.

Hogg, John E., "Host to 15,000,000 Diners," Nation's Business, (November, 1945), 44-45.

Holcomb, Robert, "The Federal Theatre in Los Angeles," The California Historical Society Quarterly, XLI:2 (June, 1962), 131-147.

Hoye, Daniel O., "Municipal Bonds," The City Employee, (April, 1932), 29.

Johansen, Dorothy O., "A Working Hypothesis for the Study of Migration," Pacific Historical Review, XXXVI:1 (February, 1967).

"Joint Cure for Unemployment and Flood Menace," Municipal League Bulletin, (February 18, 1931).

Kelso, Robert W., "Banker Control of Community Chests," Survey, (May 1, 1932).

Literary Digest, "California: No Hobo Utopia," Vol. 121, No. 9, February 15, 1936.

Lyons, Eugene, "Lament for Ham and Eggs," American Mercury, 49 (January, 1940), 95-97.

McHenry, Dean E., "Ham and Eggs." New Republic, 100 (October 25, 1939), 331-333.

McMillen, A. Wayne, "An Army of Boys on the Loose," The Survey. LXVIII:11 (September 1, 1932), 391.

McWilliams, Carey, "Pension Politics in California," The Nation, (October 1, 1949), 320-322.

Morgan, John T., "Our American Mayor George E. Cryer of Los Angeles," National Municipal Review, XVII (January, 1928), 28.

Morris, George, "A Review of California Agitational Material," Party Organizer, XI:6 (June, 1938), 30-31.

Nixon, Russell A. and Samuelson, Paul A., "Estimates of Unemployment in the United States," Review of Economic Statistics, XXII:3 (August, 1940), 101-111.

Outland, George E., "Sources of Transient Boys," Sociology and Social Research, Vol. 19,(June, 1935), 428-34.

Packard, R.M., Los Angeles Border Patrol, Nation, 142, March 4, 1936, 295.

Rowell, Edward J., "Drought Refugee and Labor Migration to California in 1936," Monthly Labor Review, 243:5 (December, 1936), 1355.

Rubinow, Sidney G., "The Democratic Front in California," The Communist, 17 (July, 1938), 663-668.

___________, "The Election Struggle in California," The Communist, 17 (October, 1938), 919-926.

Scott, R.J., "What Price Charity," City Employee, (March 1931), 17.

Shirley, F., "The Los Angeles Fire Department and the Unemployed," City Employee, (January, 1931), 35.

Stoddard, Lothrop, "Why Cities Go Broke," Forum, LXXVII (June, 1932), 375.

Symes, Lillian, "California, There She Stands," Harper's, 170 (February, 1935), 360-368.

__________, "After EPIC in California," Nation, 142 (April 22, 1936), 509-511.

Taylor, Paul S., "Again The Covered Wagon," Survey Graphic, XXIV:7 (July, 1935), 348-349.

Tyson, Dana R., "Report of Development Work Accomplished With $1,000,000 Unemployment Relief Moneys," City Employee, (November, 1931), 23.

Villard, Oswald Garrison, "Issues and Men, Los Angeles Kaleidoscope," Nation, 138, March 21, 1934.

White, Homer C., "Apple Selling Campaign an Extraordinary Success." City Employee, (April, 1931).

TWENTY YEARS LATER

> "...it is an article of literary faith with me that the first essential of good writing is that an author should have, for his book or article, a definite subject, and that he should rigidly exclude everything that does not contribute something to the exposition of it.
>
> CARL L. BECKER

It is good to return to a project of some twenty years ago. The question is asked, What new has been added? The research and writing on Los Angeles' depression decade has increased mightily. The volume is up, as important work has been done on history of unrecorded groups, neglected aspects and new developments.

But there is more to the history than the lighting of dark corners. What is involved is a deepening understanding of relations - of context with the past, the present, and the future. As one illuminates the corners, the whole room is exposed and connections are seen. For this study of the 1930s and the Great Depression three items are welcome.

In the larger setting there is the work of Irving Bernstein, whose overall study serves as a contextual setting.

Robert Willian's brief essence of the Los Angeles city government is worth examining.

And as a final general resource, one must consider the big collection of materials edited by Doyce Nunis as part memorial to Fletcher Bowron, former mayor of Los Angeles, whose term began as the 1930s became history.

Bernstein, Irving, A Caring Society - The New Deal, the Worker, and the Great Depression. Houghton Mifflin Company, Boston 1985.

Willian, Robert L. Jr., "Politics of Poverty: Los Angeles City Government and the Great Depression", Perspectives, pp. 33-45, 5 Fall 1977, California State University.

Nunis, Doyce B. Jr., editor, Los Angeles and its Environs in the 20th Century. Ward Ritchie Press, Los Angeles 1973.

BEFORE THE THIRTIES

Though the theme of sticking to the Thirties as the sole mission is valid, it must be stated that studying history in decades sharp and sudden is not really the best way. To understand the 1930s, one must grasp the Twenties, from which the Thirties flow.

Los Angeles was a "dry" city, unlike San Francisco, north of it; Los Angeles was a WASP city, almost fundamentalist; Los Angeles was a city created by the automobile.

It is hard to recall the intensity of energy that was developed around the issue of prohibition. Deep and important enough so that the U.S. Constitution was twice amended on the issue. Kenneth Rose takes a view of this city and the liquor problem in 1924 and lays a basis for understanding the city better in the Thirties. Did "Ham and Eggs" replace liquor as the cry in the streets?

Gregory Singleton has done a major pre-1930 study which deepens our knowledge of the city. A major delineation of the social, political and cultural forces is made. Of the city, he writes, "no element was more crucial to urban growth than the influence of a half-dozen Protestant denominations." Much good material is presented on voluntarism. Eventually, this study of religion in the City of the Angels discusses the Protestant Heritage and really tells us why the religious forces, in alliance with newer and later 1930 forces, finally brought about the recall of mayor Frank Shaw.

Rose, Kenneth D. "'Dry' Los Angeles and its Liquor Problem in 1924" _Southern California Quarterly_, Spring 1987 #1, pp. 51-74.

Singleton, Gregory, _Religion in the City of Angels: American Protestant Culture and Urbanization. Los Angeles 1850-1930_, UMI Research Press, Ann Arbor, Michigan 1977.

It has often been said that Los Angeles has had a love affair with the automobile. Mark Foster, in his study of urban growth and the decentralization of Los Angeles during the 1920s, lays the basis for a better grasp of the Thirties. Sometime during the 1920s, the horse was banned from downtown Los Angeles; master plans for traffic were developed. The shift from the trolley car to the auto began before 1930. The die was cast.

Foster, Mark S., "The Model-T, the Hard Sell, and Los Angeles Urban Growth: The Decentralization of Los Angeles during the 1920s", _Pacific Historical Review_ 44 (November 1975), pp. 459-984, Los Angeles.

There has to be a place in a 1930s study for the 1940s, which come out of the earlier period. We made a similar point concerning the 1920s. Marvin Brienes writes of the coming of smog. Surely we find the embryo of smog - the curse on present day Los Angeles - in that decade's massive expansion and the build-up of war industries, which gave the Los Angeles area, by 1942, some three billion dollars in war production. It was Mayor Fletcher Bowron and his administration which first began to talk of "smog".

Brienes, Marvin, "Smog Comes to Los Angeles", Southern California Quarterly, Winter 1976, pp. 515-531.

THE MEXICAN-AMERICAN CONNECTION

The greatest upsurge in scholarly work on our period (of course this is the 1930s Depression decade) is on the subject of the Mexican-American impact on our and their country, the U.S.A. The volume of the scholarship reflects the historic demography of the situation.

It would be presumptuous to claim that all the scholarship has been located. There are places unknown and works in transit. Five of the most impressive studies produced within the last twenty years are symbolic of the work done. We discuss them in alphabetic order.

Francisco Balderrama's incisive examination of the relationship between the Los Angeles Mexican Consulate and the Mexican community offers much enlightenment. In the authors words, the Mexican-American of the period "not only fought the economic crisis but also prejudice."

The centrality of the Depression is noted in the statement that the Chicanos have three great beliefs - "the virgin of Guadelupe. the Sacred Heart, and the party of Franklin Delano Roosevelt."

No one seriously interested in Los Angeles and the Great Depression can bypass this study. An additional attraction is Balderrama's extensive bibliography

Abraham Hoffman's major work on the Great Depression and its attack on Mexican-Americans through a mass deportation drive became a University of Arizona Press volume in 1974, after starting out as a UCLA dissertation. Hoffman has distinguished himself as a historian of Mexican-American relations. He has also developed a sober study of the Los Angeles water story, and we violate Carl Becker's rule by mentioning it here.

Gloria E. Miranda has produced a wide-ranging study of the Mexican immigrant family during the 1900-1945 period in Los Angeles. She adds new material to the economic and cultural aspects of a people, finding Los Angeles "among the most popular destinations" of fleeing Mexicans.

Mark Reisler's study of 40 years of Mexican immigrant labor in the United States, 1900-1940, has important material on the 1930s, which obviously loom large among the decades covered.

Robin F. Scott's dissertation covering the 1920-1950 period, traces the community's path from "acquiesence to activity" and tackles the growing political awareness. Its second chapter of nearly 200 pages is full of fascinating detail on the Depression period. There is a rich tale of struggle to hold the jobs which Anglos were taking away. Support for EPIC, Townsend's old age pension movement is also delineated. Though 20 years old, this study offers much.

Balderrama, Francisco E., _In Defense of La Raza - The Los Angeles Mexican Consulate and the Mexican Community, 1929 to 1936_, Tucson, University of Arizona Press, 1982

Hoffman, Abraham, _Unwanted Mexican-Americans in the Great Depression: Repatriation Pressure, 1929-1939_, Tucson, University of Arizona Press, 1974.

Miranda, Gloria E., "The Mexican Immigrant Family: Economic and Cultural Survival in Los Angeles, 1900-1945", pp. 39-61 in _20th Century Los Angeles - Power, Promotion, and Social Conflict_, edited by Norman M. Klein and Martin G. Schiesee, Claremont, Calif., Regina Books, 1990.

Reisler, Mark, "By the Sweat of Their Brow - Mexican Immigrant Labor in the United States, 1900-1940" Westport, Conn., Greenwood Press, 1976.

AFRO-AMERICANS

Works on Afro-Americans in the Los Angeles Depression have many citations in the basic body of this study. We want to add one of significance from 1990, written by Lonnie G. Bunche III, who notes that by the 1930s racial lines had hardened. This was in a period when the "Great Depression stunned White America, but it devastated Black America." During that decade the number of Afro-Americans in California went from 38,844 in 1930 to 63,774 in 1940. A new newspaper, the Los Angeles Sentinel, developed under Leon Washington, called for a campaign - "don't spend your money where you can't work." This essay by Bunche is rich in detail and knowledge.

Bunche III, Lonnie G., "A Past Not Necessarily Prologue: The Afro-American in Los Angeles Since 1900", pp. 101-130 in 20th Century Los Angeles - Power, Promotion, and Social Conflict, edited by Norman M. Klein and Martin G. Schiesel, Claremont, Calif., Regina Books, 1990.

ASIAN STUDIES

There is a growing wave of studies of the Asian people's coming to Los Angeles.

John Modell's discussion of the "economics and politics of racial accomodations" during the period 1900-1947 dwells in part on the Depression period. It is interesting that Asians turned to shopkeeping as an answer to unemployment. The small store owner began to be hard hit in the mid-1930s as the new mass supermarkets came into existence. Other problems developed in racial oppositions and union complications.

Donald Hata, Jr., and Nadine Ishitani Hata develop a recent study on the Japanese-American as "model minorities and indispensable scapegoats. To the mixture must be added the exclusion of immigrants. This 1990 study also concerns Korean-Americans and their survival. The grimness of the world situation and the hard times of the Depression left their mark. Korean actor Philip Ahn remembers: "I ate steamed cabbage for breakfast and a potato for supper...All day I wandered, looking for a job."

> Modell, John, The Economics and Politics of Racial Accomodations: The Japanese of Los Angeles, 1900-1947, Urbana, University of Illinois Press, 1977.

> Hata, Jr., Donald Teruo and Hata, Nadine Ishitani, "Asian-Pacific Angelenos: Model Minorities and Indispensable Scapegoats", pp. 61-100 in 20th Century Los Angeles-Power, Promotion and Social Conflict, edited by Norman M. Klein and Martin G. Schiesel, Claremont, Calif., Regina Press, 1990.

OF MANY THINGS

There are innumerable supplementary studies of the Depression Thirties. As developed in this thesis, there was a stormy movement of people looking for answers. One must look at a study by Gregory R. Woirol on a short-lived, utopian American Technotax Society in Whittier. A tax on labor saving machines, the group declared, "would solve the unemployment problem for all time to come."

Upton Sinclair's name and nomination for governor loomed large during the decade. His EPIC movement affected not only the main stream of local politics but also played havoc within his original party - the Socialist Party. Leonard Leader documents the effect.

Often lost in the record of the Thirties in Los Angeles is the story of the 1932 Olympics. John Lucas tells the story of the preparation for the global event. Said a *Los Angeles Times* editorial, "instead of the Depression discouraging the Tenth Olympiad, the Tenth Olympiad is discouraging the Depression."

A 1933 disaster involving workers in Griffith Park is dramatically presented by Abraham Hoffman. Scores died in an uncontrolled fire.

Another article delves into the "Ham and Eggs" movement. Tom Zimmerman returns to that comet-like movement which FDR called a "short cut to Utopia." Twice on the state ballot, this scheme, geared to the needs of the elderly receiving weekly stipends, nearly won. It was out of dreams and plans like this that Social Security became the law of the land.

Woirol, Gregory R., "The American Technotax Society: Whittier, California, 1934-1935", *Southern California Quarterly*, Vol. 65, No. 3, Fall 1983, pp. 213-226

Leader, Leonard, "Upton Sinclair's EPIC Switch: A Dilemma for American Socialists", *Southern California Quarterly*, Vol. 62, No. 4, Winter 1980.

Lucas, John, "Prelude to the Games of the Tenth Olympiad in Los Angeles, 1932", *Southern California Quarterly*, Vol. 64, No. 4, Winter 1982, pp. 313-318.

Hoffman, Abraham, "Griffith Park's Greatest Tragedy", Los Angeles Westerners Corral, Brand Book #16 (1982).

Zimmerman, Tom, "Ham and Eggs, Everybody", Southern California Quarterly, Vol. 62, No. 1, Spring 1980, pp. 77-96.

HUMAN ASPECTS

An example of the human element in the Great Depression is a piece by Professor Robert V. Hine, who writes that the period "may well have been the most formative historical event in my life." His description of the family crisis about the mortgage touches many chords.

Laurie Huffman discusses the WPA Project as humanistic experience, offering a partial refuge from economic woes and guilt feelings about joblessness. The woes of a collapsing society piled up, and federal programs offered supports: moments of apple selling, sewing projects, federal theater, state and city guide books (there was one for California and one for the city of Los Angeles), projects for artists and musicians. Huffman notes a WPA Historical Record which catlogued historic records. Though San Francisco is the subject of Laurie Huffman's piece, there are truths for Los Angeles too. (Studs Terkel's Hard Times is rich with Depression memories ranging throughout the country.) The experiences of getting on relief are delineated and the rise of hopes as paychecks came in for federally provided jobs.

Hine, Robert V., "Foreclosure in Los Angeles", Pacific Historian, Vol. 27, No. 4, Winter 1983, pp. 33-37, Stockton. Calif.

Huffman, Laurie, "The WPA Project as Humanistic Experience", Pacific Historian, Vol. 27, No. 4, Winter 1983, pp. 5-9, Stockton, Calif.

THE STATE ANGLE

Though one hews to the aim of excluding all material but that pertaining to Los Angeles, one cannot escape the context of the state of California and the Great Depression. We have selected three relevant articles.

Bonnie Fox Schwartz's study of social workers and the New Deal politicians in conflict discusses the Depression as seen by the caring social worker and the embattled politicians trying to build their political machines. The Branion-Williams case is a surrogate battle in this deep conflict - politicians struggling to capture the welfare machinery.

Irving G. Hendrick evaluates the public support of schools in California during the Great Depression. There is the endless battle over how much should be allotted to education - one that is still ongoing. Surprisingly, there were advances made for the education system along with defeats for the anti-education forces. School financing reform achieved much during the

Depression years.

James Leiby looks at the larger problem of relief administration in California during the Great Depression. It is the story of the coming of federal funds. Public awareness included increasing support for the notion of political responsibility. Up to 1930, private sources had dominated the system. The other big change increased the role and standing of social welfare as a professional field.

> Schwartz, Bonnie Fox, "Social Workers and New Deal Politicians in Conflict: California's Branion-Williams Case, 1933-36", _Pacific Historical Review_, Vol. 52, 1973, pp. 53-73.

> Hendrick, Irving G., "The Impact of the Great Depression on Public School Support in California", _Southern California Quarterly_, Vol. 54, 1972, pp. 177-195.

> Leiby, James, "State Welfare Administration in California", _Southern California Quarterly_, Vol. 55, Fall 1973, pp. 303-318.

PHOTOS AS RECORD

One of the great boons for reader and scholar is the growing use of the camera as history recorder. Even though Kevin Starr's volume, _Over California_, is a coffee table book, the text is rich out of the historian's knowledge. Although the subject is all of California, the 32 pages on Los Angeles are resonant concerning the city.

More pertinent is David Gebhard and Harriette von Breton's L.A. in the Thirties: 1931-1941, a photo collection of how the city looked during our critical years. Seen are the 1932 Coliseum, the 1935 Planetarium, and the 1939 Union Terminal, along with examples of WPA architecture. Many good supportive photos are here.

> Starr, Kevin, text, Morrison, Reg, photographs, Over California, San Francisco, Collins Publishers, 1990.
>
> Gebhard, David and Von Breton, Harriette, L.A. in the Thirties: 1931-1941, (City (?)) Peregrine Smith, Inc., 1975.

OF COPS, GANGSTERS AND CORRUPTION

Much of Los Angeles Depression history concerns itself with the Police Department and the mobsters. The crisis politics of the decade explodes with a bomb placed in an auto, nearly killing an investigator for the reform element, and the ouster of twice-elected Mayor Frank Shaw.

A major research work concerning those events is that of Joseph G. Woods, perhaps the best presentation in the last 20 years. It covers the period before, during, and after the Depression. This study is more than a simple examination of the history of the police, it is a chronicle of the city and provides a vital row of bricks in the edifice of what one day will be a solid history of Los Angeles.

In a chapter called "The Shaw Machine: 1933-37" the mayor is characterized as "the standard Los Angeles politician: a moderately successful small businessman of white, Protestant, Masonic, Republican convictions." As to corruption, Shaw "had been heard to say, 'where the money goes, I go.'" The Citizen News estimated that bribery reached two million dollars a month and 20% reached specific policemen.

One could easily forget that we are presenting commentary in these notes and not doing a reprise of Woods' thesis. It ranks as a must for scholars of Los Angeles history.

One turns from the excellence of Woods' work to the surprising diatribe of Fred W. Viehe, who presents what he calls "The Recall of Mayor Frank L. Shaw - A Revision". With no documentation and a complete acceptance of the Shaw side, the piece makes one wonder what happened to the critical role of scholarship. Still, it is worth reading as a partisan voice for the defenders of Frank L. Shaw but not as serious research.

Richard Whitehall tells of a time when theater screens glorified gangsters and wags quipped that Bugsy Seigel, New York mobster, came West to get into the movies.

Whitehall describes the doings of Mickey Cohen, who was involved in the back and forth of gangsterism and corrupt film dealings. At one point the industry provided a soup kitchen, free for the jobless and 35 cents for others.

Of Los Angeles law enforcement it is noted that "the police didn't fight crime; they protected it, controlling and directing vice and gambling...(the) basic philosophy of the city was that business interests took precedence."

Woods, Joseph G., "The Progressives and the Police: Urban Reform and the Profesionalization of the American Police", (Unpublished dissertation, UCLA 1973)

Whitehall, Richard, "When the Mobsters Came West: Organized Crime in Los Angeles Since 1930", pp. 131-153 in <u>20th Century Los Angeles - Power, Promotion, and Social Conflict</u>, edited by Norman M. Klein and Martin G. Schiesel, Claremont, Calif., Regina Books, 1990.

Viehe, Fred W., "The Recall of Mayor Frank L. Shaw - A Revision", <u>California History</u>, Winter 1980-81, Vol. 50, pp. 290-305.

REFORM

The movement of reform is a constant in the Los Angeles story. It is still a wide field, and there must be those to deepen the tale in the future.

One figure in the picture is John Anson Ford, whose major publication, <u>Thirty Explosive Years</u>, was cited in our original work. Yet, he wanted to say more. And in this second volume he titles the book in such a way to ensure one gets the point:

Honest Politics My Theme - The Story of a Veteran Public Official's Troubles and Triumphs.

As a regular guest in my Immaculate Heart College Los Angeles History course, Ford hit at "the cancer in politics - the method of financing it." In this volume, he characterizes the Porter administration, 1929-1933, as a disappointment, but adds that Shaw, who followed him, was "going from bad to worse."

Ford's campaign to unseat Shaw was redbaited and beaten. Only the scandals of Shaw's first term laid the basis for reform's victory in the 1938 recall. Ford has high words of praise for reformer Clifford E. Clinton. His volume, though not a polished work, is a documant of blunt and personal political opinion.

In the 20-year period from 1972 to the present there are two efforts by Thomas J. Sitton that offer significant illumination of the battle for reform in Los Angeles. Unlike Fred Viehe's partisan and anti-reform work, Sitton balances the picture.

In his 1983 study he sees Shaw as a political moderate trying to satisfy all elements and interest groups in the city. Against the Shaw alliance, Sitton sees a coalition of "moralistic, civic and social reform groups including reactionaries, liberals, communists, racketeers, and political opportunists."

The lines are not as sharp in Sitton's presentation of the forces in the 1938 recall. After all, Shaw had hailed his second term in 1937 as a victory for the New Deal of FDR. Sitton does not retreat from the facts, however, and portrays Shaw's brother "Sailor Joe" (who was in the U.S. Navy) as the great manipulator. Others saw him as "the bag man" for police and other corrupt elements.

It was the bombing of Harry Raymond's car which exposed a secret L.A. Police Department intelligence unit that worked indirectly as a political tool for the Shaw administration.

The dissertation is worth a thorough study by the student of this city in the Depression, despite its coverage of the latter years under Fletcher Bowron.

Sitton's article four years later, in 1987, tackles a "generation of urban reformers...in the 1930s." The Los Angeles scene is covered in a clear manner, with material on the struggle to defeat the incumbent city administration. He sees reform in the 1930s as a continuation of the great reform and progressive tradition from 1900 onward. There are additional insights into the recall of Shaw.

Sitton sees the 1938 recall as an important chapter in the evolution of urban reform politics. He asserts that this was "the last truly major reform movement in Los Angeles" and proof that there was continuity from earlier days.

Ford, John Anson, autobiography, Honest Politics My Theme - The Story of a Veteran Public Official's Troubles and Triumphs, New York, Vantage Press, 1978.

Sitton, Thomas Joseph, "Urban Politics and Reform in New Deal Los Angeles: The Recall of Mayor Frank L. Shaw", unpublished dissertation, U.C. Riverside, 1983.

Sitton, Tom, "Another Generation of Urban Reformers: Los Angeles in the 1930s" Western Historical Quarterly, Logan, Utah, July 1987, pp. 315-331.

Interest in Los Angeles and the Great Depression will continue, even increase. We have selected materials from the pre-1930s and, of course, the 1930s and the post-1930s. Of the future, we must await. Such a promised work is the coming fourth volume of Kevin Starr's work. We end on the note that he has called it "The Dream Endures: California, the Great Depression".

The Dream Endures...The Work Endures.

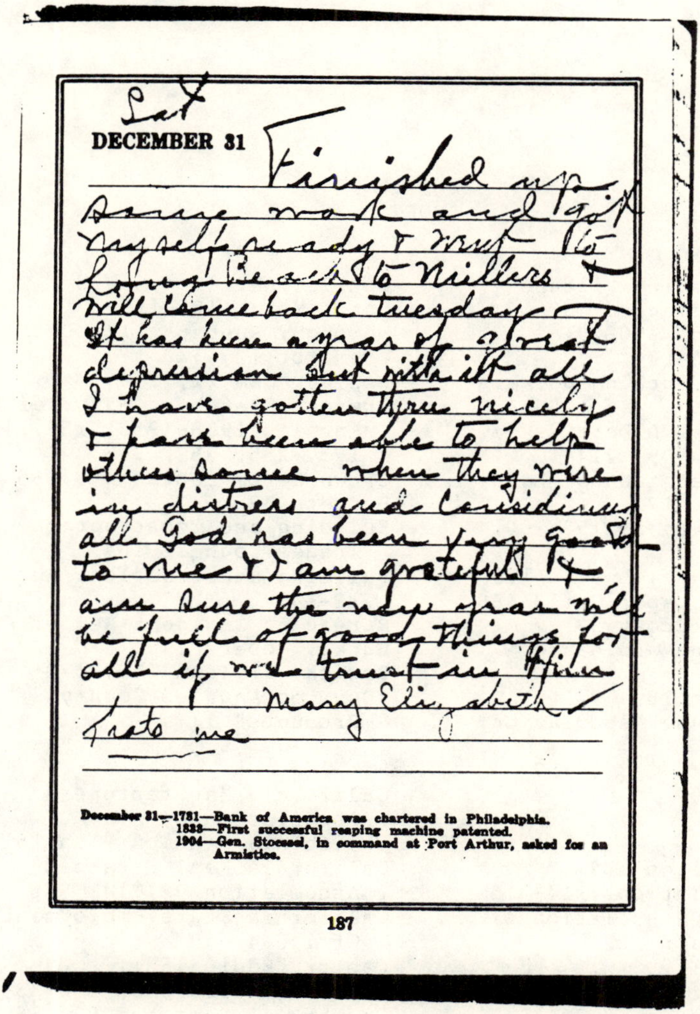
Sat
DECEMBER 31
Finished up
some work and got
myself ready & went to
Long Beach to Millers &
will come back tuesday
It has been a year of great
depression but with it all
I have gotten thru nicely
& have been able to help
others some when they were
in distress and considering
all God has been very good
to me & I am grateful &
am sure the new year will
be full of good things for
all if we trust in Him
Mary Elizabeth
Thats me

December 31—1781—Bank of America was chartered in Philadelphia.
1833—First successful reaping machine patented.
1904—Gen. Stoessel, in command at Port Arthur, asked for an Armistice.

187

"Finished up some work and got myself ready & went to Long Beach to Millers & will come back tuesday. It has been a year of great depression but with it all I have gotten through nicely & have been able to help others some when they were in distress and considering all God has been very good to me & I am grateful & am sure the new year will be full of good things for all if we trust in Him.

Mary Elizabeth

Thats me"

INDEX